W9-BZG-662

WHEN THEY WIN, YOU WIN

WHEN THEY WIN, YOU WIN

BEING A *GREAT MANAGER* IS SIMPLER THAN YOU THINK

RUSS LARAWAY

ST. MARTIN'S PRESS
NEW YORK

Although this is a work of nonfiction, the author has changed the names of certain individuals to protect their privacy and has reconstructed dialogue to the best of his recollection.

First published in the United States by St. Martin's Press, an imprint of St. Martin's Publishing Group

WHEN THEY WIN, YOU WIN. Copyright © 2022 by Russ Laraway. All rights reserved. Printed in the United States of America. For information, address St. Martin's Publishing Group, 120 Broadway, New York, NY 10271.

www.stmartins.com

Designed by Meryl Sussman Levavi

Charts by Mapping Specialists, Ltd.

The Library of Congress Cataloging-in-Publication Data is available upon request.

ISBN 978-1-250-27966-8 (hardcover)
ISBN 978-1-250-27967-5 (ebook)

Our books may be purchased in bulk for promotional, educational, or business use. Please contact your local bookseller or the Macmillan Corporate and Premium Sales Department at 1-800-221-7945, extension 5442, or by email at MacmillanSpecialMarkets@macmillan.com.

First Edition: 2022

10 9 8 7 6 5 4 3 2 1

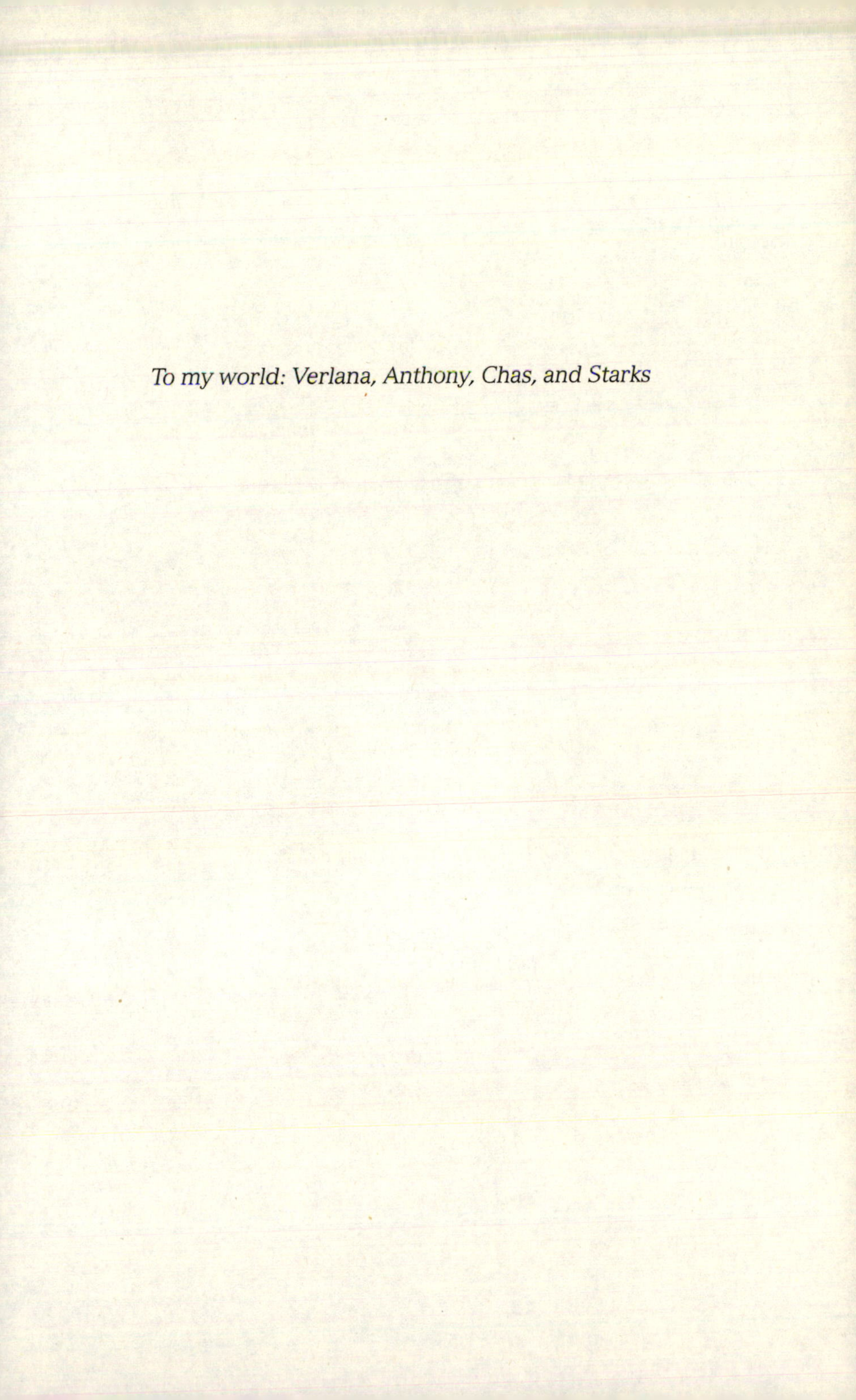

To my world: Verlana, Anthony, Chas, and Starks

Contents

Introduction

Managers are failing everywhere, and no one is helping. This is a big claim, but don't worry, I brought receipts.

Becoming a great manager takes hard work and constant practice, and even after you learn, practice, refine, and, heck, maybe even develop some expertise, you're still going to make big mistakes. That's the bad news.

The good news is that you can become a better manager, no matter what kind of person you are. It doesn't matter if you're super introverted or naturally outgoing. People with those personality types—and all types in between—just have to put in the work, and more than that, *the right kind of work*. To become a great manager you only need to learn, develop, and practice a few behaviors. Unfortunately, the world has conspired to confuse the hell out of the average manager by offering some combination of bad advice, good advice that is difficult to apply, too much advice, confusing or conflicting advice, or no advice at all. The people who promoted you often leave you to sink or swim;

the people who write management books sometimes know more about theory than practice.

This book is different. Its leadership approach is astoundingly simple. It is also proven: it predictably and measurably delivers happy, motivated employees and excellent business results. It focuses on three key elements of leadership, or "the Big 3": Direction, Coaching, and Career. Here is a brief overview of each:

1. **Direction**—Good managers ensure that every member of their team understands exactly what is expected and when it is expected.
2. **Coaching**—Good managers coach their people toward both short- and long-term success, helping them understand what they should continue to do and where and how they can improve.
3. **Career**—Good managers invest in their people's careers in a way that considers their long-term goals and aspirations beyond the four walls of the current company, and certainly beyond their next promotion.

Here are a couple examples of the difference this Big 3 leadership approach—when used together and systematically—can make. In 2011, Joe took over the Pittsburgh office of a Fortune 500 company. For years, Pittsburgh had been among the company's biggest dumpster fires. The office's culture was in shambles, and, predictably, sales were tanking. Once he arrived, Joe quickly recognized that there was solid talent on the team—even though some people needed a fresh start somewhere else—and so he set about reshaping his team. While he did, he spent time with each member, both tenured and new, ensuring they knew exactly what was expected of them in part by giving them a substantial voice in those expectations. Then he sat alongside them, day in and day out, and coached them to success. He further worked to understand every team member's short- and long-term career goals and then helped them put specific plans in place to achieve them. Less than two years later, the Pittsburgh office achieved top results in sales revenue, operations, staffing, employee retention, and profitability. For the first time in this company's history, it won the Office of the Year award.

Daniela, a tech industry colleague of mine, was a midlevel manager at a major credit card company when she took over the leadership of one of its service groups. The group had an exceedingly and unsatisfactorily high cost per contact, one of its key business measurements, and its employee satisfaction—one of a handful of measurements most companies use to understand employee engagement—was, at 55 percent, thirty points below the company average. Daniela quickly set up a series of listening sessions with one goal: to understand from the team's perspective what was wrong. Team members opened up to her quickly, recognizing their chance to change both the perception and the reality of their performance. After listening carefully and humbly to nearly all of them, Daniela had four key insights: (1) the team lacked the technological tools required to do their jobs effectively and efficiently; (2) the company had an inconsistent system for rewards and recognition; (3) they had a culture that lacked clarity on exactly what the measurable expectations were for each team; and (4) there was a lack of transparency around career progression. She appointed four working groups, one for each area, to go deep on the nature of the problem. Daniela quickly implemented several of the solutions they proposed, and within one year her division cut their cost per contact from three dollars to one dollar and raised their employee satisfaction score from 55 percent to 85 percent.

As tempting as it is to focus on where to lay the blame for a failing team, it's much more fruitful to zero in on what it takes to turn one around. It takes leaders like Daniela and Joe to come in and clarify what success looks like for each person, understand not only their strengths and weaknesses but also their hopes and dreams, and then work to enable each of them to find success. Legendary San Francisco 49ers head coach Bill Walsh summed it up nicely in his book, *The Score Takes Care of Itself.* He said that even with the best talent in the world, you cannot guarantee success, and that an excellent leader seeks to increase the probability of success by intelligently and ruthlessly pursuing solutions to the team's problems. Focus on managing your teams using the Big 3, and problems such as low pride, an unwillingness to go the extra mile, poor employee retention, low enthusiasm, and missed targets will all take care of themselves.

THE ORIGIN OF THE THREE-PART LEADERSHIP STANDARD

In 2016 I left Twitter to cofound Candor, Inc. with Kim Scott. Candor was a software company that worked with companies to put the ideas in Kim's bestselling book, *Radical Candor,* into practice. During my time there, I personally interacted with somewhere in the neighborhood of one thousand companies. When they called, I was usually the first person they talked to, and I generally started our conversations with a simple discovery question: "What problem are you trying to solve?"

Their answers were shockingly similar across industries, company sizes, and geographies. Some companies had some evidence and others just a feel, but the problem they were wrestling with nearly always came down to this: *We have an employee engagement problem related to low manager skill.* Of course, the most natural follow-up question was, "Well, can you tell me about the nature of that skill gap?" As I listened to their answers, a common set of themes began to emerge, and the problem started to feel more addressable. I ended up working directly with hundreds of these companies and sending advice via phone, email, Twitter, etc., to hundreds more. Through that process, I discovered the handful of simple practices that great managers do routinely and that less-great managers—the vast majority of us—don't.

What I learned from working with these companies fit my intuition, which made sense because most of the things I learned listening to these companies also happened to have worked for me over twenty-eight years of leading successful teams. It starts with a simple and obvious idea: the only thing that we all have in common at work is that we want to be successful. It seems reasonable, then, that the best managers help each person understand what is expected of them and then help each person find success. I've been a manager since day one of my career. I started as an officer in the US Marines, leading a 40-person infantry platoon, and rose to company commander, responsible for 175 combat Marines. Since then, I've been in a few small companies—Pathfinders, FreeMonee, and Candor, Inc.—and a few bellwether tech companies, including Google, Twitter, and Qualtrics. I received an MBA along the way from the Wharton School of Business at the University of Pennsylvania.

I have seen and solved meaningful business problems inside scaling companies, having led teams as large as 700 people globally and businesses as big as $700 million. I joined Google very shortly after its IPO; during my seven years there, its payroll went from about 2,500 employees to more than 50,000. At Twitter (and later Qualtrics), I had the experience of helping the company plan for an IPO and then continue with hair-on-fire growth afterward. At every place, Direction, Coaching, and Career have been the key ingredients to leading successful teams.

But just because I think this approach works doesn't make it so. I believe that for any management prescription to be taken seriously, the prescriber must define precisely what they mean by the word *works*. Any leadership approach can be said *to work*, **only** if it demonstrably, measurably, and predictably delivers **both** engaged employees and top- and bottom-line business results. You absolutely cannot sustainably get the latter without the former. Before I joined Qualtrics, I put together programs focused on each of the Big 3, delivered them to hundreds of companies, and solidified them based on feedback from my customers. Then, when I got to Qualtrics, I was able to formally test whether Direction, Coaching, and Career have mathematical relations to engagement and results. The answer, as you will see, was an emphatic yes.

One of the things I'm most proud of in my career is winning the 2011 Google Great Manager Award. I'm proud of it because by using the Big 3 over the course of about three years, my colleagues and I were able to help a large and mission-critical team find its footing in the upside-down-snow-globe aftermath of having been acquired.

In 2007, Google bought DoubleClick, at the time its largest acquisition ever at $3.1 billion. Back then, Google was seemingly running on ice trying to develop and scale its non-search advertising businesses. The DoubleClick acquisition finally allowed Google to build momentum and dramatically scale its display advertising operation. My job became to integrate, run, and rework the enterprise services group—approximately seven hundred people located around the globe.

I quickly learned that there was room for improvement. The DoubleClick product management team hadn't gotten along with the executive I replaced, feeling that he and his team had set the organization's goals and priorities softly, unilaterally, and opaquely. They felt stiff-armed, and there had been little collaboration as a result. Worse, the senior leadership team within the services group didn't seem fully aware of the rift, though they could sense that they were seen as not fully successful by their cross-functional counterparts. Further, I could see plain as day that this services team was being used in at least one major way that simply would not fly at Google.

Far too often, when the corporate development team completes an acquisition of a company, they incorrectly assert that the company has been "integrated" once every person from the acquired company has their laptop and email account and can print a document on the cleverly named laser printer down the hall. I call this administrative integration, and compared to the scope of the total integration problem, it's trivial. The real integration is a painstaking multiyear process of reconciling both cultures and the assorted expectations each company holds for the various functional organizations within the acquired company. The team that I took over was extremely good at putting customers first, better than any group I'd seen at Google or anywhere else, and this was clearly something we needed to maintain and build upon. At the same time, they felt underappreciated and scared about what was in store for them. They feared not only for their jobs but also their long-term career prospects.

Prior to the acquisition, DoubleClick had been a large and successful company with a culture to match, but one aspect of the culture that was meaningfully different was their attitude toward scale. This difference hit my new group right between the eyes. DoubleClick was much more willing to use people—technical support workers—to cover up both large and small product gaps, while Google was relentlessly trying to use technology to do the same thing. The process of transforming this enterprise services group to better match up with Google's culture, while also helping the cross-functional DoubleClick leaders feel like their voices were heard and their needs were met, is easy to write in a sentence but very difficult to pull off. All of this practically meant that we would need to thoroughly revise the group's direction and substantially reset expectations for nearly everyone inside the organization.

Here's an example. One of the activities that the group performed was implementation, which meant helping set up new customers and working with them to use their newly purchased products successfully. The group used a measurement called "Time to Live" (long "i" in "Live"), or TTL, to measure how long it takes from the time a customer signs a contract, until they are "live" and getting value from the product. This measurement was crucially important because the faster the customer is up and running, the quicker they are likely to be successful, the quicker we are going to be paid, and the more likely that customer will stay with us. When I took over the group, TTL was somewhere around six months, which my intuition told me seemed especially high. Worse, the measurement wasn't being performed in a consistent manner across the entire customer base, so I couldn't even be certain that the average six-month TTL was accurate.

I began to dig in and ask simple questions. As I listened, I had a hunch that we could cut TTL at least in half and standardize precisely how it was measured. Some folks were adamant that it couldn't be changed. They focused on the things we were less able to control, such as our customers lacking a sense of urgency. Others were excited by the challenge and believed there was a lot of room for improvement. But the resistant voices were much, much louder than the excited ones. The bottom line for me was that our customers bought these products to solve their most pressing business problems, and they deserved our absolute best effort to get those problems solved at the earliest possible moment.

Fast-forward about half a year, and the team was able to reduce TTL to under a month. The pattern in this TTL example is representative of those that occurred across this large, complex, highly distributed team supporting over a dozen distinct products. It's hard to convey in these pages how tiring it is to keep pushing while meeting resistance each time. We did this over and over, shedding measurements that didn't matter, focusing on the ones that did, and improving those. What a time to be a-live!

Take that example and repeat it for nearly every group and every product we were selling, implementing, and supporting. We had to clarify the team's purpose, determine our multiyear vision for success, and set measurable and meaningful targets in collaboration with our cross-functional partners. We had to nail down new expectations for every member of the group and then coach them toward success in a brand-new context. We needed to reform the leadership team to make sure every single manager in the group understood that their job was to clarify direction and coach their teammates for success. I then brought all seventy-plus managers to our Mountain View, California, headquarters to teach them the Career Conversations methodology featured in part IV of this book. We were repairing the airplane while it was midflight, but we weren't just turning one or two bolts—we were turning hundreds of them.

When we finished reshaping the operation, employee engagement had risen from unacceptably low to well above average, and the team was delivering results in a way that nearly all stakeholders were excited about, including and most importantly our customers. I traveled to Sydney to meet with our team there, and one of the senior folks, Jenny Boshell aka "Bosh," who had come in with the acquisition and remained through the transformation, pulled me aside and said, "Thank you so much for what you've done. Before you got here, this team was in a *state*." Feedback like that is very rewarding, especially considering that I had lost count of the number of mistakes I made along the way.

On the heels of the transformation, my team nominated me for the Great Manager Award. Once the team's nominations were reviewed and digested, the winners were selected by the CEO's team, and flatly you were not going to get picked by the CEO's team unless you had a track record and a reputation for driving measurable impact. But my team's nomination meant more to me than the actual award—though we'd undergone a lot of change that had been difficult for all of us, the team seemed to believe that what we'd done was not just good for Google (and it had been good for Google) but good for all of them. The award perfectly sums up my own vision for all managers, which is to be the kind of leader whose teams get incredible work done and who are totally psyched while doing it. I think you can learn to deliver these kinds of "happy results" too, and I don't think you need much more than this simple three-part leadership standard. If you're like me at all, though, you're thinking, "I'm gonna need the evidence, Russ." Lucky for you, I've got it.

3→E↔R

To put it in plain English, embrace these three (3) things—Direction, Coaching, Career—and as a manager of any organization, you will have engaged employees (E) who are delivering the expected results (R). 3→E↔R. To build this argument, we need to start with the central concept, employee engagement, and we must answer two big questions:

1. What is employee engagement, really?
2. Why should we care about it?

Once we understand the power of employee engagement and its relation to hardcore business results, the most natural next question to ask is, *How do we affect engagement?* Spoiler alert: the manager affects their team's employee engagement more than any other factor, and folks, it's not even close. Oh, and great news: you can reliably affect it for the better just by using the Big 3.

WHAT IS ENGAGEMENT AND WHY DOES IT MATTER?

As Gallup noted in its 2017 *State of the Global Workplace* report, companies in the top quartile in employee engagement deliver 17 percent better productivity and 21 percent more profitability than those in the bottom. There is a mountain of similar research to support this idea: engaged employees drive better results. This understanding is not the least bit ambiguous, though some folks are still inclined to call engagement a "soft measure." When you hear that, be aware that you are in the presence of someone who truly doesn't get it.

Let's say you're sold. "Okay Russ, I buy it. This engagement thing has a quantitative relation to results. So what does engagement really mean?" Great question. *Engagement* in this case means *measurable engagement*—not what you happen to think engagement is or what Johnny or Moira thinks engagement is. Measurable engagement is generally accepted to be a composite of a few ideas developed over thirty years of industrial and organizational (I/O) psychology, which is the scientific study of human behavior in organizations and the workplace.

If you're skeptical that a magical measurement from psychology can help you drive better results, then get in line. I've been there too. Look, I rarely bow to conventional wisdom. As far as Gretchen Rubin, author of *The Four Tendencies*, is concerned, I am a Questioner through and through. You would never get me to do something because thirty years of I/O psychology tells me to or because "so-and-so senior person wants it." I do things because they have the potential to deliver impact. Then I measure whether they really work. My team at Qualtrics systematically tracked the relationships among manager effectiveness, employee engagement, and real results, an effort that I initiated and was at the center of for a few years. To further your understanding, I've included some common measurable engagement concepts below, along with some of the questions we ask to pin them down:

- **Fulfillment**—"How fulfilled are you by the work that you do?"
- **Discretionary Effort**—"How willing are you to put in effort beyond what is expected?"
- **Pride in Employer**—"How much do you agree with the following statement: 'I am proud to work at [Employer]'?"
- **Employee Satisfaction (eSAT)**—"Overall, how satisfied or dissatisfied are you with [Employer] as a place to work?"
- **Employee Net Promoter Score (eNPS)**—"How likely are you to recommend [Employer] as a place to work?"
- **Intent to Leave/Intent to Stay**—"How much do you agree with the following statement: 'I am seriously considering leaving [Employer]'?"

Ask your employees to answer these questions on a five-point scale, tabulate the results, and you can measure engagement not only at the level of teams but also at departmental, company, industry, country, and planetary levels. We would generally say that, on the five-point scale, the top two boxes of the five-point scale are positive, the middle box is neutral, and the bottom two boxes are negative. Measurable engagement, then, is the frequency with which either of the top two boxes is selected and is expressed as a percentage, e.g., "86 percent." Inversely, disengagement is the frequency with which either of the bottom two boxes is selected.

That same 2017 Gallup *State of the Global Workplace* study measured global employee engagement to be 15 percent, which is shockingly low. In the United States, it's more than two times better—33 percent—but that's still abysmal. When you connect business results with employee engagement, these numbers indicate massive amounts of lost opportunity. Engaged employees are all in—they manufacture better products, write better marketing copy, sell better and more persistently, and create more thorough financial models and reports. For consumers, engaged employees are the ones you speak with on the customer support phone call and make it crystal clear that "we are going to solve your problem today." If you've had this experience, you know that it cements your loyalty to that product, service, or company. You also know that the opposite customer service experience—maybe, you know, the "accidental" hang-up or a rude customer service rep—leads you to look at other service providers. Engaged employees produce better business results. Better results produce wins. Winning teams engage their employees more, who in turn deliver better results in a beautiful, virtuous cycle.

You're still skeptical? Well, here are a few more examples beyond the 17 percent more productive and 21 percent more profitable stats I offered above.

Prior to Qualtrics, I did some consulting work for a major bank in Canada, and one of their ten-thousand-person business units featured a statistic indicating that a highly engaged employee drives three times more revenue than a less engaged one. The consulting firm Bain & Company, in *The Chemistry of Enthusiasm* (May 2012), found that companies with highly engaged employees grow revenue two and a half times more than those with low engagement levels. Yet another company I studied saw that 70 percent of its operating margin could be uniquely explained by its excellent employee experience. People often value employee engagement exclusively as a way to reduce expensive attrition and retraining, and while those things matter, sole focus on them shortchanges the full worth of engagement. The key point is that employee engagement is directly linked to the most important results that every company produces. It's not a "soft measurement" off to the side; it's integral.

What this all comes down to is the fact that engaged employees provide your team and your company with a competitive advantage. Based on the data, it might actually be a sustainable one, because while most companies pay lip service to the idea that *our employees are our competitive advantage,* this global engagement data helps us see that in the overwhelming majority of the cases, companies are equivocating. Their *say* and *do* are not aligned. Consequently, they are leaving piles of uncaptured opportunity laying on the floor and have been for years.

WHAT AFFECTS ENGAGEMENT?

This brings us to the next piece of the puzzle, which is the role the manager plays in producing engaged employees. In 2016, twenty-nine-year Gallup veteran Larry Emond, then the managing director for Gallup's Global Leadership Advisory, told me this: "The manager explains 70 percent of engagement." What this means is that when we observe a variance in engagement, 70 percent of that variance is statistically explained by a variance in manager quality. In other words, better engagement is a function of better management, and worse engagement is a function of worse management. Even if we arbitrarily discount that effect to 50 percent, the point still holds. Good managers develop measurably engaged employees, who produce measurably superior results. Bad managers produce the opposite. It's clear that the manager holds the keys, so please let's choose our drivers carefully and renew their licenses frequently.

Qualtrics makes software that helps businesses measure, design, and improve the "experience gaps" that their customers or employees might be feeling. According to Qualtrics's chief marketing officer Kylan Lundeen, something like 80 percent of CEOs believe their companies offer a differentiated experience to their customers, but only 8 percent of their customers feel the same way, which is the essence of the so-called *customer experience gap*. It's not just customers, though, who endure these experience gaps. "Experience Management," or XM as Qualtrics calls it, focuses on four core experiences: the customer experience (CX), the brand experience (BX), the product experience (PX), and the employee experience (EX). The employee experience gap is also massive: 81 percent of CEOs believe that employees recommend their company as a great place to work, but only 38 percent of employees would do so, according to research from Salary.com.

Similar to Gallup, Qualtrics has also found that managers, more than any other factor, have the greatest impact on engagement, the primary measurement of the EX. Qualtrics surveyed more than seventeen thousand global workers for its 2020 Workforce Study, which found that employees who received support from their managers recorded a global engagement score of 79 percent, as compared to 23 percent for those who did not—a chasmic fifty-six-point gap. A different 2020 study by Qualtrics's XM Institute, which surveyed ten thousand global respondents, discovered that the immediate manager was the single most important factor in workplace selection, more than, in descending order, the immediate team, compensation, benefits, company values, how fun it is to work in a place, workplace flexibility, and career advancement. All the usual suspects just can't hold a candle to the manager.

To sum it up succinctly, engagement matters, managers are responsible for it, and engagement is awful everywhere. Remember how we said that engagement is 15 percent globally and that the manager affects engagement more than any other factor? Put it all together and you see that managers everywhere are systematically failing.

I told you I brought receipts.

YOU JUST CAN'T SUCK AS A MANAGER

Not to put too fine of a point on all of this, but you just can't suck as a manager. If you do stink at this job—even just a little bit, by being sort of an accidental assclown (and I've been one)—it might not totally be your fault. Far too many of you were thrown into the deep end with no life vest. Or you might have been selected for your job for the wrong reason. Perhaps you simply had the most tenure on the team. Or maybe you were a great individual contributor in your old role. It's important to remember that the activities that make you successful as an individual contributor look nothing like the activities that make you successful as a manager.

Cory Christensen is a very good carpenter, but that's not why my wife and I hired him as a general contractor—twice! When deciding on a contractor, what we cared about was communication, the ability to think through problems, anticipate issues that might arise, manage and de-conflict the subcontractors, respond quickly, warn us when we were about to make a mistake, coach us through our tougher decisions or choices, hit timelines and flag them when they were in jeopardy, and help us evaluate tradeoffs. Being a builder requires different skills and activities than being a carpenter, electrician, plumber, or whatever trade might be your area of expertise.

Because mixing metaphors is my hobby, let's also think about the conductor of a symphony, Imani. She may be a talented player in her own right, but she does not play an instrument in the execution of her duties. Her job is to produce a coherent performance of a musical composition. To do that, Imani must get the right player in each seat and make certain they are all in tune before they hit the first note. Just as the legendary UCLA basketball coach John Wooden started every season by teaching his players how to lace their shoes, she can never skip this fundamental step. If there is dissonance, she must improve or replace her players, and she must make certain they all share the same understanding of the composer's intentions. The net effect of all this is a gorgeous rendering of a coherent concerto, sonata, or symphony. All of which is to say that we must be more intentional about selecting managers based on their management disposition and their leadership chops, not their prowess as individual contributors.

Selecting managers using better criteria, though, is not enough. Many companies lack formal management training, and those that have the training almost never hold the leadership standard that they teach up to measurable accountability, which means we don't know whether that particular leadership standard *works*. Compounding matters, managers are getting absolutely bombarded by "experts" with new research. Much of it is insightful and compelling, but for the average manager it's less like an à la carte lunch line and more like being hogtied in the middle of a school cafeteria where there is a multithousand-person food fight taking place. It's too much; it doesn't hang together, and it's confusing as hell. Very often, managers feel lost and alone, and because they are expected to have all the answers, they are afraid to ask for help. Worst of all is that combinatorial feeling of guilt and the frustration that you don't know how to make things any better.

Any manager who thinks honestly about their experiences will recognize one or more of these pain points. I sure do. In fact, it was with just those pain points in mind that I created this three-part leadership formula. Based on my nearly three decades of leading teams that tended to do great work and be totally psyched while doing it, the insights I gleaned from my work with *Radical Candor*, and the third-party research I've just cited, I was completely convinced that 3→E↔R was a winning idea. The only thing I was missing was the evidence.

Then, in late 2017, when Kim and I were winding down our time together at Candor, she said, "Hey, you need to look at Jared Smith's company, Qualtrics. They're doing really well . . . I think he is looking for some help with his managers." Jared and I both reported to Kim around 2005–2006 at Google, and I had a very high opinion of him. He is kind, bright, and ethical, and he enjoys hard problems. I trusted him implicitly. Beyond that, there were two important things about Jared that made me think Qualtrics might be the place I wanted to be. First, I knew he cared a lot about people management—I had seen him put in the work to refine his own personal craft. Second, he is a systems thinker. Not only is he good at conceptualizing and communicating complex systems but he understands the unique challenges and opportunities of solving systemic problems at scale. Jared and I went to lunch, and as soon as we sat down, he said, "Here's my problem. We're growing, and we're necessarily growing our management core. The more we grow, the more dependent we are on them and . . . I need help fixing our managers."

The invitation to come and help *fix managers* was extremely appealing to me. Jared understood this simple reality: that when it came to hiring and developing his managers, *what got us here won't get us there.* Qualtrics was about a year away from a planned IPO at the time, and its software was increasingly mission critical to its thousands of customers. Jared had figured out that his managers—a channel of about 150 people at the time—held the keys to Qualtrics's continuing success and that that dynamic would only increase as it scaled from hundreds to thousands and expanded its global footprint.

I was excited by the challenge that Jared presented, because I thought I was in the perfect spot in my career to help address it. I felt like my time with Candor, Inc. had meaningfully informed my context around the most common problems companies face with their managers. Further, I thought Jared might be into the idea of developing a leadership formula with proven efficacy.

As Jared and I talked, I threw out guesses: "Are you seeing that people really struggle to deliver tough feedback?"

"*Yes!*" he replied.

I continued: "Are you hearing that people are sometimes dissatisfied with their growth and development?"

"Wow, *yes,* and they leave, and we're way more surprised than we should be."

"Do you find that people are increasingly focused on large numbers of activities and less clear about how their work impacts the company's objectives?"

Again, yes.

"Ownership problems?"

"Yep, it's like you're in the building."

I'm guessing those themes, and others, sound familiar to you, too.

Jared fast-tracked me for interviews, and I started the job in January of 2018, with a charter to teach managers how to lead for both engagement and results and, of crucial importance, to measure them both so we would learn what really *works*.

Fast-forward a few years, and Qualtrics's managers have measurably improved, and consequently the company has measurably improved both engagement and results. My Qualtrics boss, Chris Beckstead, gave me this simple feedback: "You have successfully created a distinguished leadership culture." This is great for Qualtrics, but what about the tens of millions of managers in the 140 million companies out there who are still struggling to deliver these so-called happy results?

If these struggling managers keep it up, they might soon find themselves without anyone around to do the work. It's not for nothing that the phrase "people don't leave bad jobs, they leave bad bosses" has become such a cliché. Let's take a lesson from high tech, which relies the most on software engineers, along with the adjacent functions around them, including product management, design, and user research. These folks are as close to priceless as people can get in any industry. There are not a lot of them, and everyone needs them. Why does everyone need them? Martin Casado, general partner for the venture capital firm Andreessen Horowitz, points out that between 2011 and 2015, startups and high-growth tech companies typically spent twice as much as legacy companies on research and development (R&D). That's because the stock market rewards large, established companies for being able to maintain operations and produce predictable results. But those legacy companies want and need innovation, and one of the ways they achieve it is through inorganic growth, which means that they buy more innovative companies—Silicon Valley tech startups, for example. In the same time period from roughly 2011 to 2015, legacy companies spent about nine times more than growth companies to acquire innovation. The engineers create the innovations that both growth and legacy companies covet and need, and so you can plainly see how this dynamic drives up the value of software engineers.

This creates an environment conducive to extraordinary labor mobility. I was interviewing a candidate to lead engineering for Candor, Inc. who summed it up best: "This is an industry that treats engineers extremely well in that it constantly provides opportunities to work on some of the most valuable problems anywhere. I owe it to myself to ask every so often whether what I'm currently working on is the most valuable thing I could be working on. Sometimes the answer is yes—for example, I stayed at Apple for five years—and sometimes the answer is no." Said differently, these engineers have effectively limitless options. This means that even the most mediocre software engineer in Silicon Valley doesn't have to take shit from anyone.

Increasingly, this dynamic applies to sectors beyond tech. More and more people are leaving bad jobs in tech and other industries to become self-employed entrepreneurs. Freelancers, for example, can find work in other cities and states and countries without even having to move. One of my recent Lyft drivers, for example, an immigrant from Brazil, told me he also works for United Airlines. He logs in from home and handles customer issues. As the demand—or "gig"—economy continues to expand over the next decade, the trend toward freelance will only grow. From 2014 to 2018, freelance jobs grew three times faster than the workforce at large; between 2019 and 2020, they grew 22 percent, according to Upwork's seventh annual *Freelance Forward* study. The rise of remote work brought about by COVID-19 has only accelerated this trend.

This is not some futuristic pipe dream. This is all real right now, fully enabled by technology that allows people to work on their own terms. Managers who have built bad habits and neglected to invest in the people on their teams will find themselves not only drawing on shallower and shallower labor pools as potential workers opt to become their own bosses but also watching as their existing employees walk right out the door.

The platform is burning, but for too many, the fire is invisible.

WHO THIS BOOK IS FOR

It doesn't matter who you are or where you do it—if you manage people, this book can help. There are managers in every country, every industry, in companies of every size, and for *sure* at every level of the hierarchy who don't have a sound understanding of what good leadership looks like. Some were taught the wrong lessons; some weren't taught at all. Some are trying to do the right thing and often succeeding; others may be willfully ignorant. Some are fooling their bosses, hiding from accountability. Some are doing a good job, but they could be doing better still. No matter who you are, the goal is to do the things that matter the most, and I'm here to show you how.

One group I'd like to dwell on for a moment is senior managers, including the C level. Senior managers: that's right . . . don't think you're just going to hand this over to your reports like a parent handing over a pamphlet on the birds and the bees to a new teenager. Far too often the senior folks erroneously believe that their reports, who are most often also senior managers, don't need managerial basics. Julia Anas, chief people officer at Qualtrics, told me, "Candidly, I have left senior roles in my career because I was not receiving good leadership, at times including even the most basic management." One example of a senior team that didn't understand the importance of management comes from a consulting gig I did back in 2016. I was leading a training session on good coaching for a couple of hundred people at a successful Sequoia-backed tech company that was starting to hit some walls. My half-day session was one of the ingredients in their remediation recipe.

They set up their common area classroom-style and brought in a large swath of the company for the training. I'll never forget the way the senior leadership—roughly senior directors and vice presidents—behaved. They were not seated. They stood around the edges of the room, arms folded, manifesting body language like, "Oh, good, yeah, *the people* really need this. This is good for *the people*." You know who else was concerned with what's "good for the people?" Bane, Batman's archnemesis—and then he blew up a full stadium. These senior folks were obviously half in, checking an attendance box and looking for their first chance to escape. The irony, of course, is that "the people" all knew what I knew (this was not my first rodeo): those senior folks needed this stuff at least as much as "the people" did.

Dysfunctional management at the senior level spreads like a pandemic, and now we all know what *that's* like. Even small leadership missteps among senior folks echo loudly and reverberate for months. Simply said, they are highly leveraged, both for better and for worse. Don't take it from me. One of the most common bits of feedback I get when teaching leadership to folks is, "Is there any way you can get our bosses/the senior staff to do this?" Think about what's being communicated in that question. *This is good. This is valuable. This is the kind of leader I want to be. But it is downright* hard *for me to be this kind of leader unless my boss also understands the leadership standard and why it exists.*

Everyone has something to learn about how they can lead their teams better. Senior people often skip these formal learning opportunities for a variety of reasons—not invited, too busy, already know this stuff, other "more important" shit to do, etc. Just remember that the more senior you are, the easier it is for you to create misery, and because your blast radius for better or for worse is so huge, it's much easier for you to propagate that misery. If you aren't demonstrably familiar with and living the leadership standard being taught to your managers, you will look like a hypocrite. Leadership by example never goes out of style, and it's impossible to lead by example if you don't know what example you are supposed to set.

[Steps off soapbox.]

This book is also for aspiring leaders preparing for their first foray into management. You're going to get a lot of advice. Be appropriately skeptical. What is purported to be working for that manager over there (a) might not actually be what is working for them and, even if it is, (b) might not work for you. The key word, once again, is *work*.

This book is for Human Resources and People Operations folks as well. You not only manage your own teams but also, in a way, *all* the people managers, so I know you will find value in these pages. You know better than anyone how big the role is that managers play in driving engagement and shaping the employee experience—but perhaps you don't know how to meaningfully and systematically affect them at scale. Finally, it's for Learning and Development and Leadership Development pros who are looking to make their companies' and clients' managers great.

Booker T. Washington said, "If you want to lift yourself up, lift up someone else." That is the essence of this book. Most of us absolutely can become great managers. We just need to focus on the very small number of leadership behaviors that help people engage in their jobs and deliver great results. Remember, people just want to do great work and be totally psyched while doing it. Managers are the ones in the best position to make that happen. "Alone we can do so little; together we can do so much" (Helen Keller).

Let's do this; let's learn how to lead in a way that lifts our people up, and let's do it together.

PART I

The Argument for the Big 3

1

Restoring Dignity to the Office of the Manager

Big 3→Engagement↔Results (3→E↔R).

For many people, the relationships among leadership—or manager effectiveness (Big 3), employee engagement (E), and results (R)—are obvious. What is shocking to me, though, is how few companies put this understanding into practice. I have presented the 3→E↔R model I describe in this book on hundreds of occasions. When I get to the part where I say that managers explain 70 percent of engagement, people nod their heads in agreement.

So why don't teams or companies operationalize this idea? The easy answer is that it's flat-out hard. It's difficult to theoretically distill an economical number of leadership behaviors that might drive engagement and results. It's harder still to correlate those theoretical leadership behaviors with employee engagement data and then derive a set of best practices. Your average manager is too busy actually leading their teams to have the time to set up a system like this.

It's also extremely hard to muster the organizational will to allow employees to evaluate managers, which is essential because if we want to know how well a manager is leading, then we have to ask the people who are being led. They are the ones who do the real work, the ones we are all fighting to attract, develop, and retain. Some worry that when employees evaluate managers it will lead to popularity contests. Others who might be inclined to kiss up and kick down might not want the higher-ups to know about it. While it might be possible for a manager to hide from the boss, there is nowhere to hide from their employees.

If you believe the most likely place to drive such change is HR or People Ops, well, the problem there is that while most HR organizations badly want to provide the people and organizational leverage needed to drive top- and bottom-line results, they spend most of their time chasing the same kinds of low-leverage work streams as their "Personnel Department" ancestors. HR folks: in case you're not familiar with the reputation of this function, take a look at the March 2021 blockbuster Oprah Winfrey interview of Meghan Markle and Prince Harry. The interview covered a lot of ground regarding the couple's falling out with the royal family. At one point, they mentioned they went to palace HR for assistance. Here's how Meghan described the conversation:

> **Meghan to palace HR:** "I need help."
> **Palace HR response:** "My heart goes out to you because I see how bad it is, but there's nothing we can do to protect you because you're not a paid employee of the institution."

Some of us might believe this response to be technically justified, but the way the world reacted tells us a lot about the reputation of HR. I think late-night talk show host Jimmy Kimmel captured it most succinctly in his one-liner: "It's funny that the Royal Palace has HR, and it's just as unhelpful as HR every place else."

Way back in 2005, *Fast Company* magazine called HR, "at

best, a necessary evil—and at worst, a dark bureaucratic force that blindly enforces nonsensical rules, resists creativity, and impedes constructive change." They also noted that it's the function with the greatest potential, but over fifteen years later, as average tenure for the chief human resources officer (CHRO) has fallen precipitously, I think most of us agree that potential has continued to go largely unrealized.

I would argue that this reputation isn't all HR's fault; it's a symptom of a more systematic failure of leadership. As long as our senior leadership teams continue to ask for and expect all the "old stuff" that may or may not measurably impact the company's performance, CHROs and their organizations will be forced to pay attention to those things. Some are learning; I recently heard this from a colleague who stepped into the chief people officer (CPO) role at her company: "My CEO recently came to me and said that he wants me to live, think, eat, and breathe people strategy and to do so devoid of all the compliance/operation side of HR." These are the kinds of expectations CEOs should have for their CHROs and CPOs if they want to see more innovative practices emerge from the department. Without this legitimate license to innovate on people strategy, though, folks in HR are likely to keep chasing their tails, doing the same things over and over, and those things are what have led the world to believe that the function just doesn't work. Let's change that right here, right now. If you are serious about driving a results-oriented employee experience—one in which people are doing extraordinary work and are totally psyched while doing it—then your first, second, and third investment should be in making sure you have a rock-solid management core.

[Steps off soapbox.]

So, we get it. It's hard. The analysis is hard, mustering the organizational will to change is hard, but one of the biggest reasons why so few—if any—organizations measure good management is this: folks are confused. They want to draw complicated distinctions between leadership, perceived to be the magical gold standard and possessed by so few, and management, perceived to be the copper standard and easy to find. We love to say, "I think that leadership and management are very different." It sounds great when you're standing in front of a company or when you're at a cocktail party, but I don't think the distinction between the two matters even one tiny little bit. Let's take a moment to unpack that.

Here's an exercise I ask management candidates to carry out when I'm interviewing them. "I have a little task for you," I say. "I would like you to write a job description for a manager, but subject to the following constraints. First, this job description has to work for every manager at every hierarchical level in every single one of the 140 million businesses around the world. Second, you can only have two bullet points, and you should focus on duties, not attributes. Go." For fun, you might take a moment here to try this yourself. Give it five minutes and see what you come up with:

-
-

I put people through this exercise because it forces them to zero in on the essence of the job under the spartan rubric: "If you do nothing else, you must do this."

To me, the job of the manager is so freakin' simple, consisting of only two things, that it actually gets me a little hot under the collar when we overcomplicate it:

1. Deliver an aligned result.
2. Enable the success of the people on your teams.

If you only do those two things as a manager—in *any* company, *any* country, at *any* level—you will be successful, the team will be successful, and if the company collects and develops managers who do this, the company will be successful.

Most of us managers are not only *leaders* of a team but also *members* of a team. We ourselves are trying to be successful, have a meaningful career, and maximize what we get from our jobs. While I believe deeply that the job of the manager is absolutely to serve the people on the team, I think it's fair to expect that this service is only *mostly, and not fully,* altruistic, that this service to the team should lead to company, team, and therefore individual success. It's only when they win that you win.

But always remember: the manager is responsible for *everything* the team does or fails to do. Combat veteran Ben O'Rourke identifies two seminal leadership moments in a manager's career, and one of them is the moment when something goes really, really wrong. When this moment inevitably emerges, do you try to hide it or blame someone else, or do you stand up and face the music? Said differently, do you accept full and unqualified responsibility for everything your organization does or fails to do?

To deliver an aligned result, part one of our hypersimplified job description, you need to make sure each member of your team has clear direction and understands their portion of that aligned result, and therefore understands with crystal clarity what is expected of them. Lots of people talk about setting high expectations, and that is very important. In "How to Become Batman," the January 2015 episode of NPR's *Invisibilia* podcast, hosts Alix Spiegel and Lulu Miller explore the surprising effect that our expectations can have on the people around us. They start by showing evidence that people's expectations can influence how well rats run through mazes, but the episode's main course is the shocking story of Daniel Kish—a man with no eyes—who is adamant that his own high expectations and those of the people around him have helped him see. Yep. No eyes. Blind . . . and he can see.

We see this happen over and over again in education. Research shows that failing schools in under-resourced areas can make huge strides in test scores when teachers make it clear that they feel every student is both capable and expected to be successful. It's not surprising that we see the same impact on adults when managers use this behavior in the workplace.

High expectations are important, but *clear* expectations are crucial. By focusing on little more than the success of the folks on your team, you ensure that each member is pursuing their clearly articulated portion of the aligned result and that you, the manager—the one who is responsible for everything that the team does or fails to do—will deliver it. The company is then successful. Team members are successful. You are successful. So obvious, but so rarely executed.

But it gets much easier once you understand that successful leadership, defined by its ability to deliver these so-called happy results, comes down to providing employees with those three things I listed in the introduction—which are Direction, Coaching, and Career. In separate sections of this book, I will present the practical how-tos for each part of this simple and elegant standard, but for now, here is a bit more detail on what each involves:

- **Direction** in a manager's job is less about setting direction and more about ensuring direction is set. Direction setting anchors the team to an aligned result through the combination of two long-term elements, purpose and vision, and two short-term elements: (1) objectives and key results (OKRs) and (2) ruthless prioritization.
- **Coaching** enables team members to achieve those results. It comes in two forms: coaching to improve what's not working and coaching to continue what is working. The former

involves giving feedback that, no matter how hard we try, almost always induces a threat response; the latter involves helping folks explicitly understand what they have done well so they can do more of it.

- **Career** is the most overlooked element, but it is critical to employee engagement. A manager must do more than help employees succeed in the job they are doing now; they must help them discover their long-term vision for their careers and show them what actions they can take right now that will allow them to make tangible progress toward it. In doing this, you show employees that your care for them extends beyond what they can do for you or the company.

This simple framework for leading/managing naturally induces a common confusion about what management is, what leadership is, and why each matters. Our stereotypical mental models are pretty clear. A manager is a bureaucrat who manages *stuff*—processes, spreadsheets, budgets, resources. Imagine someone with a squeaky voice, thick-rimmed glasses, short-sleeve shirt with a clip-on tie, sitting behind a computer screen in a crappy cubicle with a water-stained drop ceiling in the warehouse among boxes and boxes of Dunder Mifflin paper, making sure that all the trains are on time, that factory output is up to snuff, and that all of the sterile reports are accurate, neat, clear, and left-justified, with all the figures added up correctly.

A leader, on the other hand . . . oh my; she's a visionary and a champion and a motivator. She sits atop the hill. The setting is beautiful—blue skies, a meadow in the foreground, snowcapped mountains behind her, the smell of fresh-cut grass and cotton linen sheets in the air. The leader has a visible aura around her, with a certain hard-to-explain magnetism that pulls people close. She only needs to gesture and yell, "Follow meeeee!" to inspire her people to accomplish the impossible. This "leader" archetype is ill-defined as motivational and even more ill-defined as inspirational. Leaders are out there giving TED Talks, expounding on panels, and loudly throwing out big ideas in meetings.

Implicit in these mental models is that leadership is better. Simply put, most people are excited to follow that inspirational person on top of the hill, and they think of the manager with the thick-rimmed glasses as someone to endure. They couldn't be more wrong.

In his 2017 paper "Waiting for Godot: Eight Major Problems in the Odd Field of Leadership Studies," Mats Alvesson allowed himself to wax sarcastic on people's need to make this distinction of leadership over management. It's "mainly a matter of ideological appeal and its capacity to boost the self-esteem of managers," he wrote. "Leadership fits nicely into a culture of grandiosity, where as much as possible is labelled and understood in impressive and extraordinary rather than mundane or precise ways."

I think it's important to remember that the job is called "manager," meaning that is the job you apply for: sales manager, engineering manager, etc. Almost no one applies for a job called "leader." To be great at the manager job, you have to be great at both stereotypical "management" and stereotypical, if not excessively grandiose, "leadership."

Have you ever heard of a company called General Magic? Somehow I spent thirteen years living in Silicon Valley and I never heard of it until I saw a documentary on an airplane in 2019. General Magic was founded in 1989 by Marc Porat, Bill Atkinson, and Andy Hertzfeld. It was spun out of Apple with the blessing of its then CEO John Sculley. Its *low-level* engineers included Tony Fadell and Megan Smith. Tony would go on to help create the iPod and subsequently found Nest, while Megan—after her time at Google, where she routinely did things like purchase the company Keyhole, which became the foundation for Google

Maps—ended up becoming the CTO of the United States during the Obama administration. Yes, these were General Magic's lackeys! According to legends I've never heard directly, Bill and Andy were software geniuses, and by all accounts Marc Porat could see around corners, one of the corniest phrases people regularly use in tech. The assembled team was so legendary that Tony begged and pleaded to get a job there, annoyed the absolute hell out of the HR executive, and ultimately resorted to sleeping outside the building to convey his determination to join the team.

The company was so loaded with vision and visionaries that even its rank and file recognized that it didn't need managers. When someone attempted to make one of the engineers the manager of the engineering group, they revolted, because who needs some boring pencil pusher telling you what to do? Holacracy, y'all.

General Magic IPO'd in 1995 without a single business fundamental or anything resembling one. Even so, they raked it in, raising $96 million, which they added to the $200 million they'd already pulled in from a number of other investors; this was unicorn money back then. Still with no business fundamentals, the company doubled in value as it signed up network and hardware partners such as Sony, Motorola, Matsushita, and AT&T, thanks in no small part to what might be the first recorded instance of FOMO. The CEOs of some of those companies, along with Apple CEO John Sculley, comprised a high-powered, seasoned board of directors. Everyone wanted in. We know now, with the benefit of hindsight, that they also had a winning idea, which was the iPhone. The iPhone is a thing. Maybe you've heard of it. For Android homers like me, I can tell you that Andy Rubin, founder of Android, the company acquired by Google whose software became the basis of Samsung, LG, and Google phones, also worked at General Magic.

General Magic had the vision, the talent, the great idea, and all the faith and credit they could have needed. And despite every imaginable advantage, it all ended in an epic collapse, when their stock price dropped like a hot rock on Jupiter. To be fair—or perhaps to be charitable—General Magic was way ahead of the market and market forces. Chips and networks were not in a position to support its now obviously winning idea, but I don't think this fully explains what went wrong. For four years they relentlessly missed timeline after timeline, mismanaged expectations, and failed to meet their commitments. The company had zero in the way of managerial basics, arrogantly eschewing even the most obvious managerial fundamental: logical organization. They were long on exciting leadership and short on boring-ass management. Those brilliant leaders led them to collapse and embarrassment. Instead of General Magic, we got Generally Tragic. #AmIRight? They could have used a manager or two.

I get it. It's more exciting to be around that inspirational archetype . . . for about ten minutes. Or until you add a second member to the team . . . and then a third. Pretty soon inspiration gives way to frustration because no one knows their exact job, their exact role, their unique contribution to the collective effort, or how success will be determined or measured. People don't know how they're evaluated, don't know what matters, have no sense of prioritization and no say or visibility into the company's or team's commitments. They don't know what resources are available to help them get their jobs done well. That inspirational leader has all the ideas but lacks basic tools, organization, and the processes to do what needs to be done.

It's also not that "just being the manager" is better than "just being a leader." It's great when the checkbook balances and everyone knows what success is and how it's measured, and they're all marching in perfect cadence to the beat of a tightly tuned snare drum, but if people don't know what the vision is, what their collective purpose is, and what is their individual "why," they will very likely have a hard time feeling fully connected to their work.

In order to move a group of people from point A to point B, you need both a cartographer and a navigator. Can we stipulate that maybe if you're a more junior manager you might need to be a bit more of a navigator, and if you are a senior manager you need to be more of a cartographer? Yes, but we as managers don't really get to pick and choose which one we are going to be because moving people from A to B requires us to be both.

A few years back, when I was doing work at Candor with Kim Scott, I spoke to Heather Kirkby, now the chief people officer at Recursion Pharmaceuticals. She was at Intuit at the time, having recently moved from a product management role into a leadership development role, and thought about her job in a way that strongly resonated with me. She said, "I want to restore dignity to the office of the manager."

I love that perspective because *the job is manager, and managers must lead.* Gusto, an emerging payroll 2.0 HR tech company headquartered in San Francisco, has done something legitimately clever: they have changed the name of "manager" to "people empowerer," or "PE." While I mostly dislike it when people or organizations try to get cute renaming generally accepted and understood terms, I love *this* change because it puts a key part of the manager's job directly into the title. Empowerer. Ninety-nine times out of a hundred, the job, folks, is manager—and yes, managers can and must empower people.

In his book *The Leadership Moment,* Dr. Michael Useem chronicles the cautionary tale of Wagner Dodge—a bad manager—and the fifteen-person firefighting team he led in Montana in 1949. Spoiler alert: bad management in this case led to people dying.

Wagner Dodge, or "Wag" as he was called, had been fighting fires for nine years at that point, and by all accounts he had all the technical expertise required to do the job. He had all the tools required to be a strong stereotypical leader too, but in the end it was blocking and tackling management—policy, team construction, crisp communication of direction, standard operating procedures—that led to what is now known as the Mann Gulch disaster.

Wag and his team of fifteen firefighters parachuted into a safe landing zone near Helena National Forest. As soon as they were on the ground, Wag learned that his aerial assessment of the fire had been wrong. He also learned that they did not have a map, which he had believed to be in the possession of a firefighter already on the ground. Their radio had been destroyed because of a failed equipment parachute, and they didn't have a backup. Just minutes into his mission and he was already failing Management 101. Another problem was a result of policy; the US Forest Service put teams of firefighters together based on just one variable: rest. The most rested person got put on a team, so there was no opportunity for teams to build cohesion or develop standard operating procedures. Wag's crew barely knew each other.

The fatal sequence of events is well-documented. A strong wind was moving the fire quickly and in unpredictable directions. Based on this, Wag started to move the crew to a position of safety—between the fire and the river—because the river represented an easy escape route should they need it. A big problem here, though, is that Wag failed to communicate this "why" to his crew. As the team approached the safety zone, they learned that the fire had leaped a ridgeline and blocked their path. Their best and most proximate escape route had been cut off.

Wag knew he needed to reverse course and he did so, but without saying a word to his men. Put yourself in the team's shoes. They hardly knew this leader or each other, were in an extremely dangerous, life-and-death situation, and the leader had made faulty decisions. Worst of all, they didn't fully understand "the why" of what their leader was doing because it was never communicated to them and they had no historical operating practices to fall back on.

Wag told the firefighters to drop their gear because speed was of the essence. But they couldn't outrun the blaze because of the combination of strong winds—twenty to forty miles per hour—and the unanticipated presence of highly inflammable prairie grass in their path. So Wag stopped running, lit a match to start a ring of fire in the prairie grass, and then leapt into the middle of the flames. Wag's strategy was innovative and sound, which was to burn away the fuel around him, get low to the ground, cover his face with a wet cloth, and wait for the fire to pass by. It was a desperate measure, but his experience and knowledge told him it was their only chance. This was the first time that this strategy was ever used, and it worked.

Well, it *sort of* worked. It worked for Wagner Dodge, but no one else. He created the safety ring and waved the men in, but none of them followed. The team had lost faith in Wag and his decision-making, and they acted in what they believed to be their own self-interest. In interviews after the event, one of the two other survivors said, "We thought he was nuts." They could not understand why the boss would light a fire in front of them when there was a rapidly advancing one behind them.

Wagner Dodge had the kind of credibility going into this event that allowed him to be that inspiring silhouette on the hill waving "follow me!" But his team didn't follow him, and thirteen of them died because of his awful nuts-and-bolts management. If Wag had just talked to the person immediately behind him in their column, for example, perhaps that person would have jumped in behind him—either because of trust or know-how—and then many others, perhaps all of them, would have followed. Most important though, Wag was not thoughtful about communicating direction. Barking short orders, or in Wag's case not communicating at all, does not work.

Bad management, in summary, is what led to the worst firefighting disaster in the history of the US Forest Service up till that time. Heather Kirkby is right. We need to restore dignity to the office of the manager.

But how? In order to do what Kirkby prescribes, we first have to strip the job down to its most basic tenets and get on the same page about why it matters. Only then can we start talking about what we should actually do. Reduced to its core, the manager's job is to do two things: (1) deliver an aligned result and (2) enable the individual and collective success of the people on the team. This gets done with the Big 3.

2

Big 3→Engagement↔Results (3→E↔R)

As we've previously discussed, there is a K2-sized mountain's worth of research that supports the crisp finding that "managers explain 70 percent of engagement." That sentence doesn't just describe high engagement, it also describes poor engagement. Further, I think folks sometimes overvalue other aspects of the employee experience (EX), including lower-leverage items such as perks, benefits, policies, flexible work, and facilities. Items with higher leverage include a company's mission and values, which, when taken together, are really about the best expression of culture available to us. More important still are our coworkers. Hire great cultural exemplars that other great people want to be around, and you will have done an awful lot to create a great EX. But no factor is as leveraged as the manager in delivering an extraordinary EX; for better or for worse, managers are the keepers of the employee experience.

As I've indicated, it's not surprising to most people that this relationship between engagement and results exists. What *does* surprise a lot of people is the fact that we're talking about tangible, hard business results, not just things like employee attrition.

Earnings per share, for example, the most precious result for a publicly held company, strongly correlates with employee engagement. According to a 2013 Gallup study, companies in the top decile in employee engagement saw somewhere shy of 150 percent better earnings per share (EPS) than their competitive set, and companies in the top quartile saw somewhere around 95 percent better EPS. As noted earlier, companies in the top quartile in employee engagement are 17 percent more productive and 21 percent more profitable than those in the bottom quartile.

I find that some people have a hard time drawing a straight-line connection between engaged employees and these particular kinds of results, especially old-school managers who depend more on sticks than carrots. For them, the focus on driving up engagement feels soft. Bruce Temkin and the team at Qualtrics's XM Institute illustrate this relationship beautifully with a model they call the Employee Engagement Virtuous Cycle.

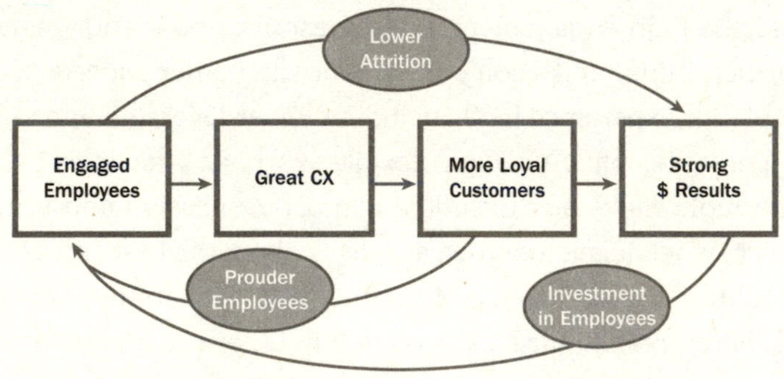

The model shows that engaged employees deliver great customer experiences (CX), and we mean that as broadly as possible. An engaged marketer works harder to explain the product or tell the story of the company's brand with just the right level of detail. An engaged software engineer designs better software with cleaner and more efficient code. An engaged sales rep shifts from being an order taker to creating a more consultative sell, perhaps manifesting the great Challenger Seller (*The Challenger Sale*, 2011) to teach, tailor, and take control. A more engaged customer service rep is more likely to go to the mat to solve your problem. If you're like me, this fits our intuition because a single frustrating customer service interaction can cause us to look elsewhere. A good experience cements our loyalty. This is crucial, because in every business I've ever seen, it's more expensive to acquire new customers than it is to keep the ones you have.

The XM Institute's model smartly captures the bidirectional impact of engagement and results. Engaged employees produce winning, and winning organizations engage employees, because who doesn't want to work for a winner? That's why they call it a virtuous cycle.

Bottom line: *affect the manager, affect the enterprise*. Said differently, the most effective intervention a senior manager or HR organization can make is at the level of managers, and in my opinion, there isn't a remotely close second place. Let that sink in. Managers, you are the keepers of engagement, and companies succeed to the extent that their employees are engaged. Better management equals better results, and that's great because the first obligation of a manager is to drive an aligned result.

But the aligned result is not enough. The full standard is *happy results*. Authoritarian leadership models are obsolete—the best people simply won't tolerate tyrants or absentee managers because they have too many other options. We spend well over half our waking lives working, so it's not a lot to ask that our leaders help us not only to succeed but to succeed in a rewarding environment.

We've confirmed this at Qualtrics by identifying the twelve behaviors that lead to happy results and then developing twelve questions that we ask employees to determine to what extent managers are demonstrating these leadership behaviors. The results of these surveys are what we call our Manager Effectiveness (ME) Index.

It's taught us some remarkable things. First, our highest performing managers—as measured by both performance ratings and quota attainment—outperformed the company average on *every one* of the twelve manager effectiveness questions (which I will share with you in the coming pages) and *dramatically* outperformed the company average on two questions in particular:

1. How frequently does your manager solicit feedback from you?
2. How consistently does your manager provide you with specific praise for good work?

This broad finding—that our highest-performing managers were outperforming the company on our Manager Effectiveness Index—was pretty exciting for obvious reasons, but it occurred to me that we'd stumbled onto something bigger. So many companies use some bogus method for determining who their best managers are, and then they typically go out and ask those arbitrarily determined top managers, "Hey, how do you do it?"

Of course, some of those managers can articulate what they believe to be their recipe for success, but many cannot. Fewer people than we realize are fully and correctly conscious about which behaviors, habits, and activities contribute to their success. Even the managers who can articulate their beliefs about why they are successful get it wrong much of the time, and when they do get it right, most likely it's by accident. This is because there is almost never any rigor, only their own experience, which is fraught with bias. But consumers of that information, looking to become better managers, go out and try to do all the things that they heard in that advice. Some of them, no doubt, are useful;

some not so much. But for the most part, those how-to consuming managers are working with bits and pieces of an anecdotal framework that may or may not help them. No one answers the question "How do we *know* this *works*?" If they become better leaders as a result of the exercise, it's sheer dumb luck.

Our finding basically meant that we could communicate a full leadership standard that would trigger better business outcomes for the team, the company, and the managers themselves. We didn't need to ask them to articulate their success secrets. We were staring at them in black and white, with numbers to back it up.

That wasn't all we found. We also found strong relationships among good leadership, employee engagement, and results that really matter, at scale. Here are some broad findings that suggest this is a leadership system that actually works.

- **Big 3→Engagement: (3→E)**: +/-2 points of manager effectiveness is worth +/-1 points of employee engagement. What this means is that we've discovered an elasticity between good leadership—or a specific set of behaviors—and employee engagement.
- **Engagement↔Results (E↔R)**:
    - **E↔R**: +5 points in employee engagement is related to about +30 points in quota attainment. I really like this statistic, not only because quota attainment for most companies is about as crucial a result as one can imagine but also because how quotas are set and whether they are attained are not determined by the fox-in-the-henhouse sales leadership team but by the independent and unswerving finance organization.
    - **E↔R**: +5 points in employee engagement is related to +5 percent in contract renewal rate. Qualtrics has great

> products that deliver real value to customers, and the company has enjoyed very strong renewal rates—a step above world-class. Sharing the specific measurements would reveal confidential information, but this point holds again: engaged engineers, product managers, designers, and user researchers are producing valuable products, and engaged customer success representatives are helping customers get the most value out of those products. Again, the key measurement—contract renewal rate—is adjudicated by the finance organization, so once again we can observe a strong relationship between objectively measured engagement and objectively measured results.

The People Analytics team at Qualtrics uncovered a couple of pages of these kinds of measurements, and to put it simply, the quantitative relationships among the Big 3 (broken down into twelve leadership behaviors), employee engagement (E), and business results (R) are real. This is the power of the 3→E↔R model. It should not come as a huge surprise, given that the broader world of employee experience research predicts that these relationships will exist. *What is unique about these findings, though, is that they add up to a simple, coherent, contiguous, and economical leadership method—the Big 3—that measurably, reliably, and predictably drives both engagement and results.* Simply, 3→E↔R.

Over my twenty-eight years of leading people, I learned that people need clear expectations, the autonomy to craft and pursue their agendas, support to achieve success, and help thinking about their careers. These can be further boiled down to the three things that managers must provide their people: Direction, Coaching, and Career. Managers who do these things well tend to have thriving, successful teams that get happy results. Those who don't tend not to. I brought this insight with me to Qualtrics, treated it as a theory, and worked closely with our People Analytics team to test the hell out of it. It held up, as you will see in the next three sections of this book, which are, appropriately enough, Direction, Coaching, and Career.

3

The Big 3 Primer

Direction, Coaching, Career. The rest of this book will cover this simple, coherent, and contiguous leadership standard in detail. Before we get to that detail, though, I want to give you a little peek into each of the three main areas. Think of this as a CliffsNotes version of the standard and how to evaluate it. I will share the kinds of questions that one might ask about you as a manager to find out how well you are meeting a given standard. I will recommend that you ask the people who report to you. Your employees' perspective is the most important because they are the ones doing the real work, they are the ones we are all fighting to attract, develop, and retain, and they are the ones most closely watching your every move. Of course, we could also ask your peers, your managers, and your cross-functional partners too, not with an eye toward punishing you but in an attempt to understand whether you are leading in a way that meaningfully shapes both engagement and results.

DIRECTION

My close friend Ryan Neading once asked me, "Why do you love maps so much?" I do love them. In fact, as I write these pages, I have about a hundred maps within two meters of me, neatly arranged in old-school timecard cubbies on my wall. After that question, though, I had to stop and think for a moment, but the answer came to me pretty quickly. I crave and require context in all aspects of life, and maps are the ultimate pictorial representations of physical context.

As an infantry officer in the US Marine Corps, I learned in painstaking detail how to do land navigation. We learned how to plot waypoints using the Universal Transverse Mercator (UTM) system, how to determine our azimuth, which is our direction of travel expressed in degrees, how to measure distance using a pace count, and how to "Left-Add, Right Subtract" to convert true north on the map to magnetic north on the ground. I was really good at it—one of the top scorers in my Basic School class. When I first deployed with my platoon in 1995, we did a patrolling exercise in the jungles of Okinawa. While dodging banana spiders and habu snakes and negotiating grueling terrain, the marine who was navigating us got us lost. I didn't really think that would happen, so I hadn't been looking over his shoulder. Finally, one of the more senior marines turned to me and said, "L. T., you're gonna need to get us back." I climbed a tree and performed a resection—which is basically a technique of using two physical points in the distance to triangulate your current position. I found our position within probably ten meters. I showed my young navigator where we were and gave him a second chance.

Here's the thing though. It is pretty darn impossible to be any good at land navigation without a high-quality map. And I've noticed over the years that even managers who are the absolute best at identifying waypoints and navigating teams from point to point often lack the awareness and skill to create one. The Direction framework that I've set forth here helps ensure that you start at the beginning—creating the map—and then walks you through to identifying waypoints and navigating from one point to the next. All of this with an eye toward arriving at the correct destination, full team intact.

It's a four-part framework that combines two long-term elements, Purpose and Vision, with two short-term elements, Objectives & Key Results (OKRs) and Priorities. Lots of managers incorrectly assume that they can skip the long-term elements, because they assume the team's purpose is obvious. *It never is.* They think that vision is only something that Zuckerberg or Elon does. Wrong.

The manager effectiveness questions that we can ask your team to find out if you are providing robust and clear direction to them are:

- *How clearly does your manager communicate what is expected of you?* The purpose of this question is simply to close the gap that frequently exists between the clarity the manager thinks she's provided to the team and the clarity that she actually has provided to the team. There is nearly always a gap, and this nearly always comes as a surprise to the manager, because the manager is relentlessly sure he or she was much clearer than they were.
- *How helpful is your manager in prioritizing your work, including helping you figure out what* not *to work on?* Prioritization is an exercise in subtraction, not addition. This is another one of those things that I've seen people nod their heads in violent agreement with and then go on chasing work streams that just don't matter, all while complaining about their poor work-life balance. Prioritization is the key

to focusing on a very small number of things that matter, being more effective at those things, and perhaps recapturing some work-life sanity. Here's the thing: overachievers abound, but they often confuse volume of work with impact. The manager can help provide that clarity and give those folks permission to do less. If the manager doesn't do that, who will?

- *How collaborative was your manager when setting your individual OKRs?* OKRs are used to help with quarterly goal-setting, and they are covered in detail in chapter 6. The only time I am likely to get accused of being a micromanager is around goal-setting time, which is usually the two or three weeks preceding a new fiscal quarter. This is because once we have clarity on the goals, I am in a much better position to grant folks the autonomy they need to achieve them. This is where you can help folks focus on the measurable goals that actually matter to the business instead of watching them create lists and lists of garbage input-oriented OKRs.
- *How collaborative was your manager when developing the team's OKRs?* When determining your team's goals—your goals, really—for the quarter, a big part of your job as manager is to gather their input. After all, it's their team too. This simple practice of asking the team "What do you believe we should be achieving together?" gives them a lot more skin in the game and a much greater feeling of ownership in the outcomes.
- *How helpful is your manager in assisting you to navigate company changes that impact you and your job?* Things change. Most people are okay with that, but they can be pushed into a threat state by the uncertainty that it introduces to their roles. *Will I still have a job? Will I get a new boss? Am I going to a different team? Is all of that effort that I just put in on that project going to go to waste? Will our stock price fall?* Folks

usually need just a little bit of help contextualizing change in the spirit of helping them find terra firma amid shifting sands. The direct manager is, by far, in the best position to do that by affirming, reiterating, or reassuring when those things are appropriate and when they're not and by ensuring that whatever is coming is communicated with clarity and that it happens quickly and humanely.

COACHING

Performance comes down to one thing: results. Great results come via great work products and good behaviors, meaning we care not only about *what* people do but *how* they do it. We coach people to either (1) continue what they are doing well or (2) improve what they can do better. Folks, that is all it is. Don't overthink it.

There are so many things a manager can do to help their team succeed. We can try to get them more resources or headcount, we can get them better tools, we can make sure they are working on the things that maximize their strengths and mitigate their weaknesses, and of course we can offer clarity on direction. The list of things we can do to help people have more success in their jobs is probably nearly limitless, but the one thing that is most available to us—and luckily it is the cheapest and most effective—is coaching.

In this section, we won't just talk about how to create more leverage by coaching your team well and frequently; we will also tackle how to coach the boss, which is a question I've been asked far too many times to count. It seems that so many people want to coach the boss in some way, but they don't know how to deliver it. We'll show you how.

Last, we're going to tackle how to show your people that you care. I recognize that this sounds utterly ridiculous to some, but trust me, the ways that many of us use to demonstrate our concern do not systematically work for everyone.

The manager effectiveness questions that we ask to find out if you are providing rock-solid coaching for your people and creating an environment where they can do the same for you are:

- *How frequently does your manager solicit feedback from you?* It's their team too. People just want to be heard, so let's just make sure every voice is heard and heard often. Ask for input, and then demonstrate that you're actually listening. Asking often and then responding in a high-quality manner is one of your best tools for building trust on your team, learning what needs to be fixed, and giving everyone a say in the team's shared path.
- *How consistently does your manager provide you with specific praise for good performance?* Praise is the best tool for providing "continue coaching," which is helping people understand what they should keep doing. We all skip this far too much. Mostly we skip it because we forget. Some of us delude ourselves into thinking that praise is some kind of ego stroke or that it is something to be withheld until something really big is delivered. "It'll mean more," is one of the lies we tell ourselves to justify our tendency toward withholding. In this book, I'm going to recommend a five-to-one praise-to-criticism ratio, as prescribed by the Positive Coaching Alliance.
- *How helpful is the feedback provided by your manager in improving your performance?* Let's knock out any worries about popularity contests right away. We expect managers to provide coaching on how to improve. It's not always sunshine and roses, and with this question we serve two purposes. First, we get a read directly from the employee on whether the manager is providing improvement coaching

and whether it's helpful. Second, we are reminding employees that we absolutely expect managers to do this.

- *How responsive is your manager to your ideas or concerns?* You have to be responsive to your team's ideas and concerns. You don't have to act on every one of their suggestions—you have to be able to exercise your own discretion in making final decisions about the team's agenda; you are, after all, the one responsible for everything the team does or fails to do. But to be an effective leader, you have to create a culture where your team believes their input is valued and heard, even if it's not always acted upon.
- *How comfortable do you feel going to your manager with a safety concern, no matter how small?* To most employees, and in the eyes of the law in most places, the manager *is* the company. People have many types of concerns, from something as obvious as an employee who is nervous to walk to their car alone after dark to a person from an underrepresented group feeling as if they are in an unsafe team environment. An employee may have concerns about another employee's intent to retaliate based on a tough interaction. These are not things to be outsourced to HR. Managers must create an environment where employees can bring forward their concerns. No matter how small they might seem to you, they are often very big to your people.
- *How much do you agree with the following statement: "My manager cares about me as a human being"?* The best managers do one thing over and over: they take the time to help people find more success. Success is the only thing we all have in common at work. The most common standards of personal care I've seen are when managers ask employees about their weekend, their kids, or their health. Not everyone wants this. Kindly, thoughtfully, diligently, and explicitly enabling their success is as close to a catholicon as we

can get in order to help folks feel like they are cared for as human beings at work. On this count, once again, I've got receipts, and you will find them in chapter 11.

CAREER

It's easy to forget this very simple reality: that coworker sitting across from you . . . that person is a human being, not just an employee.

Anyone who has seen a sci-fi space movie will be familiar with the "slingshot" approach. The ship has gone back in time or run out of fuel, and it can't achieve the speed it needs to get to where it has to go. "Unless," the commander says suspensefully, "we do a slingshot," which means using a planet's gravity to assist in a major acceleration that will launch the ship toward the far reaches of the galaxy. The engineer will worry that the forces unleashed may tear the ship apart; the science officer points out that the odds of failure are high. But ultimately everyone stacks hands and agrees that it's their only hope. That's your job—to be that gravity-assisted slingshot that launches your folks into the far reaches of their careers.

You, the manager, will likely only have this employee for quite a small window of time—two, three, four years if you're lucky. This person is on a much longer trajectory, which spans years and years—decades, really. Your job, I will posit, is to participate in and enable that *full* trajectory, not just the tiny window of time that this human is your direct report.

Helping people think intelligently about their careers is one of the most valuable activities a manager can take on, not only according to the countless anecdotes I've heard but also according to the data I'll share with you in part IV. Helping people with their careers, however, is also one of the most frequently fumbled parts of leadership. Employees usually contribute to expectation mismatches by synonymizing "career" with "the next promotion." Promotion decisions exist in a world of scarce resources, but the kinds of help that managers and others supply to allow someone to make tangible, short-run progress toward their long-range dreams is very often limitless.

If you can help people achieve their biggest dreams, not only will you dramatically transform your human relationships with your people and demonstrate that you care about them but you will also improve your company's overall metrics for growth, development, and learning.

The manager effectiveness questions that we ask your employees to learn if you are helping them think about their growth and development are:

- *How supportive is your manager of your growth and development?* Become conscious and intentional about how to do this systematically for all of your people. Avoid getting painted into the "promotion equals growth" corner, thus avoiding the inevitable disappointments that follow the ephemeral excitement of promotions.
- *(Repeat) How much do you agree with the following statement: "My manager cares about me as a human being"?* This is King Arthur's Holy Grail. Everything else falls into place if you can just help your employees understand that you care about them beyond the numbers and beyond these four walls. People are most likely to feel cared for at work if you are enabling their success. In this case, focusing on their career, we are talking about their long-term success, not just achievement of the quarterly goal coming due in just a few weeks.

Direction

- *How clearly does your manager communicate what is expected of you?*
- *How helpful is your manager in prioritizing your work, including helping you figure out what* not *to work on?*
- *How collaborative was your manager when setting your individual OKRs?*
- *How collaborative was your manager when developing the team's OKRs?*
- *How helpful is your manager in assisting you to navigate company changes that impact you and your job?*

When I worked at Twitter, I ran the SMB advertising business. SMB stands for "small and medium businesses," and our goal was to sign up pretty much every small business in the world and help them achieve their objectives using Twitter Ads. At the highest level, we had a lot of success. In my four years there, we started from scratch and ended up with hundreds of thousands of advertisers, and our revenue reached hundreds of millions of dollars. To this day, I am so proud of that team and all we got done.

That effort, though, did not come without its bumps and bruises, and I did not always live up to the expectations I set for myself. It was a pressure cooker environment, not necessarily imposed by any one leader but rather self-imposed, based on an awareness of the following fact pattern. When I started, Twitter was nine months away from its IPO, and we were acutely aware that companies such as Google and Facebook already had massive and thriving SMB advertising businesses. We knew that the analysts were going to be all over us, and we had to absolutely fly. Twitter also had a culture where teams were edited regularly. I had just come from a seven-year stint at Google, where termination of employment was not a meaningful or systematic part of the performance-management culture at the time. Within two months of showing up at Twitter, a senior marketing leader was fired. This shook me because I had worked a bit with this particular leader—and I thought they were pretty good! When I grabbed my boss, the great Richard Alfonsi—or as I like to call him, "the Fonz"—and told him how shocked I was, he simply said, "Live rounds, Russ."

Despite the high-stakes, high-pressure situation, I tried to maintain a healthy perspective. *No matter what happens here,* I thought, *no one's life is in danger, so let's just focus and get this done. This isn't the Marines.* There was a period of time when that was particularly difficult, and in retrospect I can see that it was very much my fault. I did a poor job of aligning all of the organizations and personalities that needed to come together; I failed to ensure that a common direction was set.

Let me give you a feel for the nature of the organization. I directly ran our go-to-market teams, which were tasked with marketing, sales, and customer success/support, alongside a product manager, Ravi, who quarterbacked engineering, design, and user experience. He further managed the interactions and knowledge sharing with the rest of the product and engineering teams to make sure any relevant innovations were communicated to the various research and development organizations. Importantly and customarily, I did not manage those folks directly. Ravi and I were two-in-a-box.

Further, we had geographically dispersed teams focusing on European and Asia Pacific markets. I was a rare American operating in a Silicon Valley headquarters who had deep experience running scaled businesses globally; the regional leaders we had in place were just as capable and of course had more local knowledge. All in all, there was a lot of talent, a lot of expertise, and a lot of strong personalities, and we experienced all of the challenges that go with those good things.

Beyond that, Twitter was experiencing strategic headwinds. Our user growth was stagnating, and it wasn't clear we knew how to change that. Worse, we had focused Wall Street on user growth and not revenue. So even though we'd hit our revenue goals fifteen out of the first sixteen quarters we operated, our stock price was getting hammered. At that point, our SMB business had already tapped into most of the obvious pools for advertiser growth. Stagnating user growth had significant negative implications for growing the SMB advertising business because one of our most reliable pools for finding new advertisers was among existing Twitter accounts. We had learned to recognize the signals that suggested when one of our three hundred million users was likely to be a business so we could swoop in and recruit them to advertise. When our user base wasn't growing, our SMB advertising growth necessarily slowed too, but that link was not widely recognized at Twitter's most senior levels.

Last but not least, there were some personality issues. One

of my direct reports was putting a lot of pressure on me to enact some organizational changes, because this particular person felt that the organization, which featured disjointed ownership due to the functional and regional dynamics I described above, was getting in the way of their success. Other direct reports indicated that they felt that our team was taking on a little bit more accountability for the business than some of our cross-functional and regional partners. If I'm your manager, "I am having a hard time being fully successful" are the magic words you need to say to get me to act—and act aggressively. My direct reports were pressuring me, so I put pressure on the Fonz.

I am trying to lay these sentences out as facts without having them shape your perspective on whether this organization or situation was right or wrong. I just want you to understand that the complex operating environment was typical of growing tech companies. Would I have preferred to have formal control over more of the operation? Of course, especially since these various stovepipes were primed to have orthogonal priorities, given the ambiguity inherent in starting up a business. Have you ever noticed that the people who say "reporting lines shouldn't matter" are usually the people who have the reporting line in question?

As I do everywhere I work, I felt a strong sense of ownership for the business. This *full ownership* value was infused into my blood in the Marine Corps, and it permanently altered my DNA. Importantly, though, I was formally on the hook to deliver this business. I had the quota on my head, and I was the one who sat in on our earnings preparation calls each quarter to develop our talk track around the SMB business that the CEO and CFO would deliver to Wall Street analysts.

When you add all of this up—massively heightened sense of urgency, highly complex and heavily matrixed organization, my strong feeling of accountability, and my own selfish if not natural desire to be successful—you can get a feel for what a challenging leadership environment it was. For a period of probably six months or so, I did not rise to the occasion. I could tell that I was failing, and I started to show up with an unacceptable flex: "I'm in charge."

Now to be clear, I'm sure I never said those exact words, but I expressed other words and actions that were close enough to leave people with that impression. And please let me assure you that if you feel like you need to say or imply those words, you are definitely not in charge. The sky is darkest just before dawn, and the darkest moment for me occurred at a company all-hands meeting, or "Tea Time" as they were called at Twitter. CEO Dick Costolo was hosting. I had a relationship with Dick, one that I cherish to this day. At the end of this particular Tea Time, Dick said, "I'm hearing of some cases of some of our leaders developing an 'I'm in charge' mentality, and I just want to say here to all of you, that is not how we operate."

It was an absolute gut punch, because I knew it was aimed at least partially at me. Two thousand people were squeezed into the common area on the ninth and tenth floors of our Market Street headquarters, and I had this horrible reverse *Where's Waldo?* moment. Just minutes before I'd been another face in the crowd, and with that one sentence, Dick found me with his words. I stood there dumbfounded, metaphorically in my red-and-white-striped shirt and silly hat. I say in the acknowledgments that I learned more about leadership and general management from watching Dick Costolo in action than just about anything else. In so many ways he was the perfect one to deliver this message, because for the first time I realized fully that this was on me.

We came together better as a cross-functional team primarily by developing a shared sense of expectations and a shared definition of success. After we got over the hump, and as Chief Operating Officer Adam Bain said recently, "You built a monster biz from scratch, let the record show!" We did, but ultimately our inability to fully reconcile the organizations in a way that I thought maximized success led me to the decision to leave Twitter. I left proud of what we'd done but a little bit ashamed of that period and the way I behaved. In the end, what it was that I failed to do was simple but not easy. I failed to ensure that a common direction was set for all of the stakeholders, and in that failure I jeopardized our ability to deliver an aligned result for the company.

Expectations in the workplace come in many forms. Remember, the role of the manager is first to deliver an aligned result and second to enable the success of the people on the team. The word in there that is so tricky, and ever so crucially important, is the word *aligned*. If we—and by extension, our teams—are expected to deliver an aligned result, what mechanisms exist within our organization to make sure we pull that off? This is really what direction setting is all about. Charlie Besecker is the chief revenue officer at Route, a Utah-based e-commerce company going through gangbusters growth. Chuck's prescription for expectation setting is (1) make sure you know what you expect, (2) make sure your people know what you expect, (3) have a way to measure it, and (4) manage to those expectations. I love this, not only because it's easy to remember but also because it starts with the often-skipped step: *make sure you know what you expect*. It's shocking how frequently we lead teams without even being sure what we expect.

As a manager, it's not necessarily your job to set direction, but it is absolutely your job to make sure direction is set. The difference is probably obvious, but some folks really want to argue this point. Let's be clear: if you decide you are going to "set direction yourself," you will have fulfilled your obligation to ensure direction is set. Whoopee for you. I will argue, though, that direction is absorbed and followed with much greater vigor when the folks on the team have a say in defining it. In his landmark

1954 book *The Practice of Management*, Peter Drucker said a few important things along these lines, including the assertion that subordinates should be consulted on company goals. He also noted, "When people help choose a course of action, they are more likely to see it through." When you set direction collaboratively, you also dramatically increase your chances of ticking off the first two ingredients of Chuck's prescription for expectation setting. Two birds, one stone.

My personal preference is that the team understands the broad strokes that the company is pursuing well enough that they can almost entirely set the team's direction on their own. Every good CEO I've seen in action—Ryan Smith, executive chairman of Qualtrics and owner of the Utah Jazz, Qualtrics CEO Zig Serafin, Dick Costolo and Jack Dorsey at Twitter, Google's Eric Schmidt and Larry Page—all *collaboratively* set direction and leaned heavily on input from their leaders. They tapped into the smart people around them to determine a shared company direction.

At the beginning of each year, circa 2017–2019, Ryan Smith would pull all of his C-level people, VPs, and directors offsite for a few days to build out Qualtrics's Big Bets, the company's North Star goals for the year. "Come hell or high water," Ryan is inclined to say, "we have to get these things done." His direct staff, also historically known as the Q-Staff, came into the offsite with a prepared high-level view, generally put together a few weeks in advance. This high-level view was Q-Staff's best guess—swim lanes, if you like, but even more broadly representing the location of the pool, because even the swim lanes were subject to revision at the hands of the global leadership team.

Once offsite, our group of about one hundred folks or so broke into smaller teams, each led by a Q-Staff member, then broke in half again to do the hardcore problem-solving. After lunch, the subteams reconvened and compared notes. The room was buzzing and the facilitators were *hustling*, needing to reconcile numerous perspectives into a coherent strategy for a given area of the business. For example, I had to develop the People Ops Big Bets for the year based on the input from the working team I oversaw in this exercise. Later that evening, each team presented a draft proposal of its various Big Bets, while the room of one hundred people pressure-tested them, challenging, pushing back, throwing monkey wrenches, tomatoes, and lettuce. In January of 2020, when I finished presenting my working group's thinking, Ryan commented, "This is why I love this process—you all created an agenda that my staff would never have been able to think of on our own." After that, we took our final input back from the offsite, shared it with our direct reports, and shaped a final version of our team's Big Bets. Those were then communicated at the end of January at the company's all-hands meeting and loaded into our internal goal-setting system, Odo. Everyone in the company then set their goals in alignment with those Big Bet objectives. For 2020, we started this process a few days after we returned from the 2019 December holidays, and we had it all done before the end of January.

We had to do all of our planning for 2021 in 2020 and do it all virtually because of the pandemic. Zig led what could have been a cumbersome, awkward process, skillfully bringing in hundreds of voices, making sure to capture diverse perspectives—geographic diversity, diversity in seniority, functional diversity, gender diversity, ethnic diversity—from start to finish. In the end, we stepped off in 2021 not only with a highly focused set of company goals but also with many of the operational necessities hammered out—things such as sales territories, quotas, and headcount plans for every hiring manager. All done before the new year.

All of this is to illustrate one key point: your job is to make sure direction is set, and that direction will be a higher-quality expression of your goals if you engage your people in setting that direction. You don't have to believe me, of course, but you do sort of have to believe Ryan, Zig, Dick, Jack, Larry, and Eric.

To help organize our thinking, I split direction up into four major areas, beginning with the longest lasting and least likely to change and ending with the least persistent and most likely to change regularly:

- **Purpose:** Reason for existence, possibly lasts for decades. Often more or less synonymous with mission.
- **Vision:** The mountain we are jointly trying to climb, often multiyear, often measurable.
- **OKRs:** Objectives and Key Results—quarterly, semiannual, at times annual expressions of work at all levels of the company.
- **Priorities:** Weekly and daily expressions of work.

I developed this framework for a couple reasons. First, I created it to help organize direction within a parent-child system. Each subsequent item is a child of the previous one. For example, vision is the child of purpose, OKRs are the children of vision, and priorities, most importantly, are the children of higher-level OKRs. Second, a lot of these words get mixed up, and when we're trying to understand our direction, using these words differently can lead to confusion and misalignment. Especially the word *priority*, which is the second most misused and abused word in business behind only *strategic*. For example, is it fair to say that our OKRs are our quarterly priorities? Sure, but we already have a word for our quarterly priorities, and that's "OKRs." Is the SpaceX goal "to enable life on other planets" a priority? Sure, but we already have a word for that, and it's "mission."

My theory is that people who feel easily unsettled in their

roles often fail to understand either their unique purpose within the broader context of the company or how their specific contributions support its top-line objectives—or some combination of the two. When you can draw a clear line between your daily and weekly activities and the company purpose, it's much easier to feel like you matter. Sebastian Junger, author of *Tribe*, said, "Humans don't mind hardship, in fact, they thrive on it; what they mind is not feeling necessary." Clarifying one's part of the broader organization's purpose helps people feel necessary.

A company's performance—the realization of its goals, vision, and purpose—is nothing more and nothing less than the aggregation of the performance of each person in the company. For people to feel necessary, they must understand how their work ladders up within that broader context. To understand a company's or team's broadest context possible, we start with its reason for existence. We start with *purpose*.

4

Create the Map: Purpose

First comes purpose, also sometimes called *mission*. Some assert that purpose and mission are really different, but I don't think the distinctions they draw are meaningful enough to concern ourselves with. For simplicity, I'm going to settle on the word *purpose* from here on out. To define purpose, one must ask the question, "Why does our team exist?" I've worked with a fair number of leadership teams to develop a statement of purpose, and one of the most interesting things I've observed is how much they *think* they are on the same page ex ante versus how little they are *actually* on the same page when I ask them to answer that simplest of questions.

"If you are all over the place as a leadership team," I ask them, "how likely do you think it is that your members understand what the team's purpose is?" The answer is obvious. Not likely at all. So, why develop a team purpose? Good question.

I used to be a certified CrossFit trainer, and as a newly hatched formal member of the CrossFit community, I evangelized *hard*. That evangelism led to gut-busting jokes like, "How can you tell someone does CrossFit?" . . . "They tell you!" And: "A

CrossFitter, an atheist, and a vegan walk into a bar . . . and you know this because each of them announces it immediately upon entry." These jokes touch on the reality of a certain time, say 2013–2017, that people who did CrossFit couldn't stop talking about it. In truth, though, CrossFit is extremely effective (excellent fitness outcomes), efficient (fitness outcomes manifest quickly and with a minimal time investment), and importantly, it is *tough*.

So, when I was moving into my "why you gotta do CrossFit" pitch, I always started by nudging people toward an article titled "What is Fitness?" from the October 2002 issue of *The CrossFit Journal*. Most others just said, "Come into a gym and it'll be awesome." I knew, though, that CrossFit was so damn hard that sometimes you might be in the middle of a tough workout, and you would say to yourself, *Why the fuck am I doing this?* My theory was that this question was just as frequently nonrhetorical as it was rhetorical. Do I really need to work out like this? Do I really need to pay this much money to be a member of this gym? On and on. My hunch was that if people knew the answer to that question—*Why?*—then they were more likely to fight through the pain, the failures, the soreness, the monthly bill, the setbacks, and the exhaustion because they would understand how valuable the fitness is from doing CrossFit in their everyday lives.

The article, in my view, is a stroke of genius. Greg Glassman, the founder of CrossFit, was inspired by his scientist father to think that fitness might be measurable—and therefore, subject to the scientific method of developing a theory and trying to disprove it. To start, Greg wanted to know what the definition of fitness was, and ostensibly that definition would serve as an initial working theory to test. According to Glassman, he looked everywhere but couldn't find anything useful. Somehow, no one had ever bothered to try to define fitness, and as such there was no standard by which to determine what regimens produce the best outcomes.

This article provides an answer, and it really helps folks in their moments of pain to understand why they are going to finish that workout and show up the next day. Like CrossFit, every company is capable of producing a shitty day. Every. Single. One. I've *loved* being at all the companies I ever worked at, starting with the US Marines, but at every one of them there came a time when I asked myself that same question: "What the hell am I doing this for?" I think it's important for us to anticipate this question, assume it is nonrhetorical, and make sure that the people we manage can answer it. I don't want to be that manager who shrugs his shoulders and says, "Oh, they'll figure it out." That seems like malpractice, so I teach managers to work with their teams to develop a team purpose.

Purpose is of course so much more than the answer to a negative question. Purpose is our reason for being, and I think the clearer that is to the team, the more likely they are to proactively and consciously opt in or opt out. I've generally built my career around two simple principles. The first is to find and solve hard problems with good people. The second is to do something that matters *for* something that matters. And the first and best place to look when you are evaluating whether a company can deliver on those principles is its purpose. Qualtrics's purpose, for example, is to close experience gaps. Most organizations want to deliver a great experience to their customers and employees, but they fall short. Qualtrics helps them close the gap between the intended experience and the actual experience. For me, this means that Qualtrics extracts human misery from the system. Do something that matters for something that matters? Check. Hard problems? Check. Are good people attracted to meaningful purposes? Check.

Let's look at some other companies' purpose statements. Some of them are not current, but I chose them because I think they represent very strong examples of simple statements that answer the question, *Why does this place exist?* While you read them, try to keep track of what they have in common.

COMPANY NAME	CORE PURPOSE
3M	To solve unsolved problems innovatively
Merck	To preserve and improve human life
Walmart	To give ordinary folk the chance to buy the same things as rich people
Disney	To make people happy
Coca-Cola	To refresh the world
Google	To organize the world's information and make it universally accessible and useful
Twitter	To give everyone the power to create and share ideas and information instantly without barriers
Beauty Bakerie	To be sweet, and to sweeten the lives of others

Use the space below to take a moment to reflect on the similarities you see among these core purpose statements. (Seriously, stop and take a moment to do that. I'll wait.)

When I teach this content, the first thing people notice is that these are all action statements, beginning with an infinitive. A second thing folks will notice is a lack of discrete timelines. A third similarity is that none of these statements revolves around a crisp, measurable goal. Fourth, they are short, punchy, and easy to remember—though it's worth mentioning that statements like these are often supplemented with longer, more detailed, and therefore more accountable versions. Finally, each statement successfully answers the question, "Why does this company or team exist?"

It's true, of course, that not every good purpose statement conforms precisely to all these basic rules, but those listed here are particularly successful ones, so it's useful for you to consider them as you develop your own.

It can feel like a daunting task to come up with a core purpose for your team. My first recommendation is that you don't try to do this yourself. It will be a huge swing and a miss if you do. Promise. I recommend you convene your team. Whether you're the manager of a five-person organization and you pull that group together or you have a five-hundred-person organization and you pull your eight direct reports together, working on this in collaboration with your team will lead to a better answer and better buy-in for that answer when you come up with it.

It's never too late to establish your team's purpose. If you're just starting out with a team, that's the perfect time to do this work, but it's also a relevant undertaking if you've been in your role for years. Here's a simple approach. Set up a two-hour meeting, possibly cannibalizing your existing team meeting if one exists. Set the agenda to have just one item, defining your team's core purpose.

Give the team prework to do about two weeks in advance. Ask each member to come up with their own best version of your core purpose and bring it with them to the meeting. Emphasize and insist on two things. First, that they do not collaborate—let them know they will do that together when they convene. And second, make sure they write everything down. This is important, because writing is thinking and thinking is writing. Nothing is as clear in your mind as it is after you write it down. Also, this helps ensure that everyone completes the assignment and that you will get the most diverse set of options to start with. This further maximizes your chances of tapping into the wisdom of the crowd and helps ensure that each person has a rationale for their particular version of the core purpose. A side benefit of approaching this problem in this way is that you, as the leader of the team, will gain a deeper understanding of what each person values about the team and what is most important to them.

When you meet, remember, you are answering only one question: Why do we exist? Some prompts for the team that might be useful include:

- "Who do we serve?"
- "What do we produce?"
- "Why do we produce it?"
- "Why do we matter?"
- "What (of consequence) fails to happen if we don't show up tomorrow?"
- "If we vanish, describe the crisis."
- "What is the company's purpose?"
- "What is [boss's/organization's/etc.] purpose?"

You will quickly discover that there is not a right or wrong answer to "What is our purpose?" You will also notice that some answers are "righter" and some answers are "wronger" than others, in the same way that Diet Pepsi is not healthy but is for sure healthier than regular Pepsi. The value, of course, is that by the time you are done forging this core purpose, everyone on your team or your leadership team will know exactly why each word was chosen and how you arrived at this particular statement.

To develop a purpose statement for Qualtrics's People Ops team, for example, I first assigned my direct reports some pre-work and then invited them to spend a full day in my home. First thing in the morning, right after coffee, I asked people who would normally not work directly together to pair up and reconcile their ideas about our organization's purpose. We came back together over lunch, listened to each other's ideas, and then, after we fully wrestled with them for about an hour, I assigned two or three people to finalize the statement. We ended up with three statements, all connected—a short one, a medium one, and a longer one. The short version was easy to remember; the medium one went into a higher level of detail so it could be used on a team profile page to convey our purpose to stakeholders and fellow workers. Finally, the long version allowed each subteam within People Ops to really see their part of the purpose come to life.

Here they are:

1. People Ops Purpose: To power legendary experiences . . .
2. . . . We power legendary experiences that endure beyond the employee life cycle by focusing on moments that matter and minting Qualtrics ambassadors who not only bring to life our XM vision but also embody our Qualtrics values.
3. We:
   - discover and attract talent through transformative candidate experiences, where we are all left better off than when we first met;
   - unleash data to measure, design, administer, and enhance our bar-setting employee experience;

- empower our people and their managers to lead, engage, and take action to unlock everyone's potential for success and to drive meaningful business results;
- serve as the custodians of the Qualtrics culture by casting a foundation of fairness, equity, respect, trust, and belonging.

I should warn you that most people go through this exercise with you reluctantly. Oh sure, they'll pretend to be into it; they'll all say how psyched they are to be doing it. But deep down inside, they're going to be thinking it's a waste of time. "What are we going to use this for?" they will be secretly asking themselves or their closest confidants. You'll have to push through. I've joked in the past that as I've completed this process, I suddenly become a Catholic priest, hearing everyone's confessions. "Russ, I have to be honest, I thought this was gonna be so stupid and a huge waste of time, but I actually think it was worth doing."

"Say five Hail Marys, a Glory Be, and have a shot of whiskey," I typically respond.

There's some esoteric language in those three purpose statements that might sound like buzzwords or nonsense to outsiders. Critically important, though, is the process we followed to develop them. Because of it, everyone on my leadership team is on the same page. We tussled with the words because the words really matter. As a result, not only were my leaders able to align their team's and their personal purposes with the People Ops purpose, but they could also explain it to folks deeper down in the organization.

5

Determine the Destination: Vision

On September 12, 1962, President John Fitzgerald Kennedy announced the original moonshot: "We choose to go to the moon in this decade and do other things, not because they are easy, but because they are hard, because that goal will serve to organize and measure the best of our energies and skills, because that challenge is one that we are willing to accept, one we are unwilling to postpone, and one which we intend to win."

This vision—among the most powerful in presidential history—was clear: Americans will walk on the moon before the end of the decade. It was bold—by the end of 1961, the longest an American had spent in space was about fifteen minutes, when Alan Shepard had blasted off from Cape Canaveral aboard *Freedom 7*, and only about six months before this address, John Glenn became the first person to orbit the earth. This new vision was inspiring, and it brought most Americans together. And on July 20, 1969, with one small step for man, President Kennedy's vision became a reality when Neil Armstrong and Buzz Aldrin stepped onto the moon. In just seven years, we substantially advanced our ability to explore space.

Vision is different from core purpose. While purpose is about why we exist, vision, in its most basic form, is making sure everyone has the same understanding of the common hill we are trying to climb. I think it's worth noting that a landscape with a hill often has many hills, and if you were to say to a group of followers, "Meet me on top of the hill!" the very first question they will ask is, "Which one?" Fail to articulate that and there is a high likelihood that you will end up with different people on different hills. Thus a vision statement like this, "Our vision is to be earth's most customer-centric company; to build a place where people can come to find and discover anything they might want to buy online," is preferable to something like "become the largest online retailer."

A vision statement describes the state of things at some point in the future—ideally in tangible terms, and more ideally still, in terms that are measurable or binary. Good vision statements read like descriptive sentences, and unlike the purpose statements we reviewed a few pages ago, they are not typically action oriented. They represent an ultimate and ideal end state of the current evolutionary path your team or company is on or that you want the team to be on. The simplest mental model is to think about what you want the community, team, or company you serve to look like when it's achieved its purpose, and then describe that. A snapshot of things at some specific point in the future.

A simple exercise you could do with your team is to say, "OK, it's three years from now. The CEO is holding a party in our honor. What happened that caused them to throw this extremely expensive party?" A much more heavily used and significantly less original version of this idea is for you to tell the team that it's, say, five years from now and they are featured on the cover of *Time* magazine. Their task is to write a summary of the article, which looks backward and chronicles their achievements.

To help bring the idea to life, I've selected a handful of company vision statements below. Review the list, and in the space below, identify what they all have in common.

COMPANY NAME	ENVISIONED FUTURE
Microsoft (1985)	A computer on every desktop and in every home
Walmart (1990)	Become a $125 billion company by the year 2000
Nike (1960s)	Crush Adidas
GE (1980s)	Become #1 or #2 in every market we serve
SpaceX (current)	Enable people to live on other planets
Alzheimer's Association (current)	A world without Alzheimer's
Teach for America (current)	One day, all children in this nation will have the opportunity to attain an excellent education

Notice what these vision statements have in common. First, they all clearly describe a compelling future. Second, they are all actually quite provable, i.e., measurable or binary, with the possible exception of Nike's "Crush Adidas" vision. Even with that one, though, you could imagine Nike's leadership team defining that as a massive reduction in Adidas's market share, so even though this specific statement itself is not binary or measurable, it takes only one extra step to talk about it in measurable terms. Third, they are aspirational. As a side note, in this way, they are similar to *purpose*, and as such, I think the commonality between them is the primary reason people relentlessly mix up purpose and vision. Don't do that.

With the general concepts of a good vision statement under our belts, we can then increase our sophistication around creating and communicating a strong vision for our teams. Jim Collins, author of *Built to Last*, talks about vision in two parts. First is the envisioned future, which is a simple, clear statement that describes the end state. The statements above are "envisioned future" statements. And then he recommends a much longer "vivid description," in which you are tasked with describing that future in fine detail, painting the clearest possible picture of the future that you and the team want. I agree with him that the two in combination are at their most powerful and clearest.

When working with your team to set a vision, the first thing you need to do is decide on your time horizon. I think for teams inside companies, and for most companies themselves, two to five years is about right. Tangibly—measurably—describe the state of your team, your company, or the world that you want in that time frame, and then focus everything you have toward achieving that. If the vision is big and audacious enough, you will easily be able to set goals that build up to it.

Take Walmart's vision to become a $125 billion company by

2000. For example's sake, let's say they set that vision in 1997, and let's also say they were a $100 billion company at that time. Well, if I were in their shoes, I might have set milestone targets for 1998 and 1999 that would get the company to $125 billion by 2000—perhaps $106 billion in 1998 and $115 billion in 1999, etc. Conceptually, this would be the process for any team or company. Describe the future you want, and then build the path to get there. Think, organize, and invest in strict alignment with that envisioned future.

Let's imagine an HR organization's vision. The envisioned future might be something like "happy, high-performing teams." In order, then, to construct a robust vivid description, we then might break it down into two parts.

1. Happy
2. High-Performing

In each section, we say exactly what we mean by Happy and High-Performing. For *Happy,* we can describe a future in which engagement (note to employee engagement Subject Matter Experts [SMEs] across the globe: this is a measurement, not a goal!) is market leading; a plurality of our employees report a sense of fairness, equity, inclusion, and belonging; and we have goals around our employees being vocal, public ambassadors for the company. We also set employee experience goals to move toward market leadership with two main ideas: we design, implement, measure, and improve the employee experience across the full life cycle—from candidate through alum—and we move from a quarterly cadence to continuous listening, or real-time listening. Each of these, importantly, is measurable.

Under *High-Performing,* we might set goals around manager effectiveness (ME), since we know that good leadership will most likely produce higher engagement and better results and

ME is somewhat in our control. We should also use the company vision statement, which might have a revenue and employee count goal, and then sign up to help the company beat the implied revenue productivity goal therein. For example, if the revenue goal was $100 million and the employee count goal was one hundred people, that implies productivity of $1 million per employee. As an HR team, we should be able to raise that revenue productivity by improving the employee experience through our core 3→E↔R strategy. This helps us and the organization better understand the economic value of affecting the employee experience. We could boldly say, "We'll own the delta between what is planned and what it could be."

The thing I'd like you to take away from this is that the envisioned future of *happy, high-performing teams* can easily be seen as arbitrary, capricious, words on a page—a bunch of bullshit, in other words. Someone could easily argue the yawn-inducing notion of "What does happy mean, anyway?" Importantly, we defined exactly what we meant by those ideas so we can hold ourselves accountable and own and explain our vision to our teams and cross-functional partners.

As noted above, in my experience, a lot of managers believe purpose and vision are something only the CEO does for the company. "Zuckerberg does vision, not me." I would challenge you to think differently and consider these two ideas as critical hygiene for any operating team. Also, don't allow yourself to get stuck on the semantics of mission, purpose, and vision. It's pointless and a huge waste of time. Purpose addresses the "why," and vision addresses "where we're going." Simplify and roll on. Jim Collins refers to the combination of purpose and vision as the "Core Ideology."

I've been through this exercise a few times, and without exception I've always had to gently drag skeptical people through it. I myself was doubtful when Brian Marquardt, one of my direct reports, suggested we do this for my seven-hundred-person team back in the Google days. I've been through it as a leader of an organization in need of both a purpose and vision, and I've been through it as a facilitator to help teams develop their own purposes and visions. The number of times I've seen leadership teams assemble with near certainty that they will all be on the same page only to discover that all of them are on rather different pages—and in some cases not even in the same library—is too many to count. If the leaders are not on the same page, what chance is there that the employees will be? How likely is it that they will understand what is expected of them? How can we lament folks not demonstrating a long-term ownership disposition if they don't know what we expect from them over the long run? Purpose and vision ultimately serve as the invisible leader, providing direction and guidance in the absence of specific direction and guidance. Even if they are only used a few times a year for that reason and, perhaps, during a semiannual or annual accountability session, they will have provided a valuable service for your organization.

6

Plan the Route: OKRs—Objectives and Key Results

OKRs, or Objectives and Key Results—a straightforward goal-setting system—is one of those topics that has been written about aplenty. There are two major sources that I recommend regarding OKRs. First, *Measure What Matters*, a book by venture capitalist John Doerr, is as close to the source of truth about this practice as there is. Second, Betterworks is a Silicon Valley company that builds software to help organizations develop and manage their OKRs in an aligned way, top to bottom. I don't have an opinion about their software, but their blog and the "resources" section of their website are exceptional! My task in these pages is to provide you with enough information about OKRs that you can get going with them and see how they fit into a broader framework for determining expectations, but not so much that I've rewritten *Measure What Matters* or Betterworks's mountain of content. If you want to dig deeper, you know where to go.

OKRs are a goal-setting system, and are composed of two major parts—an objective, and then underneath each objective, one or more key results. Ideally, the company develops its top-level OKRs first, and then various levels of management develop their OKRs to align to the company's. Ultimately, each individual in the company should have OKRs that explicitly link up to the company's top-level objectives. When they're done well, your teammates will never say, "I don't really understand how my work connects to the big picture."

OKRs serve both individual and organizational goals. First, they help focus and align effort around top company targets. Second, if done well and revisited frequently, they allow individuals to report real-time progress on aligned goals. Third, they provide a basis for productive coaching. When we say that a manager's job is to deliver an aligned result and enable the success of the people on their teams, the foundational idea beneath the aligned result is the OKR. That OKR invariably offers the manager a chance to enable greater success because it frequently reveals the need for a coaching intervention to improve, and it also reveals an opportunity to specifically call out great work by focusing on the things people should continue doing. Fourth, OKRs allow us to connect our purpose and vision directly to our work each quarter, each week, and each day. If our OKRs are not a function of our vision and purpose, then something is off. Either the long-term elements, purpose and vision, are not right or the OKR is disjointed from the long-term goals of the team or company. Last, OKRs offer us an opportunity to coordinate across functions more effectively and to communicate to coworkers what the heck we're doing and what we believe to be most important. This is valuable information for our partner teams to have when they, for example, want to reach out to help us with a project or to work on one of their goals. Now if we agree to help, or if we decline, we are not doing so for arbitrary reasons.

Most often, OKRs are set on a quarterly basis. You call your shot at the beginning of the quarter, check in regularly on progress over the subsequent thirteen weeks, and when the quarter closes, you grade yourself or your organization. Of course, you can set them on a multiquarter or annual basis as well. It's common, in fact, for some objectives to last for a year or more. The key here is to communicate exactly what you want to get done and when you want to get it done by. The overwhelming majority of OKRs should be set and checked on a quarterly basis, because that's the cadence most companies operate by, and those thirteen-week chunks of time tend to be both large enough to get meaningful things done and small enough to allow for course correction if success is still very far away.

To understand OKRs well, we must divide them into their constituent parts: the objective and the key result. Objectives, roughly, tend to be expressions of what we'd like to get done, using more common language. Carrying through the HR organization's example from above, an objective might be to "improve the [XYZ Corp] employee experience" or "advance our vision to be a diverse, equitable, and inclusive company." Objectives are often ambitious and significant, and they should be aligned not only to company, departmental, and cross-functional goals but also to the group's vision and purpose.

A key result (KR) describes how the team or individual will achieve the objective or how the team or individual will measure success. KRs should be measurable or binary, with the ability to clearly and unambiguously determine success or failure. They should also include a deadline. Example KRs that might support the objective "improve the [XYZ Corp] employee experience" include:

- shipping the new employee engagement survey by September 14
- raising manager effectiveness score from 83 percent to 86 percent this year
- making at least one major investment in passive and continuous listening mechanisms by the end of Q2 to more fre-

quently hear employees' needs and to act more relevantly to address them

- identifying five Moments That Matter, designing three of them using the employee-experience-journey map template, and implementing one by the end of the quarter

Example KRs that might support the objective "advance our vision to be a diverse, equitable, and inclusive company" might include:

- ensuring that by the end of the quarter, 40 percent of our total staff is from underrepresented groups
- determining, by using our own analytics and a third party, whether we have a gender pay gap, and if so, developing an action plan to close it
- closing the inclusion experience gap between majority and underrepresented groups from 12 percent to 6 percent by the end of the year

This is what calling your shot is all about. "Here's what we need to get done, here's how we'll measure it, and here's when it will be complete." Remember that most companies at their highest level are tasked with calling their shot every quarter. Public companies do this as a matter of routine. If you consider for a moment that the performance of a company is nothing more and nothing less than the accumulation of the performance of each person and team within it, then it seems reasonable that the company's ability to predict results depends on the people within the company first predicting theirs. Those predictions—from individual to company—must explicitly align. OKRs are one of the best tools to make that happen.

* * *

Here are some of the gotchas and pitfalls that I've seen over and over with OKRs:

1. **Arms race**—People incorrectly assume that because some colleague across the aisle has forty-seven OKRs, they also need to show a large volume of stuff. I once had a direct report who really struggled with focus. When he felt me pressuring him on his performance related to a few business outcomes, his threat-based response was to show me approximately twenty OKRs. Exactly zero of them articulated and called the shot on the only two business outcomes we cared about. I asked him to write two good ones and delete the rest.
2. **Ambiguous determination of success or failure**—A bad OKR leaves us without crystal clarity on exactly how we will measure or identify success. For some, this ambiguity is designed to dodge accountability. If there isn't clarity about the shot we're calling now, we might have a better chance to revise history at the end of the quarter and shape things to look like we succeeded. Call your shot clearly, and if you miss, make the conversation about what you learned in the process and how you're going to lace 'em up and try again. An example might be, "Close most of my large deals," which is significantly less clear than, "By end of quarter, close my three largest deals (company 1, company 2, company 3) in the pipeline." If you are wondering how to jumpstart a culture of accountability, then clear and unapologetic ex ante articulation of success or failure is the way; OKRs are your best tool to do this.
3. **Input oriented**—"Make a plan" and "collaborate with Taylor's team" and "meet with Gina" and "continue to help on the finance project" are inputs rather than meaningful business results. Allowing their use in OKRs is one sure path to mediocrity. If you want to annotate your OKRs to identify

some of the inputs that are required to achieve them, or if you want visibility, no problem. Just do not permit the OKR itself to be an input versus an output. In our land-navigation metaphor, "walk fast" or "shoot a good azimuth" are not useful phrases. "Reach 40.708475,-74.010846 by 2:30 P.M.," on the other hand, is clear as a bell.

4. **Esoteric Language**—Remember that OKRs serve a few purposes, and one of them is being able to communicate to interested stakeholders, such as your boss, complementary teams, or your larger organization, what the heck you're doing. Unexplained or esoteric language makes it hard for them to understand your goals. The use of esoteric language can be a problem because it can make your goals inaccessible to other stakeholders not quite as familiar with your work as you are. In order to do better, you have to try to empathize with other teams that might be trying to understand what you are doing. To keep suborganizations coordinated and linked, it's important that they clearly and simply communicate their planned objectives and measurable results.

OKRs are one of the most powerful tools for helping individuals clarify their own goals and the work required to get those things done. Remember that it is impossible to be clear with others about what you are trying to do if you are not first clear with yourself. Recall Chuck Besecker's prescription. First, know what you expect, and then tell others what you expect. This same standard applies for the people on your teams. It's only after the individuals, their managers, and their adjacent teams are crystal clear on what each expects to deliver that we can introduce a fancy word like *alignment*. If you find yourself or your company struggling to achieve this frequently elusive ghost, you can take a giant chunk out of that problem by carefully developing, syndicating, and communicating your own OKRs as well as your team's.

7

Navigate to the Destination: Ruthless Prioritization

Prioritization is an exercise in subtraction, not addition. In this four-part Direction framework, I define priorities as daily or weekly expressions of work, which should support and enable the larger expressions of work such as OKRs and the group's vision. We don't need to call quarterly expressions of work "priorities," for example, because we already have a word for those: OKRs!

How many times have you heard some version of the notion, "Do a tiny number of things really well"? How much do people talk about the need for focus and the dangers of trying to do too much? I hear these things constantly, and yet I constantly see people trying to do way too much. In the tech companies that I've worked for, we've tended to hire armies of Lisa Simpsons—people who are capable of and interested in thinking about and impacting a wide range of problems on behalf of the company. On top of that, subcultures at these companies—at best implicitly and at worst explicitly—value work volume. Legendary record producer Rick Rubin said, "Time invested making the work is irrelevant. The only criteria for evaluation is, 'Is it great?'" How many times have we seen plaudits for "nights and weekends" or "countless hours"? Wrong message! It is not the volume of work that matters.

Now, I want to clarify this point a bit because I think older-school skeptics may hear a couple of things I don't mean. First, of course it's the case that people will need to surge from time to time, say, during a tight client deadline, while planning a huge company event, or at the end-of-quarter push for the sales, legal, and accounts receivable departments. The HR teams might need to surge—and work a shit-ton of hours, let's say—around performance management season. A company might need to act quickly in response to a new market condition, like so many companies did around the COVID-19 pandemic. These all represent moments in which we might ask and expect folks to work hours beyond the norm. The problem I see far too often is that the surge becomes business as usual, which to me signals a lack of focus and planning. We used to say in the Marines, "Failure to plan on your part does not constitute an emergency on my part." The second thing I don't want old-school people to hear me say is some version of "Hard work doesn't matter." It absolutely matters. So, if you're reading this and thinking I'm saying something else, please reread this. We need to work hard, and heck, most of us *want* to work hard, but we need to work smarter to maximize and sustain impact.

People love, love, love to talk about how busy they are. Heck, I see people one-upping each other on their busyness like it's some kind of status symbol. "For once, I'd like to hear someone brag about their excellent time management skills, rather than complain about how much they can't get done," wrote Meredith Fineman in a 2013 *Harvard Business Review* article titled, "Please Stop Complaining About How Busy You Are." Hey Meredith, I am about to grant your wish.

When I was graduating from business school in 2005, I interviewed with a number of consulting firms: McKinsey, Bain,

Accenture, etc. Those were really my "if I don't get a job at Google" backup plans. I didn't really know what I wanted to be, and the best place to get a job when you don't know what you want to be, I reasoned, is in consulting.

The horrific hours in consulting and investment banking are well-documented, and as I was getting swept up in the interview process, my wife, "V" as she is known to most, stopped me one evening and asked, "So, now that you have this fancy degree" (that was dripping with sarcasm), "does this mean we're not going to see you anymore?" We had two kids with a third on the way. We talked things through, and I made a promise right then. "I will never let my career get in the way of being a good dad." More than that, I said I would be willing to stop my career dead in its tracks if I reached a point when the expected or needed time commitment was no longer compatible with showing up for my family. That was the deal, and a funny thing happened because of it. I learned to be an exceptional time manager and an excellent prioritizer. My career has never required a halt or a pause as a result of competing demands because I have become good at saying no—even in difficult contexts, like when the boss or boss's boss has strong opinions about what I should be doing. I have become really good at subtracting work that doesn't matter. Crazily enough, this simple practice, inspired by the simple idea of having dinner with my family, has led me to have much greater success than I could have ever imagined.

In 2008, I successfully recruited Archana Gilravi, a recent Wharton grad, to come work for me at Google. Archana quickly became my organization's brain, helping me keep my group's teams, processes, and investments, among many things, running on the right tracks. She was an absolute star. The only problem was that I was worried that she was working too much—she seemed to send emails at all hours of the day. In a subsequent one-to-one meeting, I broached the topic and encouraged her to subtract work. Archana never failed to deliver on the important stuff—not once—but she was also pursuing a lot of other things that just weren't as critical to me or to the operation. I offered to help her adjust her commitments and provide my perspective on what was critical and what was not. Archana is an owner through and through, and she pushed back on me hard: "No, all of those things have to be done." We chatted, debated, and argued, and, because she's about five times smarter than me, she got her way since she was, after all, doing the critical things so well.

Fast-forward a few years, and our reckoning finally arrived. Archana and her partner had a baby. Here's the thing about having a baby that all new parents learn very quickly: if you don't actively prioritize that infant's needs, you will go to jail. Suddenly you realize that those hellacious hours you were putting in at work need to change. And once you no longer have limitless hours to devote to your work, guess what you finally learn how to do? You learn how to subtract. You finally learn how to prioritize. But I would argue that most of us would live much fuller lives, and I believe we will all be much more effective in our jobs, if we learn to subtract before life makes it imperative. If you're the manager, you need to give people permission to do less. When we were in full work-from-home mode at Qualtrics as a result of the COVID pandemic, and people were redlining, CEO Zig Serafin delivered this simple message in our senior staff meeting: "You have to help people do less right now and help them focus on what really matters." Another time, just a bit later, I asked Zig, "How are you?" Instead of responding with "busy," he responded, "focused." Straight from the top, leadership by example never goes out of style.

Giving people permission to do less begins with setting a good example. If you walk around demonstrating performative workaholism by humblebragging/complaining about how you haven't had a vacation in half a year or how you always work weekends, not only are you probably terrible at managing your time but you are also likely modeling all the wrong stuff. This is leadership by (poor) example.

Instead, what great managers do is install processes to help with focus and force prioritization. Let's explore why it might be important to force prioritization. First, let's remember that many of us, like Lisa Simpson, are inclined to do too much. Second, as a guy who has consulted for thousands of companies now, I have yet to see one that's not chaotic in one form or another. So the problem lies in the combination of those two factors: there is just too much to do, and we are the kind of people who just might try to do it all. On top of that, prioritization is actually quite difficult. It is a very taxing prefrontal cortex–intensive process that takes a ton of mental energy. As such, we seek to avoid it if given the chance. It's for this reason that David Rock says in *Your Brain at Work* that you must "prioritize prioritizing." It's a silly little phrase, but if you're not forcing yourself and others to do it, you will often skip it. The leader needs to set the simple expectation that (1) we will prioritize at least every week in alignment with our goals and (2) our prioritization will be focused on a very small number of very important things.

A couple simple practices I've seen work. First, Qualtrics asks each employee to write "snippets" each Monday morning, and we further ask them to subordinate their snippets to their OKRs. In fact, as you write your snippets, the company's goal-setting platform will prompt you with, "Which OKR do you want to prioritize?" The snippets are meant to be very few in number—ideally no more than three to five—and are intended to reflect your priorities for the upcoming week. *Priorities are not a task list.* Consider this inequality: 3>2>4—"three is greater than two is greater than four" when read aloud—which is a handy way to say, "If you have more than three priorities, you have none." For me, I think about my week and try to identify the top three things I must get done, and then I try to tackle those things as quickly as possible. For transparency and coordination, the snippets at Qualtrics are also published. The entire company, for example, can see the CEO's and the CEO's staff's snippets for the week.

A second practice I love is the daily standup meeting. An outgrowth of agile software development practice, it's a short meeting—ideally fifteen minutes—where everyone stands up and articulates their priorities for that day. The idea is that if people don't get too comfortable, because they are literally standing up, the meeting will end more quickly. As a part of adjusting to a 100 percent work-from-home world during the COVID-19 pandemic, my team started using Slack for this. Each morning at 8:30, the Slackbot automatically prompted us with this question: "What are you working on today?" Then each of my direct reports and I highlighted our top priorities for that day. One small point here. You should really enforce a limit of three priorities for a day. The reason is because, duh, 3>2>4, but also because you don't want these practices to become the same arms race that I warned about in the OKRs section above. "Well, I see Alexis had five priorities yesterday, so I better show six today." If everyone is playing by the same rules, we can help ourselves by not turning priorities into task lists and falling into the same old trap of trying to do too much, most of which just doesn't matter.

In the end, prioritization is about saying no. We must all learn to say no, and we must learn to say no politely. I've coached folks on how to do this well, and I'd like to share a couple of key ideas. First, saying no politely means actually hearing out the request. I think it's best to evaluate a request in person or on Zoom (rather than email or text). The primary reason for this is because it's possible you should actually be saying yes. You can't know what your response should be unless you carefully evaluate the request. Let's assume, though, that you are managing a carefully developed, impactful agenda, and folks are coming to you with requests that are more tangential or disruptive or have less of an impact than the priorities you've already delineated. Once you evaluate the ask, it's important to explain your current priorities and goals and why it would be difficult to splice this new request into the team's workload. Heck, I even think a little apology is helpful. "I am really sorry, James, but it will be very difficult for me to help out with this request given our workload and the expectations for delivery that my boss, team, and I have set." If the requester is still persistent, offer a clean escalation path. "I'll tell you what, James. I don't think this should supplant one of my existing projects but if you want to grab your boss, I'll grab mine, and the four of us can talk through what I can possibly take off my team's punchlist to make room for this request." Finally, thank them for bringing the idea forward and consider setting an expectation for the future. "James, thanks for bringing this to my attention. Even though we're not going to get to it now, let's regroup for next quarter and see if it makes sense then for us to pursue it together."

Remember that prioritization is an exercise in subtraction, not addition. Avoid making task lists, and develop a very small number of true priorities for each day and each week. Block out interruptions and disruptions the best you can while you tackle these crucial things. Last, make sure your priorities are 100 percent a function of your OKRs. If they are not, it is fair to question whether that thing should be a priority or whether your OKRs are as good as they should be. Bottom line is that there should always be a clear relationship between the work a person does each day and the goals they have set for themselves for the quarter.

MAKING IT ALL WORK TOGETHER

I developed this Direction framework—purpose, vision, OKRs, and priorities—because it provides a set of coherent parent-child relationships that allows you to simultaneously think about long-range and the shortest-range direction in an aligned way. In the simplest terms:

- My team's purpose is a function of the company's purpose and my boss's team's purpose, et al.
- My team's vision is a function of my team's purpose and the higher organization's vision.
- My team's OKRs are a function of my team's vision and the higher organization's OKRs.
- My team and individual priorities are a function of my team's OKRs.

Here's an image to help illustrate the relationships:

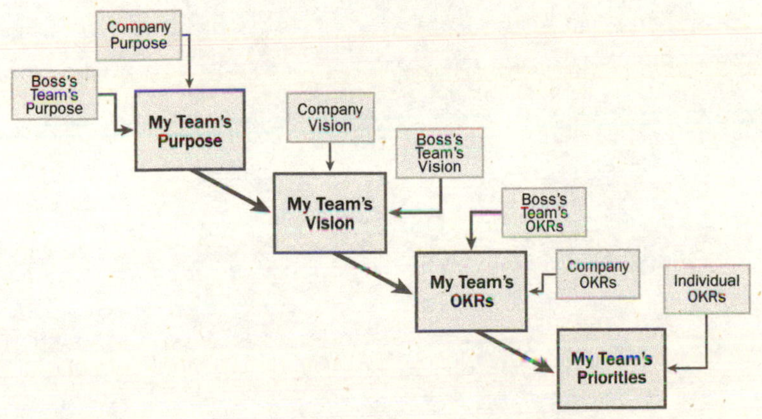

Zig Serafin, CEO of Qualtrics, summed this up well in August 2021. He was participating in a leadership series sponsored by one of our senior sales executives. Zig was asked a question from a frontline sales manager (I've paraphrased it here): "We're moving fast, growing fast, and leading a category we created, and sometimes things are very chaotic. What's your advice for how to lead in that environment?" Zig responded, "Your job as a leader is to create clarity of expectations and to be a simplifier." I couldn't have said it better: we can truly help our people find the most success by helping them focus on the few things that really matter.

PART III

Coaching

- *How frequently does your manager solicit feedback from you?*
- *How consistently does your manager provide you with specific praise for good work?*
- *How helpful is the feedback provided by your manager in improving your performance?*
- *How responsive is your manager to your ideas or concerns?*
- *How comfortable do you feel going to your manager with a safety concern, no matter how small?*
- *How much do you agree with the following statement: "My manager cares about me as a human being"?*

A Few Words on Words

Feedback. Guidance. Coaching. There are a lot of words we can use to describe this activity of helping folks get better. For some, "feedback" feels screechy, like noise-producing radio frequencies piercing one's eardrum. Some prefer "guidance" because that feels less authoritarian, like adherence to the input is more directional versus overly specific and prescriptive. For others, guidance feels paternalistic or even dogmatic, evoking a voice-of-God feeling, rather than something that allows them to take the advice as malleable or optional.

I prefer "coaching." Coaching, particularly in athletics, is where criticism of performance lives and breathes with minimal defensiveness. To me, it feels energetic and frequent and is understood to be about only one thing: getting better. But if you don't have much athletic experience or your coaches were jerks, then you might feel revulsion at the thought of receiving coaching. In what follows, I'll use these words interchangeably. You should use what makes you comfortable. All of them get at the same thing, which is enabling folks to be more successful.

8

Improve

In the fall of 1997, I was the company commander for Alpha Company, 1st Battalion, 5th Marine Regiment in Camp Pendleton, California. There is no better job in the Marine Corps than being a company commander. With about 175 combat marines, the company is the elemental combat operating unit of amphibious warfare—one of the chess pieces that generals move around the board. It's also the last time you have a shot at really knowing all of your marines. I was lucky in that I was able to command a company several years before most other officers in my peer group, well ahead of schedule.

One Friday afternoon, I secured the marines for liberty. Some might find it interesting that while it is not unusual for the marines to "have the weekends off," that time off is formally granted only after a few things have been confirmed. For example, I needed a call from my armorer saying that every single rifle and piece of serialized gear—from rocket launchers to night vision goggles—were visually accounted for. Typically, after the thumbs-up from the armory, I would hold a formation and give the marines a verbal safety brief, in which I would hammer them on the dangers of consuming too much alcohol, paying particular attention to the danger they might present to themselves and others if they drove under the influence. In short, I would tell them to be smart. Once I secured them on liberty, they would head off to Newport Beach, Las Vegas, Los Angeles, San Diego, and Tijuana.

I was one or two soda pops into my Friday night when I received a phone call from the officer of the day. Battalion officers rotated, taking about one turn each month, to stay inside the battalion headquarters overnight and be the first line of defense should anything happen, whether it's North Korea invading South Korea or a marine's relative getting injured in an accident. The officer of the day was expected to receive that call, triage the situation, and inform whoever needed to be informed.

The officer of the day (OOD) said to me: "Sir, we have a problem."

"Hit me," I responded.

He said, "One of your marines is in jail."

"Well that's pretty bad—what did he do?"

"He got drunk and punched a police officer," said the OOD.

I said, "Well okay, we have to go get him. Where is he?"

"He's in Mexico, sir."

Big f-bomb.

This presented a lot of problems, and not just for the marine but for every commander up my chain, including the general in charge of Camp Pendleton. It sounds funny to say, but this marine had created an international incident. Not one that could in any way provoke a war but one that was particularly sensitive given the tense relationships that military bases sometimes have with their neighboring communities. Marines, nicknamed "Devil Dogs" by the Germans in World War I, I'm sad to report, don't always behave exactly as we might like them to.

The OOD is armed, but he and the assistant officer of the

day—a senior noncommissioned officer—had to drive a white government van to Mexico to get our misbehaving Devil Dog, which meant they had to check their weapons back into the armory. My whole weekend was consumed with investigating so that I could make a recommendation to my boss, Lieutenant Colonel John Boggs, the battalion commander, about the punishment that should be meted out to this marine on Monday morning. Lieutenant Colonel Boggs had a few punishments available, with limitations on their severity prescribed by the Uniform Code of Military Justice (UCMJ). For example, he could demote the marine, he could suspend pay, and he could place the marine on barracks restriction—meaning no liberty for several weeks. Based on my findings, I decided to recommend the maximum punishment.

On Monday morning, I got the phone call to head up to battalion headquarters to meet with the colonel. I was expecting a customary meeting—a few stakeholders in a horseshoe around the colonel's desk, the battalion sergeant major, the officer of the day, and just a couple of others. These meetings were normally lightning fast. Then we would quickly gather up the marine so he could face his NJP, or nonjudicial punishment.

When I showed up to Colonel Boggs's office, I thought maybe I was early. No one else was there. The door was closed, and I was pretty sure it was just the sergeant major and the colonel talking in the office. Sergeant Major Scott walked out, acknowledged me, and said, "You can head on in, sir."

I walked in, and the colonel told me to close the door behind me. This was usually accompanied by "and have a seat," but not today. Today he wanted me standing. His first question seemed easy enough. "Captain Laraway, what's going on over there in Alpha Company?"

I was legitimately confused, not only by this question, but by the now obvious departure from normal process. I tried to read into the meaning, and responded, "Well sir, the marines are pretty worried about what's gonna happen here. As you know, Corporal Smith [not his real name] is a good marine and a popular one, and they all know he stepped in it pretty bad." The colonel was obviously dissatisfied with my answer, so he asked again, this time emphasizing the words *going on,* as if that would jar my understanding loose. I gave another clearly bad answer, and the colonel paused, realizing this roundabout method was not taking us where he wanted us to go, and then he levied this beauty.

"Captain Laraway, what I want to know is why your leadership is *so weak* that your marine thought it was okay to go to Tijuana, get drunk, and punch a *Federale* in the jaw." The average reader might not realize that the most competitive specialty among Marine Corps officers is infantry. Not fighter jets, not helicopters, not tanks, not artillery. Grunts. The reason it's the most competitive specialty is because it's not only the heart and soul of the Marine Corps—every other specialty exists to support the grunts—but because the infantry is the place you are most likely to get the greatest leadership challenges both immediately and for years to come. How you get chosen, of course, is based on your leadership disposition. I graduated Officer Basic School right around the top 10 percent of my class and was in the top 3 or 4 percent in leadership grading. I was put into the infantry—my first choice—because of my leadership skills, and I can assure you that there is no greater feedback thump available than to have a battalion commander, and especially one that I respected and admired so much, challenge the relative strength of my leadership capabilities.

Now, Lieutenant Colonel Boggs and I had a good relationship. Remember when I said that I was given company command several years ahead of others in my peer group? Colonel Boggs is the one who made that happen. He considered me one of his best officers, and I knew that, which made this gut punch even harder to absorb.

I left not fully convinced that this challenge was fair. After all, wasn't this marine a full-grown adult? Hadn't I given the safety brief? Didn't he make his own decision to drive to Tijuana, drink too much, and then misbehave? Did the extenuating circumstances matter—like the fact that the Mexican police officer had tried to force Corporal Smith's fiancée to give him her engagement ring to avoid some bullshit trumped-up charges?

And then it hit me. *I am responsible for everything*—everything—*that this organization does or fails to do.* Including this. Michael Jackson would have been very disappointed, because I had been looking for answers everywhere but in the mirror. Once you evacuate the victim's headspace and move into the player's headspace, you start to ask, "What could I have done differently to prevent this?" And of course, it hit me.

My safety brief.

I had been mailing in that safety brief every week. I checked the box and said the same boring crap over and over. Now you tell me—this is a group of nineteen-, twenty-, twenty-one-year-old people, and I am the only thing between them and Vegas and LA and Mexico. What do you think they heard each week? I will tell you. They heard WAH WAH WAH WAH WAH, just like Charlie Brown's teacher. I needed to use a lot more creativity to make sure that there was no gap between what was said, what was meant, what was heard, and then what actually happened.

I managed to get in contact with an old-time marine who had won the Medal of Honor. He lived close to the base, and I knew his story a little, which tragically included injuries related to a post-service DUI accident that had left him wheelchair bound. I asked him if he might be open to delivering a safety brief to my marines and then staying for a while afterward to do a bit of a fireside chat—just him and the marines—so they could hear his stories, both the heroic and the tragic. He agreed, and that day, not one marine raced off to Vegas, Los Angeles, or Mexico when I secured them for liberty. Every one of them stayed to engage with this man.

One thread runs from the Marines through every step of my career. When something bad happens off hours and it is employee related, the first sentence of the investigation usually highlights that alcohol was involved. But I am proud to say that for the remainder of my tenure—about eight months—as company commander for Alpha 1/5, we had zero of those alcohol-related incidents. I really was responsible for everything my group did or failed to do, and Colonel Boggs's tough-as-nails feedback made me see that.

TOUGH FEEDBACK AND THE BRAIN

Before we dive into this, I think it's important to understand, in the most basic terms possible, why it's so hard to give and receive feedback. I'm not a big believer in universal truths, but our resistance to coaching is so systematic, it's only natural to wonder why. Perhaps unsurprisingly, it comes back to some pretty basic physiology, so it's more of a nature and less of a nurture issue, though both play a role. I think it's important to understand the underlying physiological reality to better understand why it's so hard to give and get feedback.

The brain is well known to be a complex organ, regarded by some as one of the last remaining frontiers—space, the oceans, the brain. For our purposes here, it can be broken down into two major parts.

Composed loosely of the brainstem and the amygdala and located toward the back of the skull, the limbic system controls emotion. In evolutionary terms, it's the oldest part of the brain, which is why it's sometimes called the "lizard brain." This part of the brain is very large and very strong. It's extremely efficient in processing resources such as glucose and oxygen. This is where the fight-or-flight mechanism lives and, in the context of feedback, where threat response and defensiveness lurk—for everyone.

The second part of the brain is the prefrontal cortex, located in the front of the brain, just behind the forehead. It's young, small, relatively weak, and not as efficient in processing glucose and oxygen. This is where logic, reason, curiosity, and problem-solving live.

Most interesting, though, is the interplay between these two parts of the brain. Simply, there really isn't any. They don't work at the same time. The limbic system switches on instantly when confronted with an emotional stimulus, and most often, in the context of feedback, that stimulus tends to be a perceived threat. The prefrontal cortex requires a lot of energy to engage. So if there is a hint of a threat, these two parts of the brain not only are instantly at odds with each other but are not even on an equal playing field, because the lizard brain—older, stronger, more efficient—bathes the rest of the brain, including the prefrontal cortex, in chemicals that actively interfere with its ability to operate. One is the elephant, and the other is the rider.

If you've ever heard someone say, "I was so mad I couldn't think," they will have described very well the reality of the way these two systems work together—or more accurately don't work together.

From an evolutionary standpoint, this makes complete sense. For millions of years, those of our species that survived were the ones who ran. Humans, as individuals, are not particularly worthy adversaries against nature. In relative terms, we're not fast, we're not strong, and our senses are not particularly well tuned to see, hear, or smell threats. Our species has survived because over the course of millions of years, by and large, when we encountered something "different," we did not stand there and consider it. "Oh, my, what a beautiful tiger. I'd quite like to study its behav . . ." *gulp*. That genetic line is over. We instinctively processed threats, and we bolted.

In the modern workplace, this "running from stuff that is different" idea has two major implications. First, this is the essence of bias. See something different, run. This is why indicating that someone is exercising bias shouldn't be an insult. This is why, 100 percent of the time, when someone says "I'm completely unbiased here," they are full of shit. To have bias is to be human. The best we can do is try to raise our consciousness about it and install practices and processes that help us control it. The second major implication is that we have a very high-functioning hindbrain, lizard brain, reptilian brain. And because our jobs are so important to us, our hindbrain works overtime to protect us. There's a lot riding on our jobs and how we perform in the workplace. Thinking about Maslow's hierarchy of needs, for example, all five levels can be at least partially fulfilled by a successful career. This is why so many things incite fight-or-flight responses at work. Feedback, guidance, coaching should be about helping people be more successful. But sometimes that means calling out what should be better, which the receiver of feedback can easily interpret as "where I'm failing." And that is an idea that is likely to inspire a threat response.

Because of all of this, the most common reaction to hard feedback is defensiveness. We've been taught over the years, incorrectly, that a defensive reaction to feedback indicates we have thin skin. I don't think this is the case. Having a defensive reaction to feedback means only one thing: that we are human. Recognizing that a defensive reaction only indicates our humanity does not excuse blowing up, yelling, not listening, shutting down, or other inappropriate kinds of behavior. But at least we can understand that in the overwhelming majority of cases, when someone receives improvement feedback, it is very likely to inspire at least a silent and invisible defensive reaction—and oftentimes, as so many of us have directly experienced, a visible one.

Further, those of us who are in a position to give feedback—effectively all of us—have also been in the position of receiving it. Even though we don't want to admit it because the world has taught us not to be so darn thin-skinned, the reality is that we know that improvement-oriented coaching can feel crappy and threatening. What happens, then, is that those of us who should be giving feedback often don't. We don't do it for two major reasons, one selfless and one selfish.

The selfless reason is the idea that "I don't want to make you feel bad." Psychopaths aside, most of us have some degree of empathy, which means we can put ourselves in others' shoes and perhaps relate to feeling threatened and defensive when we get improvement feedback. The selfish reason is simply "I don't want to deal with your emotional response." Crying, yelling, dejection, pushback, arguing, the silent treatment, contempt, misdirection. It's taxing to take all of that on, but of course it's tough shit, because it is also your job as a manager, coach, friend, and colleague to do just that.

Both reasons must be overcome because the coaching must happen, and coaching won't work until they are overcome. We have an obligation to help others succeed, and feedback is the cheapest and most convenient tool in our kit. Let's remember that the purpose of coaching people up is to help them be more successful, and critical feedback highlights things folks can do better. It's a critical vector to increase success, even if it does inspire negative emotion.

CHALLENGING PEOPLE TO PERFORM BETTER

While there are no silver bullets that make improvement feedback easier, there are ways to take some of the sting out. I find that the basic idea of challenging people—because I think people like a challenge—is one such path.

Challenging people is a critical idea in Liz Wiseman's *Multipliers*. A Multiplier, as she describes it, is a leader who gets as much as two times more—more intelligence, more output, more productivity—than average from their teams. A Diminisher, by contrast, gets half as much from their teams. A key theme throughout the book is that it's often pretty uncomfortable working for a Multiplier, no picnic, but what those who worked for them said most frequently was that "my manager challenged me to do more/better than I thought I could."

There's a parallel insight that comes from sales. When the economy tanked in 2009, some salespeople somehow continued to exceed their targets. Brent Adamson and Matthew Dixon, authors of the book *The Challenger Sale*, wanted to know why that was. Through their research, they developed a handful of personas: the Lone Wolf, the Relationship Builder, the Reactive Problem Solver, the Hard Worker, and the Challenger. When they compared average performers and star performers, they discovered that average performers were spread across all five profiles. But 40 percent of star performers (those that fell into the top 20 percent of their sales orgs as measured by performance to goal) were Challengers. Even more interesting, the smallest concentration of star performers was Relationship Builders, at just 7 percent. I've always found this insight to be powerful and comforting for two reasons. The first is that so many of us have been led to believe that "sales is all about relationships." These findings directly refute that conventional wisdom. Thankfully, gone are the days when a single "sales guy" could take a buyer out for a game of golf, a steak dinner, some time at the bar, and ultimately a trip to the "gentlemen's club" and get the deal. Modern buying involves multiple people with varying perspectives and goals, people who are just trying to be successful, and they're not interested in wasting a bunch of time playing golf. The Challenger persona brings insights to the table instead, making folks smarter, fueling them with the knowledge they need to be more successful. They challenge the buying team's individual worldviews as they teach them, tailor their message to each buying team member's context, and take control of the complex buying process within that particular company. It's little wonder that these folks continued to thrive through an economic downturn.

Like Multipliers on the management side, their aim is to make people smarter and better, not necessarily liked. As I've heard Jared Smith, cofounder of Qualtrics, and Dick Costolo, former CEO of Twitter and partner at 01A, each say more times than I can count, "Managers who are trying to be liked create misery."

Robert Greenleaf, author of *The Servant as Leader*, wrote, "Great leaders . . . may have gruff, demanding, uncompromising exteriors. But deep down inside the great ones have empathy and an unqualified acceptance of the persons who go with their leadership." Demanding, uncompromising. "Emerging, a pattern is!" (Yoda, probably.)

Radical Candor, closest to my heart among all of these sources, features two key ideas as perpendicular axes on a two-by-two grid. The first is Challenge Directly, and the second, Care Personally. The theory suggests that when you do both, most specifically in the context of delivering guidance to team members, you have achieved Radical Candor, or according to the second edition, Compassionate Candor.

The list of sources that suggest challenging people to do more than they thought possible is endless. As a leader, you are tasked with making sure each team member is pursuing an aligned result. With that then secure, your job is to throw every ounce of energy into enabling the success of each person on the team. For them to be better, you must challenge them to do more than they ever thought they could. In chapter 12, I will give some tips for doing this well.

9

Continue

Improvement is one critical form of coaching. The other is praise, sometimes known as "*continue* coaching." We tend to think of praise primarily as a way to recognize folks, but that misses something deeper. The most important use of praise is in the spirit of helping people understand explicitly what they should continue doing. It's surprising for many of us to learn that most workers are not fully aware of what they are doing well and why. It's no wonder, though. Your working style, interpersonal approach, and method for delivering work products can vary in their efficacy depending on the team or company context in which we find ourselves. Offering praise that is delivered with the goal of helping people understand what to continue, which includes detail on why things *are* working, is a super high-leverage activity.

I learned this while coaching youth sports, one of the most rewarding experiences of my life. It had just a few downsides. There were coaches who thought their kid was getting drafted into Major League Baseball right out of tee-ball, there was favoritism toward the coach's kids, and there was a shocking amount of politics around the travel teams and all-star team, but even with all of that nonsense, coaching kids in athletics is one of life's great pleasures. One quick story on why.

When my two older sons were very little, we signed them up for YMCA Little Kickers soccer. My wife asked me if I was interested in "helping coach a team," and I said "sure," thinking it would require a small-time investment—perhaps I'd "get there when I could." It turned out that they were short on head coaches, so she just went ahead and signed me up for that. Thanks, V! After my initial mini panic attack for having to organize, attend, and teach at every practice, I realized that I just needed to buck up and do this thing. The first practice arrived, and I was pretty excited. I not only had my two older boys on the team but also the two older boys of close family friends, Jacob and Luke Neading. Jacob has always been a good athlete. Luke struggled a little bit physically at the time; as it turned out, it was because he had an undiagnosed vision problem. I'm happy to report it's been fixed for years now, but it no doubt contributed to a simple reality on the Green Dragons Little Kickers soccer team, which was that Luke was generally distracted and not fully engaged. He was a ball of enthusiasm in life, just not for soccer. He hustled and always gave the most effort of anyone on the team, but he was not going to be my Lionel Messi. To be clear, I didn't care about that, but I did care that the kids had fun and learned something. I wanted Luke to have a great experience, and it wasn't clear to me in the early going that he was.

Before trying a skill, like passing, I would first teach and demonstrate it and then let the kids practice it. We pretty much exclusively taught skills and positions—this was soccer on the small nets, so everything was very basic. To keep these six- and seven-year-olds engaged, I would ask them simple questions, choose someone who raised their hand, and then let them answer, trying to establish a simple cultural tenet that there are no wrong answers. Luke, as you might guess, never raised his hand.

And then one day he did. I was teaching the goalkeeper position. I asked the kids, "Who here knows what the goalie can do that no one else on the soccer team can do?" Of course, as almost all readers will know instantly, the answer is that the goalkeeper can use their hands. Easy. And it turns out that most of the kids also already knew that. But for the first time all season, finally, my pal Luke—who at this point I already loved like a nephew—raised his hand. And I mean *raised* it. It was the most enthusiastic hand-raising you've ever seen. Full arm and shoulder extension, hand waving back and forth pivoting around the wrist like Neo in *The Matrix* would do, positioning himself from his butt to his knees, and vocalizing a stereotypical "OOH! OOH! Pick me! Pick me!"

Yes, Luke! Finally! I got him engaged and he's into this! I could not wait to give Luke the floor, "Luke, yes, please tell all of us what it is that the goalie can do that no one else can do." *He's gonna nail this*, I thought.

Luke, with no irony and even greater enthusiasm than his wild, gesticulating hand-raising, earnestly announced to the team at the top of his lungs, "He can FLY! . . . and shoot FIRE!"

Kids, man. They're the best thing about life, and when coaching them, I got as much as I gave. I coached Little League baseball for a number of years for the Belmont Redwood Shores Little League (BRSLL). My favorite and best year was coaching the BRSLL AAA Phillies in 2016. I had been an assistant before, but this was my first year as a head coach, which was second in the hierarchy to the manager. Drew Healey was the manager, and we had successfully brought the BRSLL AA Yankees to a second-place finish the last time we coached together, just two years earlier. Drew played no favorites and shared my passion for developing the kids beyond baseball. But he was also competitive, and we both understood that the kids wanted to win. Our aim was to create a *development first, but winning matters* culture. Our kids and their parents had all enjoyed the experience with the AA Yankees, and so I was looking forward to joining forces with Drew again coaching the AAA Phillies.

Before this special season, we attended a semi-mandatory seminar delivered by the Positive Coaching Alliance. To my surprise, it turned out to be one of the best uses of a Saturday in my life. They covered a bunch of topics, but the most interesting was around praise. They guided us toward a five-to-one praise-to-criticism ratio. They were careful to say, "it's not five to zero, it's five to one" to make the point that correcting the kids was also critical to developing them. The bigger point was far more interesting, though. The reality was that the kids were doing tons more right than wrong, and that you, as a coach, needed to highlight the things they did right to give them the best chance of repeating those things. I took this to heart immediately. It just made intuitive sense to me, and so it entered "the Book."

"Coach Russ, can we do some Book!?"

While the kids practiced, I kept notes about the things they did well. I wrote down who was early and on time to practice. I wrote down who counted loudly during stretching, walking around holding my book and pencil in an exaggerated fashion so the kids knew I was documenting their behavior, effort, and technique. As they fielded ground balls, I wrote down who moved their feet instead of just reaching and who covered the ground ball in their glove with their throwing hand, etc. Then at the midpoint of practice, I'd call the kids to the infield to review what each did well, by name and relative to team standards. When talking about who was early or on time for practice, if you were not on time, your name was not called during that section of the Book. This, by the way, is so much more powerful than calling out the kids who were late. James, for example, was one of our kids that was 100 percent heart and effort, and he was routinely late to practice. He was excused because he had a conflicting piano lesson that his mom had discussed with Drew and me. James was not penalized for being late, but he was also not called out for being on time, because he was not on time. James gave his mom and dad a mountain of shit over being on time to practice. Think about that for a moment. This ten-year-old kid is pushing his parents to get him to practice on time because it's valued and rewarded. Of course we all cracked the code—he was probably just looking for an excuse to get out of piano—but the point still holds. This practice of highlighting regularly what the kids did well drove behavior better than anything I've ever seen in twenty-eight years of managing people. They knew I was watching, and they knew that if they kept their heads down, moved their feet, and covered that grounder when it got in their glove, I was not only gonna do "some Book" with them in the middle and end of practice but I was also going to write about it on the team website that night.

I suspect there is a lot of complicated psychology at play in this example, but we're laypeople, so let's agree not to overcomplicate this. The practice of keeping "the Book" forced us as coaches to articulate team standards. Counting loudly during stretching, for example, was a clearly articulated standard. As the kids' focus on counting loudly gave way to half-assing their hamstring stretches, we adjusted our praise to focus on both—proper stretching technique *and* counting loudly. Everything was on the table, from timeliness and effort to the technical standards for hitting, fielding, and running the bases. We publicly acknowledged when the kids performed up to the standards—in the moment and during "the Book"—and in doing so, we were able to constantly reiterate and reinforce those standards.

I thought about this in a work context. My first realization was that kids are nothing more and nothing less than small people.

It's tempting to think that praise is a dark art that somehow only works on kids, but I challenged myself to imagine for a minute that adults are more like kids than maybe I believed. Then I thought about other reasons leaders might not routinely and regularly give praise to their teams. I recalled that some leaders have this weird instinct to withhold praise, like somehow it will mean more when it finally comes. Some also withhold it to avoid the perception that this praise instance is somehow indicative of their judgment on total performance. Maybe someone is underperforming, for example, and it feels risky or confusing to offer them praise in a downside performance management context.

All of these are understandable, but I think they are incorrect. The most important realization I had was that most of us are not walking around firing people willy-nilly, left and right. This means, nearly by definition, that people are doing a hell of a lot more right than they are doing wrong. So, if you can get past your notions that praise is an ego stroke or something to be withheld, and you can see that it's your best, most available, lowest-cost, low-threat behavior driver, then you realize that you should use it all the time. Imagine a team culture where you hear very often, "What I loved about the way you ran that meeting . . . " or, "What surprised me about this campaign you built . . . " or, "I think the reason that customer meeting went as well as it did was because you . . ." Imagine *that* culture, which is to imagine a culture where everyone on your team loves coming to work. Put this phrase in your quiver right now: "You know what I love about X . . . ?" Use it liberally.

I think it's worth reminding you here about one of our findings at Qualtrics. You recall that our top-performing managers, by performance ratings and quota attainment, outperformed the average of each of the twelve manager effectiveness questions. But they dramatically—by double digits—outperformed the average on two questions. One of them was, *"How consis-*

tently does your manager provide you with specific praise for good work?" In a company that has outperformed its category (a category that it created), the leaders who outperform their peers dramatically outperform on this particular leadership tactic. In other words, think twice before withholding praise because of some cockamamie contrived nonsense you've come up with to justify holding back. Say it, explain it, mean it. You and your teams will perform better.

10

Coaching the Boss

FEEDBACK UP THE CHAIN

Having worked with thousands of people on how to give better feedback, I've learned that most of them need a lot of advice on giving feedback to their bosses. This can be really hard because of the real or perceived risk of giving the boss a tough message. Remember, no matter how "chill" a manager thinks they are, there will almost always be a power differential in the relationship. Managers control or influence elements that are critical for an employee's prospects and trajectory—things like pay, promotion, time off, access to new opportunities—and most people are not interested in getting on the wrong side of that equation. The best managers recognize this and seek to minimize or even squash that power differential—they definitely do not accentuate or flaunt it.

If you believe at all the premise of this book—that the manager is the primary driver and curator of the employee's experience—then it's reasonable to assume that things may reach a point where the employee feels like she just needs to say something to the manager. Managers are human beings, and hence the teams and the systems they operate will always have some flaws.

Before I lay out the simple four-step framework for giving feedback up the chain, I want to offer one simple idea: your manager is a person, and this person wants to be successful. If you understand that you have a role to play in helping that manager be more successful—and that you're not going in there to kick them in the shins—you've already set yourself up to have a much better outcome.

A brief note on the watercooler and gossip. For a variety of reasons most likely related to the power differential I described above, people are disinclined to give managers the feedback those managers need in order to be successful. I have seen, however, people more than willing to discuss the manager's shortcomings with their colleagues—from well-intentioned advice seeking to injurious character assassination. My theory is that gossip is really just the act of choosing to transact in other people's information, and some people think that transacting in that information increases their status. Just remember that when you are talking *about* someone and not *to* someone, you are not helping them. You are also not helping yourself to have the best experience you can have at work. A better way is to give your manager feedback directly.

Step 1: Account for Your Risk

If you work for a retaliator, do not give them the feedback. End of process, except your next step should be to polish up your résumé (*never* more than one page, by the way!) and start looking around for a new situation. Life is too short to work for someone whom you believe will not hear you, your ideas, your needs and wants, and it is way too short to live in fear. Sure, there are scads of assclown managers out there, but there are also plenty of great ones who will work to understand what you have to offer—even if it's extremely hard for them to hear.

The vast majority of managers aren't retaliators. They might seem like they are because they're human—if you work for Skynet, this particular detail could be worth double checking—and are likely to manifest a little bit of a defensive reaction. The most common defensive reaction is to try to find out *who is saying what,* particularly in cases where the feedback is not given directly. This is a bad instinct on the manager's part because it's almost always the case that they want to know who is saying these things in order to at least partially invalidate the feedback. Often, it will be couched in the context of customizing the action plan—"Well, if I know it's Blaise and Maria who are saying this, then I can follow up with them directly"—but more often than not, that information is used to explain the feedback away. Remember, one of the most persistent and nefarious forms of bias is our ability to absorb the signal that suggests we're crushing it and our difficulty in absorbing feedback that suggests we're not. Realize that the instinct to learn "who said what" is a normal, though flawed, defensive reaction and not necessarily indicative of a retaliatory disposition.

Step 2: Gather the Boss's Unique Context

You are not right. Let that sink in, please. You are not right. You *think* you are right, but you are not right. You have an important and valid perspective, but again—I'll reiterate—you are not right. Even though you are sure you're right, even though you've talked about it with your coworkers and they've corroborated everything you've said, I'll make the point one last time—you are not right.

Lieutenant Colonel John Boggs, my battalion commander at 1st Battalion, 5th Marine Regiment, used to ask his officers,

"What do you know, and who are you telling?" to emphasize the need to share, not hoard, information. He constantly hammered us with that question. I would walk into his office, talk about some set of issues, brainstorm some action, and leave with him saying, "What do you know, and who are you telling?" The need for managers to share what they know is a critical idea, but even the best managers will fail pretty often to share everything they know with everyone who needs to know—or even *should* know. For this reason, I think it's important for you not to assume the boss knows nothing about the issue you're about to lay at their feet. Don't assume the boss has their head up their ass, is incompetent, or is unfamiliar with the facts. They might have simply neglected to share something with you. You just don't know, and lucky for us, we've discovered a foolproof way to know stuff. Ask.

It goes something like this.

"Hey boss, I have been spending a lot of time thinking about Issue X, and I was wondering if you wouldn't mind sharing your perspective on it." Now shut up and listen. Clarify and listen. Listen and clarify. Don't argue, don't push back, just actively listen. "So what I think I hear you saying is that the reason Issue X is the way it is is because of reasons A, B, and C. Do I have that right?" Rinse and repeat until you believe you firmly understand the boss's position and unique context. The simple prescription in this step is to assume the boss knows more, not less.

So now you've done your job—you've gathered the boss's unique context, and now you need to decide if you should proceed. Maybe you learned that Issue X isn't even on her radar. Then you need to ask yourself: should it be? Maybe Issue X looks like a clown car to you, but you learn from the boss that it's the way it is for some good reasons. Maybe Issue X is some other person's pet project. Maybe you learned that there are massive structural obstacles to tackling Issue X, and the return on investment (ROI) of addressing it is quite low. But then there's also the possibility that what you've learned about Issue X solidifies your feeling that you have a perspective that can really move the needle on the way the boss is thinking about it. You have to decide at that moment whether to gracefully exit with "Thanks a ton, I have what I need" or push into step 3, ask permission. If you have a real opportunity to help make the team and hence the company more successful, then you should.

Step 3: Ask Permission

Asking for permission is the greatest risk mitigation strategy ever created for the workplace. I do it all the time. Once I understand someone's perspective and see that mine is slightly different, I might ask, "Do you mind if I push your thinking a little bit?" One hundred percent of the times I've asked this question, the response has been "Yes," and most often an enthusiastic "*Yes!*" I think people tend to respond favorably to this question because it signals that we're about to learn. It signals that the boss is engaged and is going to help you get better. While I won't claim that this is some kind of defense-diffusing panacea, I have found this little tactic to be a great way to open up someone's mind for some improvement coaching.

In this case, you're providing feedback up the chain, so you might say something like this: "Bossfriend, thanks for walking me through that. I think I see things a little bit differently, and I was wondering if you are open to hearing that?" Boom.

If the manager says, "No," then go all the way back to the step about polishing up the résumé. In my experience, however, people are receptive. Most will say, "Yep," and off you go. The good news is that the door is now open. The bad news is that you are going to have to walk through it. You're committed.

Step 4: Just Do It

It's go time. You've done everything right. You've managed your risk, you've gathered the boss's unique context, you've asked permission, and I'm going to argue that now you *must* give the feedback. Why would I argue that? Because you have reason to believe that everyone around you—your team, the company, your manager—will be more successful if you add your perspective to the mix. If you believe a part of your job is to enable the success of others, then it just makes sense that you are obliged to act.

HEY, WHAT'S A GREAT WAY TO KNOW STUFF? ASK.

Let's talk about Serena Williams for a moment. For most of her career she's been the best tennis player in the world, a stretch of dominance that I believe deserves to be discussed among the top five or so all-time greatest athletic achievements. She was great, and for at least a decade the greatest, and still, as of today, the greatest ever—and it's not even close.

Serena Williams has had a number of different coaches. People who help her with service, with backhand, forehand, strategy, nutrition, flexibility, agility, strength, endurance. I was able to count at least a half dozen different people who have explicitly been asked to help her improve over the years. I suspect it's many more. An important question we might pose is, who asked them to help? Well, it was Serena, you sillies.

So, let's get this clear. The best ever at her craft has actively and explicitly asked and *paid* people to come in and criticize her work as a matter of course. Huh. The best in the world pays for criticism. . . . The next question is obvious.

Are you the best in the world at your job? The probability

is that you are not, and that's okay, but if the best ever thinks it's important to get more eyes on her work, then why shouldn't you? Even better, you have people all around you, including those on your team, who are observing your behaviors and evaluating your work products; if you ask skillfully enough, respond thoughtfully enough, and demonstrate a persistence and authenticity in your desire to hear their perspectives, you can tap into all of that wisdom for *free*. You don't even have to pay for that coaching. If it's good enough for Serena, it's good enough for you.

The "Feedback up the Chain" section above serves as a reality check for the sheer amount of work involved just to give feedback to the boss who is not asking. Imagine a world where your people do not have to guess about the risk involved in giving you tough feedback, where they know that their input will be carefully considered, respected, valued, trusted, and acted upon. I've become fond of saying that the best managers *assault* the power differential that sits between the boss and the employee. Assault it. Dismantle it. Imagine a world where you invite challenges to the status quo—to how your team operates, how you lead the team, how your team is addressing whatever market opportunity it is pursuing—so seamlessly that it starts to happen naturally. Imagine how much better that team will perform because you are ensuring that every voice and every idea is heard in service of finding the best solutions. Imagine how much ownership a team feels when each member's voice is heard and valued.

The way to get here is to ask, ask, and ask some more. After you ask, listen. After you listen, act. People will start to see the pattern: my manager listens to me, values the input, occasionally makes changes based on the input, and *then I don't get fired but instead get applauded*. Pretty soon, folks will begin to speak more freely because they believe they are in an environment where getting to the best answer, no matter where it comes from, is important.

I believe that Kim Scott's four-step process for soliciting feedback is the most important idea in *Radical Candor*. This process was inspired by Andy Grove, who was the CEO of Intel for many years and is well known for giving excellent leadership advice. Regarding Kim's process, I will not fully rehash it here—Kim does it really well in the book. Instead, I will offer some tidbits I learned from teaching this content to thousands of people.

1. **Have a go-to question.** A go-to question is a question you can ask regularly that might elicit some feedback. It worked for Andy Grove, of course, but in teaching this content, I learned that a go-to question can get stale pretty fast and isn't the only way to go. I think we should vary our questions based on context. We're getting signals all the time—engagement surveys, clues from colleagues, other managers, sideways glances, surprising reactions—that should offer us clues about what we should be asking about. I've reached a pseudo-conclusion that it's better to help people learn how to *construct* a question rather than just prescribe that they work one out to use frequently, so I'll ask you, in the following space, to identify what each of the following questions has in common:
   - What could be better on this team?
   - If this was your budget, how would you spend it?
   - How can I help you be even more successful?
   - What do I need to do to better build trust with you?
   - If you had a magic wand and could change one thing in the way we interact, what would that be?
   - What improvements would you make to our team meeting?
   - Why do you think the team's engagement is sinking?

- What opportunities do you think the team is missing in the way we go to market?
- What could have been better about my presentation to the customer?
- What am I doing right now that is not helping you?

They have three things in common.

- First, each is open-ended, and therefore really hard to answer with a simple yes or no. Let's be really clear, though. There are no silver bullets for getting folks to open up. Even with an open-ended question, it's possible to exit the conversation without answering what might feel like an uncomfortable question—but we at least increase our chances by asking questions this way.
- Second, each is specific. The worst question to ask when you want feedback is the most common one: "Hey, can I get some feedback?" It's too broad and, hence, too hard to grab hold of. Meetings are a great place to start asking questions. We spend arguably way too much time in them, and hey, did you know the only person who ever thinks the team meeting is totally rad is the person running the team meeting? If you are being thoughtful about your team and how it works, you should have some theories about various processes and relationships that might need a little hacking. If you really do want everything to be better, suddenly it becomes much easier to see the areas that others might not only want to improve but can also help to improve. Those are the things you should be asking about.
- Last, each question invites a challenge to the current state. Not a single one invites you to affirm what you are already doing. Each one is effectively seeking insight on how to make things better. Whether it's your personal style or things happening on the team, there's no difference—after all, you as the manager are responsible for everything the team does or fails to do.

2. **Embrace the discomfort.** This is really a prescription centered on listening. I've worked in companies loaded with insecure overachievers, people in their thirties and forties

who are still trying to get an A. It's like Goose said to Maverick in *Top Gun*: "Every time we go up there, it's like you're flying against a ghost. It makes me nervous." Insecure overachievers, and most other kinds, have this one really bad habit. As soon as they ask a question, they start answering it, because, I suppose, they need to show everyone how much stuff they know. The problem is that when they do that, no one else wants to answer. You have two ears and one mouth, folks. Take that as a signal from the universe as to how much you're supposed to use each.

3. **Listen with the intent to understand and not respond.** Easier said than done. Simple, but not easy. The key skill here is active listening, and the key skill in active listening is repeating back what you heard. So, what I think I hear myself saying is that the key skill in active listening is repeating back what I think I heard. Do I have that right? If all else fails, and you start to panic because of your threat response, just fall back on this and really use it to clarify what you're hearing. Beware of asking for examples. Yes, we've all been taught that we need to *bring examples* to tough conversations, especially in more acute or punitive performance management situations, but we need to realize that *asking* for them, while probably a well-meaning and growth-oriented act, might feel like a cross-examination or a challenge to someone who is your junior. You might, entirely by accident, be saying *"Prove it."* You can get the same thing accomplished by using active listening *and* going out of your way to manifest a curious tone and body language. Take notes, get excited, enthusiastically use *"Say more"* to make it clear that you are tracking, absorbing, trying to understand, and you'll also signal to your report that you are absolutely loving the insight they are providing.

4. **Reward the candor.** I've put this question to hundreds of groups I've led in workshops: "Someone took that risk, gave you the feedback, and now they are feeling exposed, and so I ask you, good people, what's the greatest reward you can give someone who did that?" Nearly 100 percent of the time, the audience will lunge at "Say thanks!" Before I thoroughly diss this response, I want to expand on the broader point that I think gratitude is underutilized in the workplace. I once heard Danny Ainge, former GM for the Boston Celtics and current CEO of Basketball Operations for the Utah Jazz, give a fireside chat. He said a number of compelling things, but chief among them was that he believes gratitude is a leadership trait. I had never once thought about it like that, but after quite a bit of reflection, I agree with him. Gratitude is awesome and too frequently absent. Most of the time, we're far too focused on what we don't have, what we didn't get, or, worse, what that other person got. Steph Curry once noted, "One thing my pops always told me is you never count another man's money." Gratitude is wonderful, but it's not the best reward you can give someone after they've taken the risk of speaking up. Heck, if you don't mean it, which is often the case, it's not even a halfway decent reward. Let's say the feedback you got really stings and you're a little bit pissed, or maybe you got crappy feedback. I'm okay with gratitude as one *possible* reward, but let's not do anything inauthentic. The *greatest* reward is to follow up. And just to be clear, following up does not necessarily mean you enact whatever suggestion you heard! As the person responsible for everything the team does or fails to do, you will need to exercise your own managerial discretion, but you must *always* follow up. If you decide not to enact the suggestion, it's important to communicate why and encour-

> age folks to continue to push you and the team to be better. All of that said, the input you get from your teams almost always has something valuable in it that you can use. Christa Quarles, the former CEO of OpenTable and all-around badass, espouses what she calls "the 5 Percent Rule." When someone is giving you improvement feedback, hunt for at least 5 percent that you can use. Brilliant. She knows that it's hard for people to absorb feedback that suggests they need to be better, so she sets the bar incredibly low. Find 5 percent. Just 5 percent. Of course there's almost always way more than 5 percent available for you to take on board and make improvements, but start at a paltry, measly 5 percent. If 5 percent feels like too much, (a) you are hopeless, and (b) you need to invent the 4 percent rule, and so on.

It doesn't have to be that hard, though. All that matters is that you are authentically inspired to tap into the teams' brains to make things better. If you want to improve, it will come through.

Here's a story from my time at Twitter. One rainy San Francisco afternoon in 2013, I was sitting in a conference room by myself. It was one of those moments when the other person hadn't shown up, so I had a chance to just hide out, capitalize on the quiet time, and crank. Dick Costolo, CEO at the time, walked by the room, saw me, and popped in.

"Hey, congratulations, I saw that the advertisers are spending more on average, so they must be getting more value from advertising on Twitter!"

Dick always prioritized his "walk-around time" for a number of reasons, but chief among them was that he knew his context was constantly warped by his direct reports. He understood how dangerous it was to listen *only* to them, the small number of old-timers, or the people he played golf and basketball with. He understood what many senior people fail to understand, which is that you have to work hard and open way up to get what is really going on at your company. Only listen to a few people, and you will know a tiny fraction of reality. Only solicit the good news or discourage your questioners and bearers of bad news, and you'll never really know what's up.

This moment—when Dick congratulated me—was a big moment. I knew instantly he'd been given the wrong information, and I knew the risks of telling him that directly. But I also knew what he as CEO expected, which was for me to tell him exactly what I thought, and to his credit he didn't care about window dressing or positioning. Lucky for me, because guess who has two thumbs and is terrible at window dressing and positioning? [*Thumbs pointed at my face*] This guy.

The context on this matters a bunch. Remember, I'd joined Twitter during the countdown to its 2013 IPO. When I arrived in 2012, the SMB advertising business I ran had no people, no products, and no customers. *Go!* The marketing folks I hired quickly built a machine that brought in thousands of new advertisers with no human intervention. Our problem, however, was that it was extremely difficult to show those advertisers clear return on investment. On the one hand, people love to say that SMB advertisers are less sophisticated. On the other hand, they are extremely rational: if you can make them two dollars for every dollar they spend and show them how you'll do it in simple terms, they will spend and spend and spend.

Our products at the time struggled to both deliver and communicate obvious ROI, so we were losing a large number of our advertisers within just a few months. This is not a sustainable or healthy business, and we all knew it. We were also keen to fix it. I knew when Dick walked in that conference room how badly everyone wanted the narrative to be that we were delivering more and clearer value to advertisers and that as a result they were spending more. The problem is that I had done my own listening and understood that we were seeing something very different. My marketing wizards—Anne, Joe, and Vinay—had devised a new strategy recently with the objective of acquiring new advertisers who were already predisposed to spend more. Bigger budgets, larger SMBs, if you will. That practice was what was driving higher average spend, not a newfound realization of value.

So there it is, hanging in the air, some good news that I know Dick wants to be true but that I know is false. Worse, I know he's been duped—probably not intentionally, of course, but the person who interpreted the dashboard for him was one step away from the business and had every incentive to shape the CEO's context toward the idea that the products were delivering more value. They were not.

I knew what Dick expected around shooting straight, and I knew that by delivering him a truer version of reality than he had received, I was likely going to make things a little uncomfortable for some of my partners. So I said, "Dick, I don't want to drop any dimes on anyone here."

Dick chose to remind me he's a sophisticated manager and that he wouldn't walk into the product person's office and shout, "Russ told me you are wrong!"

"Of course you won't do that, Dick, but these relationships need to work, and I just can't have it so that folks around me feel like I'm tattling to you."

"They won't," he assured me.

With that assurance, and my deep understanding that my first obligation is to shareholders, and that the worst thing for our customers and our shareholders is for us to let up on our efforts to build an ROI machine, I gave the CEO a version of the facts that hewed much closer to the truth. We weren't systematically creating better or clearer ROI, I told him. We were acquiring advertisers with bigger budgets. The data showed that this increasing average spend was being misinterpreted.

There is a lot to unpack in this story, but Dick modeled so many important behaviors, and that's what I want to focus on. First, his walk-around time didn't just carry him to comfortable places in the company. He went everywhere. Second, he had developed a clear understanding with me that I was never to pull any punches with him. He'd rather I give him my rawest version of reality than some heavily positioned bullshit good news version of it. He also didn't mind being wrong. In fact, he seemed to love it. Third, he understood his own need to get better information, but not at the expense of blowing up all the relationships needed for our various cross-functional teams to find success.

The bottom line was that I could really say it exactly as I saw it, with no wrapping paper, and Dick would never punish that. In fact, I believed it was riskier to withhold my perspective than to deliver it plainly. He expected that kind of input because he saw it as a way to get closer and closer to the most elusive idea in all of business: the truth.

11

Showing That You Care About People as Human Beings

One of the twelve questions we base our manager effectiveness score on is "How much do you agree with the following statement: 'My manager cares about me as a human being'?" While the correlation between positive answers and employee engagement is not as strong as it is with some of the other twelve, this question *is* strongly correlated with intent to leave ("How much do you agree with the following statement: I am seriously considering leaving [Employer]"). The implications are clear: If you feel like your manager cares about you as a human being, you are more likely to stay at your company. If you don't feel like your manager cares about you as a human being, you are more likely to leave. I think this is worth a minute of our time.

"Care Personally" is the label Kim Scott put on one of the two axes of the two-by-two grid that defines Radical Candor. But as she and I began to consult and train people on the model and how to use it, we noticed something interesting. Folks would routinely forget about the personal care part. Over and over again, someone would walk up to us and say something like this (I'm exaggerating for effect, but not much): "You will love this.

My boss is an asshole, so I marched up those stairs and did not knock on his door. No, I *kicked* it in [*pantomimes kicking the door in like a martial arts master*] and told him what an incredible shithead he is and how much everyone hates him. Man, it felt good to be radically candid." I don't have to tell you that there is no personal care on display in that story.

I got curious about why this was. As a manager, I already believed deeply in personal care. In fact, at one point Kim told me that everything she learned about caring for people at work she learned counterintuitively, from her former infantry marine, 2 percent Neanderthal employee: me. She's always saying hyperbolically generous stuff like that—she's the best person to have in your corner. But the point is, as I said in the introduction, I believe in this idea deeply, and I just couldn't understand why people were so inclined to ignore it. The answer, as it turned out, was staring me right in the face. It was simply a matter of focus and know-how. People generally have so much anxiety about the tough conversation that the big win to them is mustering the courage to have it. At that moment, nothing else matters but delivering that tough message. Further, folks probably believe that personal care is generally in their hearts and that they don't have to do anything special to manifest it visibly or tangibly.

Most of us hear the phrase "care about people" and intuitively understand what it means, but I've learned that it's not that intuitive or easy to understand when we talk about caring about people *at work*. Kim and I once had a long laugh because an engineer at some tech company asked us, "So, *how DO you* care personally?" Hilarious! The tech industry loves to chuckle at its low-EQ, massively introverted engineering groups, even though they are responsible for nearly every ounce of every tech company's competitive advantage. Turns out, though, that this is actually an extraordinary question, and I didn't realize it for months and months. People really don't know how to show personal care *at work*, and most lack either the self-awareness or the courage to say so.

Recognizing this, I devised an exercise for our workshops that was explicitly designed to force people to articulate personal care. It went like this. I gave everyone eight minutes to "write down a story about a time you received Radical Candor at work." By this time in the workshop, I would have explained the model in full, so it was a reasonable request. This was a carefully developed sentence. First, it was very important to me that they were the *recipients* of Radical Candor. I assumed most of their stories would feature improvement feedback, and that a byproduct of the exercise might be to normalize the idea that we all have stuff to work on. I specifically did not want to give the students a chance to wax prosaically about their big win giving tough feedback. Instead, I wanted them all to be on an equal footing as the goat (not the G.O.A.T.) of their stories. Second, it was important that this example happened at work. I was not interested in your spouse giving you "Radical Candor" about not taking out the trash or some other safe version of the model. I really wanted people to articulate a time they messed up at work and someone called them on it, and I wanted them to feel the psychological safety to do that.

The second part of the exercise was called "turn, pair, and share." Each participant grabbed a partner, and for four minutes each—eight minutes total—they told their stories to one another. As was explained to me by a teaching professional, this step is really a quality assurance measure to prevent all the extroverts from jumping up to the microphone; it helps to ensure that the stuff that does get shared in the impending third step of the exercise, when volunteers are invited to the front to tell their stories, will generally be of a very high quality. Having everyone share their story raises the chances that the less-likely-to-share introverts will be encouraged to address the whole group. Should they all elect not to come forward, at least they will have had a chance to share their stories with someone.

But regardless of who stepped up to the microphone, whether extrovert or introvert, the stories they shared predictably had a crystal-clear focus on hard feedback or "direct challenge," in RC parlance. As I expected, no one said anything about personal care, which was, in fact, the whole point of the exercise.

After everyone had finished speaking, I would ask for a round of applause from the audience and gently direct the storyteller "to stay put because I had some questions about their story." Always intentional, I used the opportunity to model active listening. "So what I heard in your story is that the direct challenge was X and Y and Z, did I get that right?" Once we agreed on the clearest version of the hard feedback, I would say, "But what I didn't quite hear in your story was the *care personally*. How would you characterize that?" You'd think that after I asked that question of the first volunteer's story, the next three people would pick up on the idea and proactively include personal care in their stories. But by and large, fascinatingly, they did not. So I would facilitate it out of them.

This exercise ended up serving a lot of purposes. People were able to convey how valuable the hard feedback had been for them, which allowed me to make the point that each audience member should walk out of the workshop intending to be an upstander—providing that kind of value to those around them—versus being a bystander and offering no value. It allowed me to clarify the model and, in particular, emphasize the notion of caring personally: "It ain't RC without CP."

By 2018, I had probably been through this exercise some six hundred times. The most important thing those six hundred people taught me was something I'd absolutely not set out to learn. It happened quite organically and entirely by accident. I learned the "Universal Care Personally Playbook at Work," or the UCP-PAW, which rolls off the tongue much better.

When I would ask folks, "Where's the *care personally* in your story?" they would often start with sort of a lazy, conventionally wise version of personal care, something like, "Well, we had a long relationship." I would challenge them, "But in that specific coaching moment, what in your boss's actions led you to believe she was showing you she cared personally?" Other substandard answers included, "Well, my manager always asked about my weekends and was genuinely interested in my kids' big soccer tournaments." I don't dispute that this kind of interaction might feel like the manager is invested in you personally, but what about managers who don't give a shit about your soccer weekend *or* your kids? Do they need to inauthentically pretend to care about them in an attempt to show personal care for you? What about an extremely private employee who doesn't care to share any details of their personal life with the boss? There are a lot more of both of those than you think . . . or at least than I thought. Others lunged at the fact that their boss was concerned about their health. Again, most managers are not doctors, and very often people are not excited to share their maladies with the boss. Happy hours, axe-throwing, or bowling offsites . . . these are all lazy examples of caring personally.

Some of these things work. I do many of them because they work for me, and over the years I've learned to more explicitly gauge if they work for my employees. The biggest problem, though, is that what works for some flat out doesn't work for others. I've known great managers—and great people—who really dislike children. Yep. I've known employees who have experienced deep anxiety over their boss's interest in their personal lives and didn't know how to respectfully say "Butt out." The problem is obvious. An example comes from Bill, a European manager I worked with some time ago. Bill could not wrap his head around the idea that asking about and engaging in people's personal lives was not the only way to demonstrate that he cared about them personally. Bill was in my class when this came up. I had thirty-five people in the class, and I requested a show of hands of who would prefer it if their manager asked them about their personal lives. Fifteen raised their hands. Then I queried who would prefer it if their manager didn't ask. Twenty hands went up to say "Butt out." Bill saw this happen live and still couldn't believe it. Bias is so powerful.

After six hundred repetitions of challenging people to think harder and get to the essence of how they knew the feedback giver cared about them as a human being, a bold and simple word cloud began to emerge. Three words in particular came up over and over and over and over, and none of them were "offsites" or "health" or "weekends." Those three words?

Time. Help. Success.

If I put them into a simple sentence that represents—from the perspective of six hundred real people—the UCP-PAW, it's "That person took the *time* to *help* me be more *successful.*" "Success" in this case tends to have two distinct meanings. The coach had either helped them be better at their specific job in the here and now or was currently helping them to be successful vis-à-vis some future dream or goal. Time. Help. Success.

What I realized through this process is that there's really only one thing everyone has in common at work. Along these lines, I'd like to emphasize an area that we commonly associate with showing that we care but in reality has risk. We are not all at work to learn about or share the details of our personal lives, even though, of course, some are. Often people withhold things from the boss that are deeply personal. Probing from said boss, no matter how well intentioned, can feel like taking a lie detector test, and it can induce a ton of anxiety. I once had an employee share with me that he was transgender in the course of a very personal conversation. He stopped and said, "I just want you to know I've never told anyone at work that I'm trans—you're the first person I've ever said that to. . . . I just got talking and it sorta came out, and wow, now I came out at work! I need assurance that you will not share that deeply personal and private detail." Naturally, I honored the request.

A part of my leadership still includes really trying to know my people personally. I love to inquire about their families or their weekends, and I am always fully available to support them through their most trying times, work or not. I now recognize that this comes with a certain amount of risk. While it works well for me, it doesn't work well for everyone, and rather than just assume that everyone loves my attempts to get to know them on a more personal level, I've learned to ask if that sort of engagement is welcome or not.

All of this leads us to the most important question: What is the only thing that every single person at work has in common?

Everyone wants to be successful. That's the only thing. Some of you will read this and think of a coworker who maybe is not trying as hard as you think they should to be successful, but the reality is that they almost certainly want to and just don't know how to do it or don't even realize that they are not being fully successful. So yeah, some are not trying as hard as they can, but the only thing every single person in the building *wants* is success. It's little wonder that those six hundred people in the workshops ultimately said that what makes them feel cared about at work is when someone takes the time to help them be more successful.

Time. Help. Success.

So with all of that said, we can see that that simple question from a few pages ago, posed by a stereotypically introverted engineer and primed to be dismissed as something that only someone with zero people skills would ask, was among the most key questions imaginable—and one that badly needed to be answered.

12

Coaching Mechanics

STRUCTURING FEEDBACK

Whether you're delivering improve (critical) or continue (praise) coaching (feedback, guidance), using an effective structure for the impending conversation can help you deliver a cleaner, clearer message, but there is no existing nostrum that will diffuse the natural defensive reaction most humans have to criticism. We only have coping mechanisms for working around and through the threat response.

Remember, we are all at work to drive an aligned result. Good organizations not only care about *whether* you deliver the result but also *how* you get those results, which are the methods or behaviors. So managing and evaluating performance is fundamentally about two things: results and behaviors. Results can be measurable, such as sales quota attainment, factory production, generated sales leads, renewed customers, or total number of hires. They can also be binary, such as the delivery of a work product, which itself likely serves some measurable result. Methods, as I noted earlier, are generally behaviors. Good companies have a few sources of behavioral expectations. At the most basic level, there is a code of conduct and a respectful workplace policy. More interesting is when we clearly define our company's core values and then expect people to manifest the behaviors that motivate those values. Some companies have broad behavioral guidelines by level. You expect, for example, a very junior person to deliver their work on time and correctly, but a very senior person might be expected to deliver system-wide effects or impact so substantial that it sends shockwaves through the entire company. The most common behavioral standards are some version of "Career Stage Profiles," a tool used to articulate expectations that vary where role and level intersect. What is expected of a customer service representative at, say, level 2, and then how does that change when I'm promoted to level 3? As a side note, I am not a huge fan of Career Stage Profiles, because they tend to become checklists for promotion instead of guidelines for growth; they are frequently weaponized for securing a guaranteed promotion. Just make sure you use them wisely.

The best coaching structure I've seen is the SBI model, which comes from the Center for Creative Leadership. SBI stands for Situation-Behavior-Impact.

- **Situation**—Describe the situation (or context, scenario, or interaction type) and be specific about when and where the behavior occurred.
- **Behavior**—Describe the observable behavior. Ideally, the behaviors in question come from a source, such as a handbook, a list of core values, or a set of level and functional guidelines. Steer clear of projecting or interpreting, and stick with what you have observed.
- **Impact**—Describe what you believe to be the impact of the behavior. In this case, we might be talking about the impact on others.

While this structure is sound and elegant, I've found it to be insufficient in many cases because behaviors are not the only things we need to evaluate people on or help them improve or repeat in order to find success. We also have to work on, well . . . *the work.*

Yes, you read that right. The Center for Creative Leadership has been around for half a century, and they carefully developed the SBI model through painstaking research, trial, and error. They've achieved broad-based adoption of the model in 3,000 organizations in 160 countries, impacting 500,000 people, and here comes Russ Laraway, who on a Thursday in October, made up the SBI counterpart. I call it SWI, which means: Situation-Work-Impact. SWI.

- **Situation**—Describe the situation (or context, scenario, or typical interaction type), and be specific about which work product you are describing.
- **Work**—Describe how well the work product builds to results: the code, the copy, the customer service tickets, the sales pitch, the presentation slides, the presentation delivery, the financial model, the candidate experience strategy, etc.
- **Impact**—Describe the impact of the work on the business and on others. Why does this work matter? What result does it contribute to? How well do you believe it contributes, or how poorly?

I want to be clear, neither SBI nor SWI is sufficient alone because one omits the idea of providing feedback on the work and the other omits behavioral feedback. SBI and SWI together offer a portfolio of feedback-structuring techniques that will cover an overwhelming majority of coaching scenarios.

Let me walk you through an example using SBI. Jasmine

uses her sense of humor in the team meeting. In scenario 1, Jasmine's behavior is disruptive, so the coaching will be around improvement. In scenario 2, Jasmine's behavior defuses a tense situation, so the coaching will be around praise. An important detail to notice is that a sense of humor is not inherently bad or inherently good. The situation, context, and the way the behavior manifests are all critical variables.

One of the common questions I receive about structuring feedback is, "How do I get started?" I've seen people, often unconsciously, spend so much time talking *about* the impending conversation that they don't leave themselves enough time to actually *have* the conversation. That's why I prefer a minimalist opening salvo.

At one of my speaking gigs, I was lucky enough to hear Mallory Weggemann tell her story, which beautifully articulates why an opening preamble is not worth much investment. It makes such a powerful point that I'm going to interrupt my story about Jasmine to share it with you.

Mallory was a competitive swimmer, but in 2008 her legs became paralyzed after she received an injection to treat post-shingles back pain. Just four months later, she began training as a Paralympic swimmer. She quickly rose to the top of the sport, and was named World Disabled Swimmer of the Year in 2009 and 2010. In the 2010 IPC Swimming World Championships, the last world games before the 2012 Paralympics, she won gold in every single event. The pinnacle was visible and in reach. She would go on to the 2012 games, likely sweep every event, and round out one of the most extraordinary examples of human resiliency and achievement that has ever been seen.

An important detail on Paralympic sports. Athletes are classified based on their specific level of impairment. Like most things in life, these impairments sit on a continuum. There are varying levels of paralysis, for example, and it would be unfair for someone with partial paralysis, say, to compete against people with full and complete paralysis. Mallory broke all those world records in 2009 and 2010 and won all those gold medals under an "S7" classification based on her level of impairment. But when she arrived at the 2012 Paralympic games, she received some shocking news. She had been reclassified as an S8. "Do you know what every competitor classified as an S8 had in common?" Mallory asked. By the time I saw her speak, she'd become a highly refined raconteur and knew the value of pausing and letting the silence wash over us. She sat in her wheelchair on the stage, statuesque and completely in charge of the room. Every single one of us was on the edge of our seats.

"They have the use of their legs."

It would not have surprised me if at that moment every member of the audience grabbed torches and pitchforks and streamed out of the building toward the Paralympic Games headquarters, because Mallory, as we all could plainly see, did not have the use of her legs.

Upon receiving the reclassification news, she became dejected and despondent, and understandably told her coach that she would not compete.

Her coach, though, talked her through it. He said that there was an appeals process to follow and that they would work to get her reclassified as an S7. After a multiday ordeal, he had the decision. He returned from his final meeting with the Paralympic Games officials, greeted her, and suggested they find a private area so they could talk.

When Mallory told us about this moment, she said, "You know how when someone has good news for you, you can just tell? They have upbeat body language, an upbeat tone of voice, they exchange a bunch of pleasantries, smiles, etc.?" And then she offered the key insight. "Well, that day, in this moment, there was none of that, and before my coach spoke a word, I knew our appeal was unsuccessful."

This basic insight instantly resonated with me. People can tell when you have tough news or need to open up a difficult conversation. You give all kinds of signals, and there is no point in delaying. Their threat response is already building, and no opening statement will reverse that. It's go time, time to get on with it, to get into the meat of the conversation as quickly as you can. With that in mind, I offer a simple, one-sentence prescription to bridge the gap from silence to SB/WI.

"I think I'm seeing some behavior that I believe is getting in your way. Are you in a spot where you can hear that right now?"

By asking this question, you are effectively flagging that this might be a tough conversation and requesting permission to have it. And you are doing it in a way that gets you quickly into the real conversation. It gets you out of talking *about* the coaching and into *providing* it. The answer will almost always be yes, regardless of whether they are actually in an appropriate mindset. People often ask, "Well, what if they do say 'no'?" In that case, you honor that response. I might say something along the lines of, "OK, no problem, I get it. When is a good time for us to catch up on this? Will tomorrow morning work for you?" You just want to keep it on the books, because hard conversations have a way of magically disappearing. The "escape and evade" approach to tough feedback, though common, is not a strategy for getting better or helping others around you get better.

Back to Jasmine, who manifested her sense of humor in the team meeting. In the first scenario it was disruptive, so the coaching is oriented toward improvement.

"Hey Jasmine! I think I noticed something today that might represent an opportunity for you to be better here. Are you in a place where you can hear that?"

"Yes, let's chat."

"Cool, so today in the team meeting [Situation], when you kept hammering jokes pretty regularly—I counted maybe seven [Behavior]—I felt like it was pretty disruptive, and more specifically, we were not able to complete the agenda. Now we need to have two meetings instead of one to make this decision [Impact]. What are your thoughts about that?"

That last part is important. Rather than starting with an inauthentic "How do you think things went in the team meeting?" and hoping beyond hope that Jasmine will self-diagnose, lay out your perspective. But because you understand that your perspective is not *the* truth but only *your* truth, it is important to ask Jasmine about her feelings on the matter. Remember, the Talmud says that "we do not see things as they are. We see things as we are." For this reason, it's important to gather the other person's perspective and try to understand it. I prefer this order, though, because it feels more authentic. I asked for the meeting, and so it seems appropriate that I lead it off. To call the meeting, have a perspective, and then to not lead with it can feel manipulative or inauthentic. Open with your perspective, then use the conversation to gather the critically important other side of the story. My truth is not the truth. Your truth is not the truth. My one wish for humanity might just be that we can all adopt this simple idea. What might this look like in practice?

I have had to do a number of investigations over the years around a number of different topics. I vividly remember a favoritism claim from years ago. The accuser came to me to indicate, roughly, that the organization he was part of was not dishing out the best opportunities based on some sensible rubric but whether or not the opportunity assigner and the opportunity receiver went to the same church. The accuser had data and other witnesses, leading me to walk out of that room as convinced as the accuser that we had a favoritism problem to solve. I was sure

I'd go ask a bunch of witnesses some questions, and that would be that.

Of course, the opposite happened. I learned that the only thing the company was guilty of was poor communication around how the opportunities were distributed. Despite the accuser's certainty that the leaders worshipped and hung out together, I learned that was not the case. On top of that, the opportunities *were* being distributed based on reasonable logic and via a neutral third-party organization. To solve our problem and wrap this one up, I asked that neutral third-party group to make some small refinements to their distribution rubric. I also asked them, along with the accuser's leadership team, to convey more explicitly the "why" and "how" of opportunity distribution. The claim had helped me and others shine a light on opportunities for improvement, for sure, but the simplest way that I can state the outcome of the investigation is that there was not a shred of objective evidence that any favoritism transpired.

That really shook me. I had walked out of my initial meeting with the accuser sure that he was right. By the end of my work, it was clear that he was not, even though his perspective was understandable and even reasonable based on the information he had. I have since coined a simple phrase that I use to help communicate the idea that *your* truth is not *the* truth. "The next time that the first version I hear about an event is the truth will be the first time." To be clear, I do not think for a second that the accuser was lying to me or trying to mislead me. He truly believed what he saw and strung a bunch of observations together to create a narrative. This is a well-understood dynamic that rests somewhere between logical fallacy and a kind of apophenia—seeing patterns where no such patterns exist—called narrative fallacy, where we interpret a set of facts as a story by threading them together into an imagined chain of causes and effects.

To put this into perspective, we don't *know* some of the most basic things about the physical world. For example, there is disagreement among scientists about whether gravity is a force or a depression in the space-time fabric. Further, we are pretty sure that electrons, protons, and neutrons—the building blocks of atoms, which are the building blocks of elements, which are the building blocks of compounds, which are the building blocks of matter—are made up of particles. Still, we theorize, but lack certainty about the presence of certain particles—perhaps as many as half of the total particles we believe exist. And just to hammer the point home, we hypothesize that 99.9999 percent (you get it) of the universe is made up of so-called dark matter, but we aren't remotely sure. This is basically *all* of the universe we're talking about here, and we don't know what it's made of. So the idea that we *know* something about whether someone's work or behavior is right or wrong, or that any one of us possesses the truth about some topic at work, is, for me, asymptotic with impossible.

Imagine for a moment that some topic, idea, behavioral problem, work product, or other issue can be represented by a sphere, a physical sphere that sits between you and me. In this mental model, you and I disagree about the nature of the sphere. The sphere shape, by the way, is particularly useful in this metaphor because a sphere can intuitively and easily be viewed from an infinite number of perspectives. I always imagine the perspectives are perpendicular to the surface of the sphere or to the tangent of the outline of the sphere, which is, of course, a circle.

Like all good conversations, this one starts with a shared objective. We are both trying to understand the true nature of the sphere. It starts, perhaps, with me sharing my perspective. Here's what I see. I can describe my half or so of the sphere with crystal clarity. Its color ranges from blue to green moving from left to right. It's reflective, and I can see things behind me by using it like a mirror. I see some scratches on the top left quadrant, some imperfections in the lower right quadrant that look like perhaps it rolled over fine gravel. The lighting illuminates the right side of the sphere quite well but begins to cast a shadow as we move past the vertical center line. Because we have a shared objective to understand the true nature of the sphere, once I've described my perspective, the most important thing for me to do is understand yours.

I might ask, "What do you notice?" and then I will listen carefully as you describe your side of the sphere, asking for clarifying details if I feel you've omitted them, acting genuinely curious, and trying genuinely to understand what your side looks like. Perhaps your description inspires me to enhance or expand upon my own, etc. Of course, we're both aware that we are lacking a clear view of the extreme right, left, top, and bottom of the sphere, and so just the two of us probably won't be able to even approach understanding its full and true nature.

Of course this isn't at all what would happen if the sphere were an issue and we were at work. A person would come to the conversation with a full command of their side of the sphere and with the objective to make you understand it. They would come bearing arms to persuade you that their side adequately offers the understanding we need. They would likely assume a lot about your side of the sphere, and they wouldn't be particularly interested in hearing your description. The most nefarious force I see when two people come together to debate is the desire to win.

"I'll talk to him and get him on board" is a benign-sounding version of this. There are no enemies in the building. Great teams debate with the shared objective of understanding the true nature of the sphere, not the objective of convincing the other party that their view of the sphere is representative of its true nature. We shouldn't be trying to win against each other in the workplace. We should be trying to win against our competitors. We say all the time that we want a culture of debate, but what I think we really want is a culture of dialectic.

All of this builds to a simple idea: when you offer someone feedback, the best you can offer is what you see. You cannot offer them truth, right, or wrong. What you see, however, while limited, is extremely valuable. When you offer your perspective to the feedback receiver, you should label your perspective as exactly that: what you see. Use that opportunity to share what you believe you are seeing with the utmost clarity. Ideally, you'll use the SBI or SWI framework and then serve the ball across to the other person so you can try to understand what they see. Now we are having a conversation, and now we are going to begin to understand one another. Feedback is most often a two-way collaborative negotiation. It should be a dialogue and not a set of overlapping monologues.

Let's shift gears to *continue coaching* and check in on our friend, Jasmine. In this scenario, her humor is useful.

"Hey, Jasmine! I wanted to take a few minutes to call out something I saw you do today that I really liked. You got a sec?"

"For that? Hell, yeah!"

"Cool, so today in the team meeting, you no doubt felt the tension in the room as we talked about the results from the engagement survey [Situation], and I just have to say that your joke was perfectly timed. I mean, wow, it really seemed to cut right through the tension [Behavior] and help everyone get back on track to solving the problem [Impact]. I just wanted to take a minute to say thanks for the strong assist in there."

This example uses exactly the same structure for the *continue*-style feedback that we used for *improvement*-style feedback. Even in this praise, we are careful to make this about what we believe we saw; we're not trying to indicate truth. Perhaps most important, we're not making any of this about Jasmine's sense of humor, generally, as a personality attribute.

Imagine for a moment that you go back to the original example and, instead of coaching Jasmine about the specific behavioral manifestation in context, you focus more generally on her sense of humor. For example, "Jasmine, your sense of humor is a real issue here." This creates all kinds of problems. First, even though the original feedback isn't all rainbows, butterflies, unicorns, and sunshine, this version will likely feel more like a personal attack if for no other reason than it has a sense of permanence. Jasmine, no doubt, possesses countless examples from her life in which her sense of humor has served her well, so she likely won't even experience this feedback as credible. Most of all, this sort of arrogant—in this case *ontologically arrogant*, since it presumes that *your* truth is *the* truth—feedback shuts off any possibility for the praise scenario. Imagine that both of these scenarios play out sequentially over the course of a few weeks. The disruptive one occurs first, and instead of carefully identifying your observation about Jasmine's behavioral manifestation of humor in context, you just say, "Your sense of humor is a problem." Fast-forward two weeks, and now her sense of humor saves the day. You can imagine how confusing those two messages would be.

Exercising basic discipline around the structure of feedback helps you sidestep these and other predictable problems.

GIVING THE COACHING IN THE MOMENT

Professional athletic coaches spend nearly every waking moment thinking about how they can help their athletes be better, collaborating with others on the same effort, and offering feedback to their athletes in real time. Let's take a look at Coach Matt and his gymnast, Starks.

Let's say Starks is at practice, working on his vault. Starks steps onto the long blue vault runway, which is eighty-two feet long. The runway generally has a tape measure running alongside it so that each gymnast can carefully choose the distance that allows them to gradually increase speed and hit the springboard at exactly the right number of steps. Starks hits the springboard with prodigious power, launches himself off the vault table, and performs a Kasamatsu (Kas), which is, at least to me, an incomprehensible combination of aerial twisting and flipping. He then lands on a pile of blue mats, turns to Coach Matt, and without uttering a word, listens for input.

Coach Matt might say something like "You over-rotated" or "You didn't get enough power off the vault table." Starks nods and heads back to the line to do another repetition.

This is really an SWI example. The situation and impact are both understood, with the situation being that particular vault repetition, possibly a pattern, and the impact being point deductions for any deviation from a perfect Kas.

This example also serves another purpose, as it demonstrates the importance of timely feedback. Let's say this series of events transpired at the beginning of practice, say, 6:00 P.M. on a Monday in March. I want you to imagine that instead of offering Starks his correction immediately following that particular vault repetition, Coach Matt instead waits until Starks's six-month review. Ridiculous, right? Of course. "Okay Starks, remember that vault repetition four months ago?"

Let's say that Coach Matt does a "performance wrap-up" Friday night before the guys all get the weekend off. Better? I agree, but not really. Okay, okay, forget that Friday-night nonsense. How about Coach Matt gives everyone their coaching points at the end of practice, say, 9:00 P.M. Now are we good? Of course not. We're obviously circling around the idea of giving coaching in a temporally proximate way. One of the reasons this is important is because it helps cut down on all that wasteful preamble I just mentioned. In Starks's example, Coach Matt didn't even need to describe the situation. They both had perfect context and were immediately able to get to problem-solving, and of course, as Kim Scott notes in *Radical Candor,* giving the feedback right away "helps them fix it faster." We recognize that in the gymnastics example, Starks is ostensibly going to get another repetition in like five minutes, so it's crucially important that the feedback happens right away. In most other contexts, the work or opportunities for behavior unfold a bit more slowly, but you still want to give your coaching as close to the event as possible.

When I started working at Qualtrics, many folks there knew I'd worked with Kim on *Radical Candor* stuff. Kim was on the board of directors at the Q, and thanks to Jared Smith's personal generosity, every new hire gets a copy of her book. It so happens that I am mentioned in the book a half dozen times or so, and Kim and I also cohosted a moderately popular podcast.

The day I joined, Alexis Lopez sidled up next to me while we were walking down the hall and said, "Hi, I'm Alexis. I'm going to be on your team." Until very recently, I did not know what happened next. If you'd asked me, I would have told you my response was charming and magnanimous, that I was generous with my time, stopping everything to focus solely on my new, precious teammate. But Alexis and I were talking about this recently while recording an internal podcast, and she reminded me that the reality was that I barely uttered a word and kind of brushed her off. Embarrassing. I know I am something of an acquired taste, but I never thought I was that much of a train wreck.

Anyway, cut to about six months later, when, modeling feedback culture perfectly, Alexis said to me, "Hey, you're being a little bit of a hypocrite." I loved it because I knew she trusted that she could shoot me straight. So I'm all smiles, genuinely excited to get her input.

"Really? How so?"

"You are all over the Radical Candor podcast, book, and videos talking about feedback this, feedback that, and we've been working together for six months, and you haven't criticized me *once*." Importantly, Alexis is one of those rare birds who truly loves to get coaching around how she can be better. I asked her once why she thinks that is, and she replied, "If someone is willing to tell me how they think I can be better, why would I not want to hear that?" Genius.

I laughed in response and was actually relieved that this is what she thought. Because in my mind, I had done *nothing but* criticize her work since I showed up, more of a series of SWI scenarios. The reality was that Alexis is both the Adam and the Eve of all things HR at Qualtrics, which means that she founded or cofounded nearly every thread of Qualtrics's HR capability. From compensation analysis to performance management, promotions, engagement surveys, diversity and inclusion, and people analytics, she wound up each of those cars, set them down, and let them rip. Others have since picked them up, wound them up again, tinkered with them, etc., but all can be traced back to Alexis. She intelligently designed processes in close collaboration with key senior folks and executed them with varying levels of help along the way, but she was generally on an island for a lot of the work. The processes worked well but were, in my view, imperfect, particularly for the next phase of scale that I was specifically brought in to help us gear up for.

So, for six months, I asked her lots of questions and together we changed . . . everything. In one case, we assembled an eight-person team for months to make major revisions to a critical set of HR processes around performance management, compensation, and promotion, all of which she had originally founded. My concern during that time was that she thought I considered her professionally weak because I believed all her work needed to be revised. In reality, she didn't see our shared goal of improving the things she'd built as anything resembling criticism. Let's be super clear, though—if the purpose of improvement coaching is to help people discover what they can do better, I did little more than that for our first several months together. Alexis, luckily, has never thought of her work as a reflection of herself or her values. To her, it's just work, and whether it is good or bad doesn't imply anything about who *she* is. What an incredibly mature perspective; far too many people allow their work to affect how they feel about themselves. She does not. Alexis only cares about getting better, so to her, none of the effort to fix her stuff was criticism; it was a gold mine, like I was giving her the answers to the test. My focus on helping her improve the work, coupled with her absolute thirst to be better, created an environment where she got better, I got better, the work got better, and we were all just psyched to be doing it.

PART IV

Career

- *How supportive is your manager of your growth and development?*
- *How much do you agree with the following statement: "My manager cares about me as a human being"?*

The Career Conversations model that I am about to lay out is a game changer in the employee-boss relationship. A long time ago, I received a simple piece of advice from author and tech executive Sheryl Sandberg: "When thinking about your career, you have to have a long-term vision and an eighteen-month plan." The Career Conversations model I developed, which I will share with you in detail in the next chapters, helps you clarify both with the people you manage. It is extremely effective—both for your employees, who will benefit from it throughout their careers, and for your organization, which will see it reflected in employee experience measurements.

A couple of years ago, I helped a colleague named Antonio execute it at his company. I received this email from him in March 2021. "Hi Russ, you might not remember, but we spoke on the phone for thirty minutes about career conversations, and I'm still deeply grateful for your generosity and the bond that those conversations created between my team and me." In April 2021, I heard from Adam, a manager I had worked with closely a decade earlier. He wrote, "Hey Russ—I hope you're doing well! Wanted to share something. I've been using your Career Conversations framework for the past ten years or so with my directs. At my current company, in collaboration with our L&D team, we're starting to teach the framework to all managers—around a thousand people across the company. I'm optimistic that, in addition to teaching a skill and helping the recipients, it'll have a positive impact on the culture. Take care!"

I have a large number of these anecdotes available, but I also want to offer some data that suggests there is real magic in working through this full model with your teams. As with so much of the employee experience, it is much more than a "nice-to-do"—there are strong correlations with results.

When Heather Carpenter, Qualtrics's Experience Business Partner for the Americas region, was working with a manager who wanted to deploy the Career Conversations process in her organization but was receiving some pushback because of the time investment it involved, she said to herself, "Let's get the data." The People Analytics team did some analysis and discovered that, yes, executing the full model with your people makes a big difference—and those are their words, not mine. The first question they asked survey respondents was, "Have you worked with your manager to develop a Career Action Plan?" As you will soon understand, developing a Career Action Plan (CAP) definitionally means completing the full Career Conversations process. Managers for whom the answer was "yes" had overall manager effectiveness scores that were an average of 19 percentage points higher than the scores of those who answered "no." As for the question, "How supportive is your manager of your growth and development?" we found that managers who'd completed CAPs with their reports scored higher than those who hadn't by an average of 23 percentage points.

We then asked people who'd had these Career Conversations with their managers if they found them helpful for their careers. Of them, 74 percent indicated that the Career Conversations were indeed helpful, and their managers scored 36 percentage points higher on their overall manager effectiveness scores. When we asked that same 74 percent, "How supportive is your manager of your growth and development?" they scored their managers 48 percentage points higher than the small subset who indicated that the Career Conversations were not helpful.

Most interesting was the fact that managers who completed the CAP process scored meaningfully higher on every single individual manager effectiveness question than managers who did not. There are many explanations for this. It could be that managers who are willing to invest this much time in career development are more naturally inclined to invest more time in both direction setting and coaching. It's also possible that completing the CAP with employees is so leveraged that those managers enjoy a "halo effect" and often receive the benefit of the doubt. It could also be that those managers, now understanding the career aspirations of each employee in depth, are able to customize and tailor their interactions with their employees to be more human and less official—and, of course, more relevant. The bottom line, though, is clear. Employees whose managers invested fully in Career Conversations were more engaged and felt systematically better about their relationships with their managers than employees whose managers did not.

There are many ways for managers to improve their relationships with their employees. But there may be no better way to show them that you care about them as human beings than by engaging deeply with their long-term career aspirations. Doing so will grow and develop your people while driving up employee engagement, retention, and results.

A lack of growth and development, or their close cousins learning and development (L&D), are among the top reasons high performers cite for leaving companies. Many believe the solution to this problem is training. Learning-related problems? Training answers! I've come to believe that training aimed at solving the growth and development problem is most frequently a major red herring.

By some measures, formal, centralized L&D investment is mostly wasted. "Research shows that employees forget up to 75 percent of the material taught and revert back to old practices, wasting the bulk of that investment, with little progress made," wrote Dr. Gabriella Rosen Kellerman of BetterUp in her article "The Path to Individual Transformation in the Workplace." Torch Leadership Labs is an emerging company with a similar idea—to personalize individual learning—and they raised $25 million in February 2021. I could point you to a mountain of other research that supports that conclusion, but a slightly different and enormously fun way to view the gap between the perceived and actual value of training is that BetterUp has reached a $1.73 billion valuation in 2021 based on the theory that centralized L&D doesn't work! Doctor Kellerman's position is simply that learning must be in context, which means the person best suited to quarterback any employee's growth and development is their manager. Have I mentioned that the manager is holding the keys?

My own experience confirms this. The logic for so much of the curricula that centralized L&D functions produce turns out to be specious—it *seems* like it should matter, but in practice it turns out to be so general that employees don't find it relevant to their own unique circumstances. For reference, when I was at Google from 2005 to 2012, we had seemingly limitless resources; the company was effectively printing money. Heavy investments were made in L&D because employees were saying in exit interviews and Googlegeist surveys that "learning, growth, and development" was a problem. But despite all of that investment, the scores on career-related questions and growth-and-development-related questions continued to decline, quarter after quarter.

My seven-hundred-person organization was no different. But instead of repeating the same ineffective stuff, I developed a new model for Career Conversations and rolled it out to all eighty of my managers. I insisted they actually do it, and when they did, we changed the slope of the curve on those questions! We were the only large organization in the company to reverse that negative trend. From an L&D perspective, the critical difference with our new model was that we applied learning, growth, and all those other related buzzwords to the context of a person's long-term career vision.

There are a few critical ideas that support the Career Action Plan as it relates to L&D:

1. Most "development and growth" comes from challenging work, day in and day out, not from training.
2. People can accept a little bit of role stagnation, temporarily, if they feel that their manager/organization has their progression front of mind. Progression should be mostly a function of their long-term career vision.
3. Specific job-related training, i.e., how to do this current job, is a critical discipline and needs to be owned by the function in which that job is performed. For example, sales enablement

should sit in sales, engineering enablement should be in engineering, and neither should be in a central "training" function. This training is crucial for low-tenure new hires but rarely affects the scoring or mindset for "learning and development" for tenured employees with lots of on-the-job experience or who have reached the top of their productivity curve.

4. Other nonfunctional, non-job-enablement training is sometimes useful, but it should be in the context of an individual's path, specifically a path to a long-term vision. Otherwise, it tends to fall flat, and the investment is wasted.

Career Conversations are exactly what they sound like—discussions about someone's career with an emphasis on their long-term aspirations. When done well, these should connect a person's historical life story with their futuristic wildest dreams by gaining a detailed understanding of who they are and what motivates them, both day to day and over the arc of their entire hoped-for career. I never want to portray this kind of thing as easy. Michelle Obama nailed it in *Becoming*, when she said, "I recognize the universal challenge of squaring who you are, with where you come from and where you wanna go." When you do know where you want to go, you can begin to plan your path to get there, starting right now.

Here's a simple metaphor to help us get started: The dream job, or career vision, is a lighthouse in the distance, perhaps miles away. At first, the only way you can identify it is from its flashing light. Looking closer, you can make out its tall, cylindrical shape. I think it's white. Maybe a red roof, hard to say. Windows on the side? Wait, is that a bird on top or just the lighthouse keeper who has bird legs? We're pretty sure it's a lighthouse, but we can't say much more right now.

We have a number of ways to bring this lighthouse into focus. Maybe some binoculars, maybe a telephoto lens, or maybe just taking a few steps in that direction. Bottom line is that we have to do some work to be able to describe that lighthouse in the distance in any kind of useful detail.

The next major thing we must understand is the path behind us. How did we get to this place at this moment in time? We are standing here staring at a lighthouse for some reason. Importantly, we need to understand the hilltops we climbed, the rocks we stumbled over, the valleys we crossed. We need to understand the forks in the road and why we chose fork A over fork B. There's a lot to forkin' understand there. We need to understand what was great and what was terrible. Learning from that path behind helps us chart a better, smarter, probably more direct but certainly more rewarding path from here—this moment in time—to there, our precious lighthouse in the distance.

Only now, with the lighthouse in focus, are we in a position to connect the path behind us to our path forward. As in precise military drill, we're going to take a full thirty-inch step forward, together. We might have to get out the machete and cut a path. Could be thickets and woods. Could be ice. Could be a U-turn. It can be perilous, but the most important thing is that we clear the way and drop a big-ass flagstone down just in front of us. We will not get to that lighthouse today, and by the looks of things, we probably will not get to that lighthouse tomorrow or next week, and that's okay, but we want some reasonable assurance that the progress we are making right now, in this moment, is relevant and in the right direction. We could probably drop that flagstone almost anywhere in the 180-degree field of view bisected by the lighthouse, but we probably want to avoid the other 180 degrees behind us. I say probably because we might look 10 or 15 degrees behind us and spy a smooth, luge-like path to the lighthouse. Every once in a while, the calculated decision to go backward in order to go forward more quickly is the right move. I've done it. Most important is that even when we decide to go back a little bit, we still have that lighthouse in full view, and getting to it is the reason we make any decision from this point forward. Focus on the lighthouse in the distance. Understand the path behind us. Connect them up.

When it comes to long-term vision and supporting people in their careers beyond these four walls, it is common to ask, Why should managers do this? Why should they have these conversations with their team? Why should they invest this much in, explicitly, the idea that people *will leave this place*?

Besides the fact that a real human is sitting in that chair across from you, and that your job is to enable the success of the people on your teams, the number one reason that managers should have Career Conversations with the folks on their teams is that people need . . . so . . . damn . . . much . . . help with this. I've had hundreds and hundreds of Career Conversations, and I've witnessed a multitude of self-defeating tendencies. Flawed thinking, deprioritization, people trying to live their parents' dreams . . . it's all bad, and people need help. We all do. Lots of people can help. Friends, family, other colleagues, but if I'm a manager, I don't want to leave it to chance that folks will get this help for themselves.

Reason number two: the people on your team and in your organization are absolutely thinking about such things as the next step in their career. If your best people leave you and the company, it is very likely because they feel a lack in the area of growth and development. They are actively considering all of their options within and beyond your company and your team. A 2016 study from LinkedIn Talent Solutions found that people's number-one motive for changing jobs is career opportunity. Usually, there is far more opportunity right here, right now in the current role than is immediately obvious. That's because the manager hasn't taken the time to make this clear to the employee, and the manager couldn't do so because they don't really know who the employee is. Managers are just not investing the right way, almost certainly allowing the "career conversation" to be about the next promotion or the next pay raise, definitively short-term ideas, which won't matter really at all in the larger scheme. None of it is really about their growth and development and, more specifically, growth toward something that matters.

So you have a choice. You can choose not to engage and be surprised when someone hands in their resignation, Monday-morning quarterbacking your decision to bury your head in the sand—or you can be a part of that conversation from the beginning and contribute to your valued employee's decision-making as a trusted advisor. It might still be the right thing for them to leave, but at least you've had some time to prepare for their departure. It's also possible that someone is suffering from a little "grass is greener" syndrome. When I worked at Twitter, I had an extraordinary marketing lead, Anne Mercogliano. Anne came and told me she was leaving one day. I had a good sense of what her career aspirations were because I had invested in her using Career Conversations, and it was really obvious to me that this opportunity she was planning to leave for was not the right one for her. We talked about it at length, and ultimately she agreed. "You only leave Twitter once," I told her, which was advice that David Rosenblatt, the former CEO of DoubleClick, Twitter board member, and CEO of 1stDibs once gave me when I was thinking about leaving Google. Knowing where Anne wanted to be in the long run, knowing what she deeply valued, I was able to help her avoid a huge career mistake. She stayed not because I thought it was important to retain her at all costs but because we agreed that this just wasn't her best option given her path behind her and her lighthouse in the distance. As it turned out, we both left Twitter around the same time, and the opportunity she pursued then was awesome—much more befitting of the kinds of challenges she's great at tackling, and with a company that was much more promising. Anne's path has been filled with jobs she loves, jobs that maximize her strength. She's now the CEO of Gretchen Rubin Media, helping take Gretchen's important work to the masses.

Maybe, though, now is the right time for someone to leave your team, and maybe the next step they are planning to take makes a ton of sense given their long-term career aspirations. They need to know it's okay—safe—to be clear about their intentions. But if you are participating in the process, perhaps that next step can be within your current company, enabling an overall retention of talent even if it feels like a loss for your team. But hey, if it's time for someone to move on, if you have proven trustworthy and invested in the process, maybe you can reduce the time that there's a gap in your operation and backfill much more quickly. You can save the company cycles in trying to retain this person by saying, "I really believe it's time for her to seize this opportunity." Skip the financial save, which will likely only delay the inevitable by about six months as most financial saves end in short-run attrition anyway. We can follow Sting's poetic advice here, "If you love someone, set them free."

In short, your choices are:

1. to participate, be helpful, and be prepared, or
2. to be unhelpful and get blindsided.

Amazingly, some of us will still choose door number two.

Finally, and extremely importantly, isn't your job as a leader to help people grow? I hope this is an obvious "yes" to you. Day-to-day task management is not enough to inspire the people on your teams. Management is absolutely *not* solely about the tasks. It is also about hearts and minds. In fact, when I developed this module working with Candor, Inc., I called it "Leading with Heart." Helping the people on your team grow toward their dreams is the kind of differentiated and leveraged activity that makes people want to work for you, that makes them feel like you have their backs, like you are a human being who actually cares about them. Helping your people grow is a crucial activity for you to undertake as a manager.

Let's assume you're right here with me. "Russ, I agree. My job is to help people grow, and I do it every day." I think leaders who have their own hearts and minds in the right places can still get this "helping people grow" idea wrong and often do, because they never ask the most important question. Yes, we agree your job is to help people grow, but you have to constantly ask yourself: "Help them grow *into what*?"

If you are not clear on the answer to that question, then isn't all of this "help them grow" talk entirely arbitrary? You want to help them grow into who they want to be and not who you need them to be or who you think they should be.

As you might guess, I get asked for a lot of career advice, and as you also might guess, I love providing it. It's a passion. But having gone through this model so many times, I cannot in good conscience give someone a shred of advice until I get some clarity on the job or the vision they have for themselves at the pinnacle of their career.

Career Conversations are all about growth, yes, but critically, growth toward a dream. The path is (1) to the lighthouse and (2) (mostly) forward. These conversations will enable you to *really help* the people on your teams, to be a leader who invests in the team, and to be the kind of manager that makes work more rewarding and more fun.

Provided, of course, that you are doing it right. There are four big ways that people get career conversations wrong.

13

The Problems with Career Conversations Today

PROBLEM 1: CAREER CONVERSATIONS FIGHT CLUB

In the book/movie *Fight Club,* Tyler Durden taught us that the first rule about Fight Club is that you do not talk about Fight Club. Fun fact: this is also the second rule about Fight Club, and there are only four rules! In other words, 50 percent of the Fight Club rules are about not talking about Fight Club. Confidentiality seems important to the group, and, clearly, suppressing any and all discussion about Fight Club works for that organization—but it doesn't work for having impactful career conversations.

In my view, the single biggest problem with career conversations is that there are no career conversations. Good for Fight Club, bad for employee growth and development. This lack of career conversations is not always intentional, and so this characterization is not a judgment, just a fact.

Oftentimes, leaders just don't know they're supposed to be having these types of conversations—ones that deepen their understanding of what makes their people tick, about their lives beyond their current roles. Other times, leaders are under pressure to deliver against quarterly goals, and these longer-range conversations simply don't factor into their leadership mix. In almost every company I've worked in, managers are running around with their hair on fire just dealing with yesterday, today, and, if they are lucky, tomorrow. They are so busy trying to deliver the quarter, ship a product, close the accounting books, or launch the campaign that the idea of a higher-leverage set of conversations that don't immediately impact a one-day radius from today seems like a poor use of time. At the very least, this kind of conversation can easily and understandably slip lower down on their priority lists. Remember, when it comes to prioritization, 3>2>4; if you have more than three priorities, you have none. But the practical outcome is that the days slide by, giving way to weeks. Weeks give way to months, months to quarters. Soon critical talent is leaving your team, and some are headed to crappy opportunities.

Even if it crosses leaders' minds to have deeper, more meaningful career conversations, they often don't know exactly what to do. Sure, there are a couple of books on the topic—like this one—but this kind of thing is taught infrequently, even at some of the great companies that care deeply about the growth and development of people, and in some circles it is even actively resisted. Focusing on the teaching part of that last statement, for example, L&D professionals might manifest a "not invented here" mentality, preferring instead their own agendas about what will work, their own priorities around what needs attention.

Even worse is that leaders often *think* they're having deep, meaningful, impactful career conversations when they're really just having imposter conversations. For example, some leaders believe they are having career conversations because they're having performance reviews. Performance reviews tend to be mostly backward-looking appraisals of the most immediate observed performance. When it comes to someone's career, we should be focused mostly on the future.

Performance reviews are not only an insufficient substitute for real career conversations, there's also reason to believe they don't even serve their primary purpose. GE, long recognized in the industry as a pioneer of formal performance review processes, is now leading the way in reevaluating the approach. If performance reviews aren't such a good way to review performance, what on earth would lead us to believe that they are good for something else?

Performance reviews tend to suffer, paradoxically, from both recency and primacy bias. Regarding recency bias, review cycles are designed to be six or twelve months, but very often the feedback is heavily focused on the last six weeks or so. This is understandable, but it can feel unfair to an employee who believes they had a big achievement way back in the review period. Primacy bias is really about managers "saving up" their feedback. Getting feedback on things that happened potentially as far back as eleven months ago doesn't feel particularly useful to employees, but sometimes this stuff shows up because that manager's gotta write *something*. Of course, if the feedback is in any way adverse, it can feel downright unfair, especially if it's dated. Many companies are following GE's example and scrapping their annual or semiannual review process in favor of more frequent, continuous feedback. (Side note, I am actually a strong believer in a semiannual performance review cycle for a large number of carefully considered reasons beyond the scope of this book. I'm hammering the review here only to make the point that the career conversation and performance reviews are just not the same, and in my opinion they are hardly even related.)

So I am going to offer a new first rule about career conversations: *do* talk about career conversations. We need to educate managers on the importance and proper process for doing this.

PROBLEM 2: SHORT-TERM FOCUS AND PROMOTION OBSESSION

If career conversations are happening at all, they are frequently carried out with an excessively short-term focus. John Maynard Keynes was a famous economist who argued that governments should intervene and solve problems for the short run because, as he wrote, "in the long run, we are all dead." When people resist thinking about their long-term career vision, I think that they roughly use Keynes's logic—what's the point?

However, when it comes to career planning, the long run is a paramount consideration. Consider this exchange from the 1990s sitcom *Seinfeld*, in which Jerry and his best friend and loveable loser George Costanza come up with the essence of our plan here.

Jerry: If every instinct you have is wrong, then the opposite would have to be right.

George: Yes, I will do the opposite. I used to sit here and do nothing, and regret it for the rest of the day, so now I will do the opposite, and I will do something!

We've been trained to focus on the short run, specifically that next promotion, but we're going to do the opposite and focus on the long run now, because in this case, working through long-term career aspirations helps us make better decisions about the short and medium run as well. I do not favor putting arbitrary time boundaries around this kind of thinking, i.e., "What is your ten-year plan?" I believe we should instead think about long-term career aspirations within the pesky constraint of a whole lifetime. The bottom line is that this notion of a "ten-year plan" is just arbitrary, tends to promote shorter-term thinking, and is only slightly more addressable than the long-term vision.

When it comes to discussing their careers, people often instinctively focus on their current role, on new projects that might interest them or offer some growth, or maybe even on that next role. These are easier time horizons to think about, and there is some value to working those things through, but we have to be careful about having these conversations *outside* the context of a long-term career aspiration, or worse (and as happens frequently) as a substitute. You as a manager do need to be able to address the short term, but the point is that these conversations should always formally and explicitly contemplate a long-term career vision.

Stephen Covey cautioned that "some habits of ineffectiveness are rooted in our social conditioning toward quick-fix, short-term thinking." One example of excessive short-term focus I've seen is the idea that promotion equals career development. I don't have enough room to indicate the extent to which this perspective is badly flawed, but I see it over and over in promotion-obsessed companies and with promotion-obsessed individuals. The weight that any single promotion tends to have on the landscape of "career" is often perceived to be far heavier than reality. People imagine an ACME anvil, and I see a canary feather.

Earlier in the book, I mentioned my role at Twitter, where I led the SMB advertising business. One of the go-to-market teams I oversaw was our sales organization, which helped onboard and optimize advertisers so they could get the most value out of Twitter Ads and, of course, hopefully spend more money. Great people, great team.

The team was very junior, as this was more or less an entry-level sales job. Some on the team had a little bit of experience, but mostly it was made up of super-high-potential, bright, energetic, hardworking people in their first or second real job. As a result of the team's juniority, there was an expectation that promotions would come fast and furious. For the record, this wasn't an altogether unreasonable expectation. A side note on a peeve of mine: I think too much is made of "those damn millennials" and their unwieldy expectations of being a "vice president after being in the job for six months." As I say to most people, "Those are your employees, and they think about life and work differently. You have a choice: you can complain, or you can figure out how to work with them. I recommend embracing them and figuring it out because they'll be running things soon." Never mind the problem with applying population-level dynamic tendencies to individuals. That's called stereotyping, and it is just as wrong to do that for a generation as it is for, say, an underrepresented group. It creates the exact same problem—making some prejudgment on an individual because they belong to some category. When my millennial employees put in the work, they had high expectations for reward. I was okay with that. Slight digression, but please just stop complaining about millennials. Okay, boomer?

As in any organization, the promotion problem here was that not everyone got promoted at the exact moment when they thought they should. For our young sales team, I was probably more like a "work dad," or maybe more accurately "work grandpa." I didn't directly manage any of them, or even directly manage their direct managers for that matter. They were in my organization, and for a time, I was quite literally the only guy with kids old enough to walk and talk, so when someone would get news they didn't like about getting passed over for promotion, they might roll into my office hours to chat or set up a one-to-one. I was usually well prepared by their manager. We were all okay talking to these folks about the promotion decision, the promotion and performance calibration process, etc. Those discussions were useful and instructive to all of us, but most interesting to me was the preconversation setup. For example, any preparatory materials I received about the discussion—the calendar invitation, the email they would send me for context, or the brief hallway conversation to set things up—almost always contained something like, "I want to chat with you about my career."

No you don't. You want to talk to me about your promotion.

Wait . . . what's the difference?

Promotions, at their absolute best—absolute *best*—represent incremental personal growth, an increase in scope that comes with new challenges and responsibilities and requires new thinking. That's good! Who doesn't love a new challenge? Growth! Learning! Development! Great. Additionally, a promotion is a really nice, formal recognition for a job consistently well done. Companies only have so many formal levers they can pull to say "Thanks," and promotion tends to be one of the most meaningful. A promotion is something you can tell your family and friends about. Both of my promotions at Google, for example, were extremely meaningful, and I won't pretend for even a half of a heartbeat that they weren't. When I was promoted to director in 2007, my wife rented a limo, and she, my dad, my sister, my boys, and a couple of friends picked me up at the office and took me to my favorite sushi restaurant. In the Marines, we always made a big deal out of promotions that, frankly, were mostly a function of time and not so much merit.

Those feelings, though, like so many other things that feel great in the moment, are usually ephemeral. You enjoy a nice glow for about a week, and then it's back to business as usual, with the promotion offering no clarity on what the future holds, what it should hold, and how to get there.

At its worst, a promotion is nothing. A nominal title change with virtually no change to anything else. Sometimes, a promotion is just formalizing the fact that you've been doing the job already. At most places I've worked, we've said that to get promoted, you have to be doing the next-level job well for six months or more.

Normally, promotions fall somewhere in between; they represent a rare, formal recognition of a job well done that includes a pay increase, a title change, and the opportunity to signal upward mobility on LinkedIn or your résumé. I get that those things matter to people for an array of reasons. But we shouldn't be confused that real career growth tells a clear story through intentional scope increase and skill development, all within the context of a long-term career aspiration, and to get those things, promotions are absolutely not necessary.

Career conversations mandate that we wrangle the future so that we can bring it into better focus and deal with it explicitly. And there is nothing about a promotion per se that is rooted in a compelling, shared understanding of the future.

PROBLEM 3: CHECK-IN-THE-BOX MENTALITY

I have a story to tell you; maybe you've heard it before. It's called "The Ridiculousness of the IDP." Ah, the IDP, or the individual development plan. As someone who cares about people, champions people's careers, and tries like the dickens to help improve people's thinking about their careers, the IDP is my Thanos or Lex Luthor, the lovechild of Doc Ock and Venom, and if you aren't into superheroes the way I am, let's just say it's my archnemesis.

"But Russ," you say, "it has the word 'development' in it!"

"Right, but catgut is made from sheep intestines, head cheese is a meat product, a horned toad is a lizard, and a velvet ant is a wasp."

"Ummm . . ."

"What's in a name?"

Nestle in, children, it's story time.

Once upon a time, the Chief Whatchamahoozit (CWO) at Company XYZ, Inc., gathered her VPs together to look at employee engagement survey scores. A common question asked in employee engagement surveys is, "How much do you agree with the following statement: 'I am seriously considering leaving Company XYZ'?" Right there on the slides it could plainly be seen that an alarming percentage of current employees were seriously considering leaving. XYZ had some good analysts gathering experience data, and it was obvious that "development" and "career" were the reasons employees didn't want to stay.

The employees' eyes darted, casting sideways glances around the room, settling finally, like one hundred movie-premiere spotlights converging on one tiny focal point, on the HR leader. Very much to his credit, the HR leader, a hero named HR Guy (HRG), was passionate about growth and development, and so, manifesting his executive table stakes bias for action, he said, "Maybe we should have everyone do an IDP."

There was a deafening silence in the room as "IDP" echoed around in everyone's heads. One VP's brow unfurrowed. Another VP's eyebrows arched in a hopeful way. And still another's eyes opened wide. Several more sat up in their chairs. Hope.

"Great idea! IDPs! Let's gather our directors and give them the good news!" the VPs all shouted in unison.

All of them except HRG skipped out of the conference room arm in arm, straight down their yellow brick hallway. Still seated, arms folded, with a look of great satisfaction on his face, maybe even a wry smile, HRG silently nodded to himself in approval. "IDPs, baby. Problem solved."

The VPs scattered across the campus and convened their directors. VP Radha said, "I need everyone in your organization to do an IDP."

"OK, boss, by when?" asked Director Juliana.

"Next Friday," VP Radha responded.

Director Juliana strode straight into her staff meeting and hijacked the agenda. "We need everyone in the org to have their IDPs done," she announced.

The managers asked a few context questions, but they were generally on board. Manager Omar asked, "When do we need this done by?"

"Next Wednesday," Director Juliana replied, giving herself a little breathing room in case her folks dillydallied.

"Got it," Manager Omar replied. Manager Omar made haste back to the team cubicles.

"Gather 'round, team!" he called excitedly. Team members slowly removed their headphones, put on their shoes, paused their NBA live streams, and gathered around Manager Omar. He said, "Gang, I need your IDPs done."

"Not a bad idea, Manager Omar," said Individual Contributor (IC) Rodrigo, which he didn't really mean, but he was playing the game. "When do you want it by?"

"Monday," Manager Omar said, leaving nothing to chance. An unspoken "Who will be done first?" competition was underway, with everyone trying to get their respective organizations across the finish line first.

"Roger that," agreed IC Rodrigo. The rest of the team followed Rod's lead, committing to hammer out their IDPs over the weekend. Rod went out Friday night and strangely, at the ripe old age of twenty-five, did his first-ever keg stand at an absolute rager. Through the bleary eyes of Saturday morning, he started working on his IDP, and he finished it up Sunday evening. Rod's a good guy, very detail oriented, so he made sure he filled in all the spaces on the sheet. Every "i" was dotted and every "t" was crossed. Rod was so thorough, he sometimes even dotted his t's and crossed his i's, a real overachiever. Rod's IDP featured all the usual suspects, such as "I want to be the team lead" as his "career goal," and "I've got to stop caring so much" as a development area. Monday came. Rod and everyone else said, "We're 100 percent compliant on IDPs," and on it went, all the way up the chain.

Manager Omar gave a thumbs-up to Director Juliana. Director Juliana gave her thumbs-up to VP Radha, who turned around and gave his thumbs-up to the CWO. Everyone had their IDPs done and done early. "Wow," HRG thought, super pleased with himself. "Surely—and at last—I'm gonna go from HR leader to chief people officer." Company XYZ was 100 percent compliant on IDP completion. Success.

Meanwhile, no one up the chain had any idea what was in any of the IDPs. No one actually read them, and worse, no one—and I mean no one—ever looked at a single one of those IDPs again. Not even Rodrigo, who had tried sort of hard to do a good job. Success? More like suck-cess.

Six months later, they all reconvened in their swank conference room to reexamine the engagement scores. "Intent to leave" had increased, and the employee experience analysis continued to suggest that growth, learning, and development were the primary drivers behind folks' intent to move on. Nothing had changed because employees and managers, by and large, just checked a box and filled in some forms. This is a sad story, I think we can all agree—I'm crying as I write this.

While this story is fictional, I lived a version of it myself. At the beginning of part IV, recall, I talked about how Google poured seemingly endless amounts of money into learning programs that were aimed at fixing all the things departing employees said were wrong. What this cautionary tale and the Google story have in common is that you can waste a lot of time and money on activities that fail to deliver the results you need. This is an illness plaguing most companies—high visibility, low-impact activity. Let's stop that cycle now.

PROBLEM 4: CAREER *FROGGER*

We plan a lot of stuff. We plan end-of-year baseball parties. We plan end-of-school-year gifts for teachers. We plan family reunions. We plan our families. We plan our meals. We plan weddings . . . big time. We plan our weekends and our vacations. Those are fun. But despite all of this planning, when it comes to the thing we spend most of our waking hours on—our careers—we're surprisingly unstructured and haphazard.

Sometimes we don't plan because we don't know exactly how. Other times we offer ourselves the excuse that "I don't know what I want to be when I grow up." Well, I'm here to tell you that isn't an excuse, because, hey, everyone has a dream.

If we focus on our careers at all, we do so with no real intentionality, with no grounding in anything logical, and without a shred of analytical thinking, likely because the world has not ever offered us even a halfway decent analytical framework to help us *do* the thinking! Often we take a *Frogger* approach: get to that next open space as quickly as possible, avoid a car—*whoa*, avoid that speeding truck, timer counting down providing an anxiety-inducing sense of urgency. If you get a split second, you look ahead to be a bit more strategic, but your focus quickly comes back to the current location and the next hop. Again, you quickly hop to the next open space. There are some alligators somewhere, but you'll deal with them when you're closer. You evaluate: where am I now, and where's the next open space? You evaluate again: where am I now, and where's the next open space? And again: where am I now, and where's the next open space?

These so-called plans are almost never grounded in a compelling future or an examined sense of one's past. In *Frogger*, you get to the other side of the road, which is apparently what most chickens are after. Is that what we are? Frogchickens? The other side of the road, in this case, looks exactly like the side you were just on, and oh, by the way, the next task is to cross another identical road.

With all of this reactivity, it's impossible to arrive at any sort of relevant conclusion about what someone—manager or employee—should do right now in service to their career aspirations.

Sergeant Steve Luhrsen, who eventually became Colonel Steve Luhrsen, captained our Marine ROTC unit marksmanship team back in the 1990s. He was truly a fountain of wisdom—street smarts meets homely country sagacity. For example, a friend of mine, Mike Moran, and I were once held up at gunpoint in downtown Columbia, South Carolina, while on our way to a keg party. Mike and I told our tale at the kegger, and the party hosts were kind enough to let us drink for free.

A few days later, we were recounting the story to Sergeant Luhrsen and some others. The gunman was definitely drunk, and a number of the upperclassmen in the room made fun of us, pantomiming a highly inebriated person, barely able to stand or speak, holding up a stick and dispossessing us of our wallets. We were embarrassed that we'd done nothing, and their ribbing was making us feel worse. "The gun was just a little .25-caliber Raven," Mike admitted, suggesting that the threat was not so great because that bullet was basically a BB. Sergeant Luhrsen, who could probably catch a bullet in his teeth, chew it, and say, "Good source of iron," answered, "Yeah, a little .25-caliber Raven that'll kill you deader than shit." His point was simple: our wallets, and especially Mike's Velcro one, were not worth the risk to our lives.

Sergeant Luhrsen's wisdom would make an incredible book, but with respect to this CAP process, he had one shining piece of advice. One time we were working on some kind of complex exercise when Sergeant Luhrsen walked up to me and said, "Laraway, what's your plan?"

Confused, I said, "What do you mean?"

"What's your *plan*?" he said as if emphasizing the word "plan" would suddenly jar me into understanding.

"I don't really have one," I said, sensing strongly this was the wrong answer.

"Not good enough. In everything, Laraway, you must have a plan. Look at me. I always have a plan. *My plans almost always suck, but at least I have a plan.*"

His point, simply, was that a plan is never etched in stone. When we assemble a plan, no one orders a headstone, has their plan engraved on it, and sets it up at their future gravesite. A plan, Sergeant Luhrsen highlighted, is little more than a platform from which to deviate. Act or be acted upon. Mike Tyson famously said that "everyone has a plan until they get punched in the mouth." Sure, your plan might ultimately suck. That's fine—change your plan. What's not okay, as Sergeant Luhrsen will colorfully remind you, is to have no plan, because then you are wandering aimlessly, just like Frogger, jumping from open hole in traffic to open hole in traffic, heading nowhere special.

WE CAN DO BETTER: THE US MARINES AND COMMANDER'S INTENT

I'm going to pull some more wisdom from the Marine Corps. One reason that the US military in general and the US Marine Corps specifically are so successful is that they know how to systematically push decision-making to the most junior folks in the organization, as these folks tend to be closest to the most relevant facts on the ground. A fire team leader—often a twentyish-year-old corporal—leads three marines and is trained to make life-and-death operational decisions and make them faster than the people shooting at him and his marines. There is a famous story from World War II in which Erwin Rommel, the German tank commander, was outmaneuvered by a US sergeant because Adolf Hitler was attending a wedding and was not available to approve one of Rommel's decisions.

Agility really matters because battlefields are such a chaotic mess. The Marines call this chaos "the fog of war," which describes not only the literal fog on the battlefield—smoke from explosions, vehicle exhaust, flying soil, sandstorms, etc.—but the figurative fog that manifests as jammed weapons, lost ammunition, malfunctioning radios, twisted ankles, and the need to shout complex instructions through brain-rattling noise. The fog of war is, simply, ambiguity and chaos. To ensure that even a twenty-year-old corporal knows what to do in such a confusing and high-stakes—literally life-and-death—environment, every operation that the Marine Corps undertakes is guided by a detailed set of plans that are laid out in five paragraphs covering Situation, Mission, Execution, Administration and Logistics, and Command and Signal, or SMEAC. Each of these orders carefully articulates what your team is supposed to be doing and what the teams around you are supposed to be doing. The problem is this: as Helmuth von Moltke, the famous nineteenth-century head of the Prussian army and military strategist, put it, "No battle plan survives first contact with the enemy."

I'm sure you've heard some version of this before. We know what Sergeant Luhrsen and Mike Tyson said about plans. Some people invoke Murphy's Law: whatever can go wrong, will go wrong. Agile software development companies constantly adjust their plans as the world disrupts them. Even the Scottish bard Robert Burns nailed it with, "The best laid schemes o' Mice an' Men. Gang aft agley." The idea that even our most carefully laid plans rarely stand up to the rigors of the real world seems to be well understood and generally well accepted—from warfare to athletics to shipping technology products. So, if all their plans go awry, how on earth do those young marines on the battlefield know what to do? Enter *commander's intent.* A mandatory part of the SMEAC orders, commander's intent is a succinct statement by a commander that describes the end state of the battlefield, or the envisioned future the commander wants to see when the operation is all said and done. Those young marines, shouldering enormous responsibility in the midst of character-testing chaos, can take decisive, winning action right now, even when their plans have been rendered useless, because they know what the end state is supposed to look like.

I'm not the first to think of using commander's intent outside of the five-paragraph order. In 2010, *Harvard Business Review* published an article titled "Manage Uncertainty with Commander's Intent." There is a lot of uncertainty in our careers. There is a lot of *now* before *then*, but we can't let that be an excuse for inaction. Let's manage some of that uncertainty with commander's intent.

We can take relevant action right now—the present—because we have a clear vision to work toward—the future.

LONG-TERM VISION AND AN EIGHTEEN-MONTH PLAN

Perhaps fifteen years ago, when we were both at Google, Sheryl Sandberg was talking to me about career development. Recall from earlier in the book that she said, "You have to have a long-term vision and an eighteen-month plan."

She mentioned this to me in response to a couple of errors she'd observed people making in thinking about their careers. They either did no planning at all—see "Problem 4: Career *Frogger*" above—or they tried to plan every step of the way. Well, we know how many carefully laid schemes "gang aft agley," as the poet put it. That's what happened to Sheryl. She had every step of her career planned brick by brick—she has a pattern of overachievement in her life, after all. "If I would have stayed with that plan I laid out for myself as a young woman," she admitted, "I would have never taken this Google opportunity."

Whether you prefer the Marines, the *Harvard Business*

Review, or an ultra-accomplished Silicon Valley executive, the charter is clear: having a clear understanding of your long-term vision allows you to take relevant action right now.

OVERVIEW OF THE PROCESS

In practice, career work comes down to three structured conversations from which you and your employee converge on a plan. They should occur within a period of about three weeks (but it's common for them to stretch out longer, and that's okay too). I will describe each part of the process in detail, but here is a brief overview:

- **Start with the Past—Life Story.** In the first conversation, make an effort to understand the employee's motivations and values, the things that drive them. You should focus on their major pivots and transitions, including athletics choices, hobby choices, study choices, and work choices. Why did they make those choices? What did those transitions teach them about what they love and hate about their work? This is the *path behind* that led this human being to this moment in time.
- **Talk about the Future—Dreams.** Conversation 2 is where you ask questions designed to discover where this person wants to be at the pinnacle of their career. Some are skeptical that our younger workers know what they want to be when they grow up. Others worry that it's too early in a career to home in on a single vision. Don't use those worries as excuses; nothing is irrevocable at this stage, and we will cover how to overcome these objections.
- **Plan for the Present—Career Action Plan.** With a firm understanding of the past and the future, now you can begin to build a relevant and thoughtful action plan, with clear

timelines and explicit owners for each action. Most often the manager or employee will "own" the action item, but sometimes you're pulling in other folks too. Expect little to happen if you don't fill in the blanks of *who* will do *what* by *when*. We can see the path behind us, we can see the lighthouse in the distance, and now we just need to start swinging our machete through the vegetation so we can *cut a path* that connects the two.

Once we understand the past and the future, we'll know what we need to do right now.

14

Conversation 1: Life Story and the Things That Make People Tick

VALUES MISMATCH, CULTURE MISMATCH

In 2012, when I left Google, I joined a forty-person startup called FreeMonee. Yes, you can laugh at that name, everyone else does! FreeMonee no longer exists, but I will take to my grave that it was founded upon a good idea. Its thesis went like this: the primary objective of a coupon is to drive incremental foot traffic, ideally getting you to spend more than you had intended—but coupon redemption is very low in the United States, maybe 0.1 percent or less. Digital coupons are redeemed at a rate that's somewhere between 0.5 and 2 percent—still fairly low, especially when you consider that there is another option to drive foot traffic: gift cards.

Gift cards redeem at a rate of like 80 to 98 percent. If you're like me, you're wondering who the hell those 20 percent of people are who don't redeem their gift cards. It's like they're throwing away free money!! Wait a minute. Hold on.

Free . . . money . . . ?

Free money
Freemoney
FreeMoney
FreeMonee!

Now it makes sense. Okay, maybe that name is simply unjustifiable, but here's how it worked: it started with the recruitment of credit card partners, because the first thing we needed to do was analyze—anonymously—credit card usage at scale. For example, we could see that certain cardholders would visit, say, Target on average eighteen times a year. It would be extremely valuable for Target to get them into the store one or two more times a year. One way you might do that is to give those customers a gift card, especially since the gift card was far more likely to inspire the extra trip than some measly coupon.

Next up were the marketing partners, the people to whom it was my job to sell. In this example, the marketing partner is Target. Target knows its analytics and could say with a high degree of certainty that offering a Target loyalist, say, fifteen dollars would not only mean that they would make an incremental trip to the store but also that the trip would almost certainly be profitable, meaning they would spend more than fifteen dollars. We were also able to help in this analysis and recommend the right amount for the right consumer at the right time. At least that was the idea—our technology was never quite that good.

But here was the magic: the Target gift card would not be a physical gift card. It would appear on your credit card statement. So in this example, you would receive a notification that you've gotten a fifteen-dollar Target gift card. When you went to Target and spent fifteen dollars, the credit would be automatically applied.

This is a fairly complicated model and rather hard to execute, which was probably the company's critical vulnerability in the end, but I felt good about the thinking and the bones of the model. Further, the CEO was an experienced guy with a successful track record of producing substantial exits. His public profiles used to say something like "seven successful exits producing billions in value." It was true. The guy was really good at taking these ideas and turning them into nice exits for shareholders. At that time, my primary career vision was to be a CEO, so I thought this would be a guy I could learn from.

Before I joined, I had been at Google for seven years. I loved my time there, and they had invested a lot in me to signal their desire for me to stay, and that really meant a lot to me. But when I looked at my path there, it seemed as though I had topped out. The company was really good and really good to me, and I was very proud to work there. But I had just reached a point where I felt like things were getting too easy.

My job was a good one. It was called "industry director," and at a high level, I was responsible for leading a team that managed a couple hundred accounts, including Microsoft, Oracle, Citrix, IBM, Symantec, and Adobe, and over $700 million in revenue. Before I got there, the team was flailing, missing targets, and producing negative year-on-year growth.

At first I thought it was bonkers that the sales leadership team gave me this job, given that I had never once in my life had a quota at any level. The reason I got it was because the large customer sales organization was learning that, as you scale, sales are a lot less about the art of the sale and much more about the science. Being a whiz in a customer meeting is a lot less useful at senior levels than understanding the blocking and tackling aspects of running a team. They were seeing other non-sales people crush these roles, and pattern matching suggested I could fit the mold. John McAteer, who would become my boss, took a chance on me, and no one was more surprised than I was.

Fast-forward nine months—just nine months—and we were beating quota, back to double-digit year-on-year growth. I was just about to pull my biceps tendon by patting myself on the back when I paused and thought, *That was too easy*. And then it hit me.

Google was a perpetual motion machine. Sure, I might be able to apply some oil to the machine, but it was hard to really feel like I mattered to the company. Senior management knew they could trust me to run things well and take good care of our people. But to this perpetual motion revenue machine, I just didn't matter. I started to look to my left, my right, and above. The next role up, called a "sector lead," was not a real job. It was an administrative construct because the next *real* job, which was head of sales for the Americas, simply could not have all twenty-plus industry directors, like me, reporting to her. Every single job I'd had at Google up to that point had felt like the challenge I was handed was more than I could tackle and more than I deserved. I thrived on the challenge—my entire career has been about hard problems with good people. But now I had reached a point at which the company could not produce a stretch assignment for me in a reasonable time frame.

So I picked my head up and made exactly the wrong move. Mistake number one was answering a headhunter call. It feels good to get headhunted, but it's a fundamentally reactive disposition when planning your next step. Far better to proactively identify the best next roles and then pursue them.

Most embarrassing was my failure to understand the culture at FreeMonee—particularly as I am someone who is supposed to know a thing or two about culture. To give you just one minor example, I once received feedback from the CEO that he didn't like the way I dressed. The company was populated by a bunch of ex-Oracle people who had determined that the key to success in sales is a dry-cleaned shirt, wool pants, and shiny shoes. "We are not going to have a blue jeans sales culture," he said to me. Aside from the fact that lots of sales folks in tech were wearing nice shoes, nice jeans, a blazer, and an oxford, I had just come from a place that was pretty successful and had published on its website as one of its core values, "You don't have to wear a suit to be serious."

On the more important end, the leadership team was (mostly) accidentally misleading our various partners. I'd walked by the office of a couple leaders one day and heard them saying something about an unsustainable burn rate. I inserted myself into the conversation. "Well, the good news is that we just raised over $30 million, so we should be good, right?" One of the leaders said, "Well, we subsidize a lot . . . we put a lot of offers into the marketplace on behalf of our customers. That's very expensive to do."

"OK, well—that's easy to solve, let's just dial back our subsidies."

"We can't."

"Why not?"

"Because our financial institution partners expect a certain level of activity, and if we stop the subsidies, they will be pissed."

"Let's talk to them, tell them we can't survive like this."

"We can't because they don't know we're subsidizing; they think these are real sales, real offers from merchants."

"Say again?"

"The banks . . . they think we've signed all these merchants [marketing partners] that we're putting in offers for."

"How did that happen?"

"We had to do it. If they knew we didn't have any merchants, this business would have never achieved liftoff."

I was really worried about this. But as a senior person on the team, I felt like it was my duty to try to make this better. I asked the CEO whether we might be exaggerating a bit, trying to use the least accusatory language I could come up with. "This is how you get a network business going," he replied in his defense.

He wasn't wrong. History records that many successful

companies have exaggerated their way into existence. In *ESPN: The Uncensored History,* Michael Freeman tells the story of how Bill Rasmussen got traction in the late 1970s when starting ESPN. The simplest version is that Bill and his team told the NCAA that they had the satellite provider lined up, and they told the satellite provider, RCA Americom, they had the appropriate financing to rent time on their system. Both were exaggerations and bluffs, but luckily both came through at the eleventh hour, and ESPN was born. Alas, history mostly forgets the thousands of companies that crashed and burned as a result of their truth stretching. I want to win, but I never want to win like that. I was there for six months before moving over to Twitter.

My first interview at Twitter was with Dick Costolo, the CEO. I was preparing to exit FreeMonee, so everything was fresh, and I decided—for no good reason—to feature this experience prominently. "Well, what did you learn?" he asked me. My answer was so simple. "I learned," I told him, "that I should never take another job unless I am beyond certain that our values line up." To this day, I pick companies based on mission and values. . . . Hard problems, good people. That's it. Not all lessons have to be this painful. You can help your reports take steps to avoid such pain by engaging in the Life Story Conversation and gaining clarity on what they truly value in their work.

GETTING TO VALUES IS HARD

Stephen Covey said that "personal leadership is the process of keeping your vision and values before you and aligning your life to be congruent with them." But to align your life and your career with your values, you have to know what they are. Ideally, one could simply make a list of values and be done, but this doesn't work for everyone.

Before I go any further, I want to clear up any potential

semantic confusion. This exercise is about values, but not necessarily about ethics-type values, family values, or religious values of any kind. While ethics are obviously important, what we're trying to do here is gain clarity on what you care about . . . *at work*. What are the things that keep you inspired, motivated, interested, and engaged? I mention this because a fair number of people have a hard time getting past the word *values* because of those other connotations. I'm asking you not to overthink it. Values, in this case, are the things you value in your vocation. Easy.

Now to the problem. Interestingly, many people aren't totally sure what they value in their work. As a result, a practical problem with getting to meaningful values is that "every patient lies." That is the mantra of Dr. Gregory House, MD, who, if you don't remember, is easily the greatest diagnostician in the history of medicine—at least on TV. Whenever he and his team were developing a challenging diagnosis for a six-sigma mystery illness, they routinely disregarded the patient's medical history because, as they would say, "every patient lies." When it comes to getting underneath the things that someone values, the things that motivate someone, the things that make them tick, I maintain the same. Every patient lies.

They don't always lie on purpose, of course. The most pressing problem that I've observed is that most people are simply not fully aware of their own values. There is a long, at times confusing, continuum of awareness. Some are vaguely aware, and others are not even remotely aware of the things they really care about in their careers and their work. Further, many are often confused by the relationship among

A. their own values,
B. the values they think they *should* have, and
C. the values that family and friends expect them to have.

This understandable confusion can cause a gap between your true values and your stated values. Every patient lies.

To bring this to life, let's focus on a couple of values that, in my experience, seldom coexist. Think back to your days in school and consider the difference between *learning* and *getting good grades*. Which did you value? In the case of *learning,* the idea is that you enjoy learning for learning's sake—for the pursuit of knowledge or skills. Learning has no borders, whereas a class for which a letter grade is obtained does have borders, and those borders are created by a syllabus. Learning is also about the journey, and the outcome of having learned something is a sufficient outcome. In the case of *grades,* the outcome—a numerical measurement of the extent to which you were successful in the class—is the focus. One expects to put in hard work—or not—but if one performs against the stated standards, they expect to get rewarded. If *learning* happens during that process, *great!* But this value, as separate and distinct from *learning,* is about getting an A.

Assume for a moment that you are probably biased toward one over the other. Which is more important to you? Give this just a couple minutes of thought before carrying on with the text.

In thinking this question through, people will often have two distinct reactions. First, many will want to reach for *learning* because it feels so much more noble. *The pursuit of knowledge. Didn't Mark Twain write some shit about that being important? Or Aristotle? I read the* Wall Street Journal *and the* Economist. *I just like to learn. Anyway, I'm all about the pursuit of knowledge . . . at least at cocktail parties, where I also love to discuss the very meaningful distinction between leadership and management.* A second reaction might be to think back to what your parents emphasized when you were in school. Having gone through this process with hundreds of coworkers (I will now refer to these coworkers as my patients), I can tell you that the surest approach is to take the patient back to elementary school and probe their parents' attitudes toward education. We find very frequently that there was an incentive structure in the home—fifty dollars for straight A's, for example—that tended to heavily emphasize grades over learning. Interestingly, I estimate that about 75 percent of the people with whom I've had this conversation ultimately decide that they are biased toward *grades* over *learning*. It's not a bad thing. It tends to explain a focus on outputs or results. There are a lot of places in business where this focus is extremely important, like in sales or marketing.

It shouldn't come as a surprise that people have been trained by their parents and by schools to think about inputs and outcomes. Study hard, get A's. Bust your ass on the ACT, make sure you hit some extracurriculars, get into Stanford. Go to Silicon Valley or Wall Street and make a shit-ton of money. I could construct that statement one hundred ways and still make the same point. For so many, life is set up that way.

This reality makes sense to most of us, and yet so many people want the answer to be *learning*—so much so that they lie. I've spent a great deal of time thinking about this; I have even gone so far as to construct the "Getting to Values" portion of this career management methodology to control for this tendency.

I think the first answer to the question "Why would someone lie?" is that it's often unintentional. Most people have never stopped to consider or articulate their full set of values in the professional context. Some can clearly articulate one value. "My number one job requirement is autonomy." Ask them for number two, and they draw a blank. "What is a value, anyway?" they might ask. People are good at articulating life values—*I value time with my partner or my children,* for example—but these are not exactly what we're looking for in this particular context.

The second answer, though, is really not much more complicated than this: People are people. They have fear. They seek approval. Their instinct is self-preservation. They have dreams, aspirations, goals for how they want to behave and how they want their coworkers to behave. They care about how they are perceived. When talking with the boss or the boss's boss, there is always a power differential. I don't care how much of a chill bro or ya-ya sisterhood kind of manager you think you are, how much you believe you are your reports' friend, you still control—or at least influence—meaningful things to them, such as compensation, promotions, assignments, projects, and firing, just to name a few. As a result, folks might not be ready to show up and just start laying bare their souls. They might be a little bit guarded with you, a bit oriented toward saying things that position them in the best possible light.

Below is a model denoting three major sources of stated values, or the values that one will articulate when asked. There could be more, but that doesn't matter.

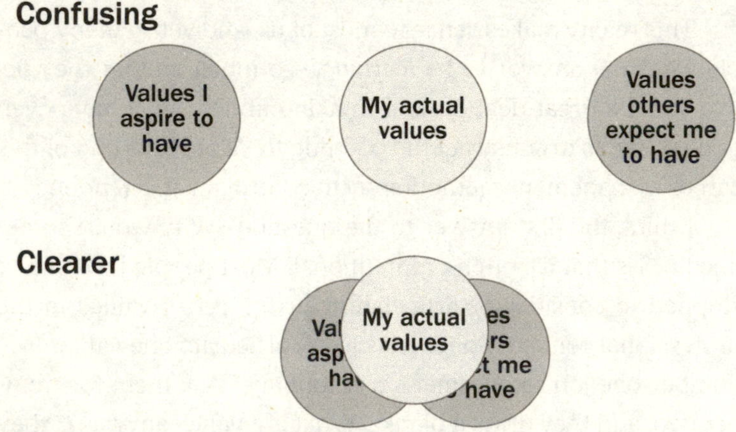

Overlap equals clarity. When your acquired and aspirational values line up with your real values, it's much easier to understand what you want. But that isn't always the case. The best way to uncover people's real values is through an exercise I call the Life Story Conversation. The next section is written to help a manager facilitate the conversation, but at the risk of stating the obvious, there's absolutely no reason that you can't find a friend and take turns facilitating each other through these conversations. In fact, this is exactly how I teach this at companies. Participants pair up and spend one hour in which Person A is the "manager" and Person B is the "employee," and then they switch roles for a second hour. So grab at least two copies of the book, a friend, and a couple seats at Starbucks and have at it. Or hand a copy to your manager and ask for an intervention. But in all cases, buy extra copies, please.

THE LIFE STORY CONVERSATION

In its most basic form, you carry out a Life Story Conversation by asking someone to tell you about their life. As they do, you pay careful attention to their choices, decisions, and pivot points, identifying patterns and common themes. Ultimately, you should be able to tease out five to ten "core values" and articulate them and the evidence for them back to the employee, giving both of you a shared, highly textured understanding of what makes them tick. This activity helps both of us—the employee and you, their manager—to not only relevantly shape their long-term career vision but also help guide the critical steps they will take on their way to that vision.

I've had career conversations with hundreds of people now, and the Life Story Conversation was the last part of the process I put into place. At first, I just tried to help people nail down their long-term visions and short-term plans, but as I conducted more and more of these conversations, I started to notice some problems.

The first was that as often as not, people's long-term vision statements didn't make sense based on what I knew about them.

Maybe someone would say that their dream in life was to run a substantial part of a large organization, and yet I knew that they were completely frustrated by the slowness of large companies and their inability to make any impact within them. I often found myself furrowing my brow, and I realized that I didn't have what I needed to be a true thought partner to my employees in their career plans, that I was missing a critical piece of a complicated jigsaw puzzle. Worse, this missing piece seemed to be a corner piece—maybe even *all four* corner pieces.

So, to rectify this, whenever I detected some kind of dissonance between what I thought someone valued and what they stated to be their long-term career vision, I would say, "Can we take a step back here? This doesn't quite add up for me."

Every Patient Lies, but Not About Their Life Story

At first, I would just ask something like, "What do you really care about in your career?" Not a horrible question, actually, and if that's all you've got, you can get some value from it. But I quickly realized that relying solely on this question left us with a pretty dull, thoroughly non-nuanced, and often downright wrong view of what the respondent cares about.

Remember our lesson from Doctor House. "Every patient lies." Most often, our people just can't articulate a set of things that really matter to them. They might not know what kinds of things are relevant. "I value ethical practices." Well, that's great, but so does pretty much everyone not named Nixon, and this probably doesn't offer us any unique benefit in thinking about our careers, other than perhaps "Steer clear of Enron." Also possible is that they don't know themselves that well. I have seen countless instances where the person I was listening to "had never really thought about that."

Take Stella, for example. She was a compliant patient, a doctor's favorite kind; she fully engaged with the process. Early on, she talked about a transition she had decided to make around the beginning of high school. She said, "Well, I was in cheerleading, but then I actually gave that up and joined the swim team in tenth grade, and I loved that activity so much more than cheerleading."

She was preparing to keep on truckin' through her high school years, but I knew that we had probably just plowed over a key insight about what makes her tick. I backed her up. "Can we pause for just a second? I have a question about that," I interjected. "You said that you loved swimming so much more than cheerleading, right?"

"Right."

"Why?"

And what happened next is the kind of thing that causes me to leap out of bed in the morning because I love this work so much. Stella averted her eyes, effectively shutting down her visual cortex so that she could better engage her prefrontal cortex to answer this question, and said: "Huh, I don't know. I never really thought about that."

Let that sink in for a moment. *I don't know. I never really thought about that.* What she said *next* was absolute gold. "Well, okay, um . . . I loved cheerleading. I really did. We had so much fun . . . the girls were great. We actually worked pretty hard, and honestly, it was a good and natural outlet for life after gymnastics. I guess it scratched an itch. But the reason swimming was so much better . . . I mean we worked *so hard*. We were in the pool at 5:00 A.M. most days swimming lap after lap, but the key for me was that all of that hard work manifested in tangible outcomes. I would end up on the podium more often, or even if I didn't podium I would usually reduce my times and set personal records."

This was a clear insight that ultimately proved to be a pattern throughout her life, and this value had manifested as early as high school. Even better, she hadn't even known this about herself.

If I had just asked Stella, "What kinds of things make you tick?" I'm not sure she would have ever mentioned this "hard work leads to tangible outcomes" idea. Even if she were inclined to say, "Hard work leads to tangible outcomes," how much credibility would either of us put into that? That's the kind of cool-sounding yet thoroughly clichéd shit people write on their résumés all the time but has no real meaning. Conversely, now Stella and I shared a rich, detailed, and textured understanding that, for real, her whole life, she has valued tangible outcomes as the fruits of her hard work. Gold.

Another case I'd like to highlight here: Erin and I had a great Life Story Conversation. Throughout it I probed and prodded with "Tell me more about X?" and "What did you love about Y?" and "Why did you make that change then?" I had a great view of her life and career, and a strong sense of the things she deeply valued. I thought I knew what made her tick. So I ended the conversation with the question I use to end every single one of these conversations.

"What else?"

That is my go-to open-ended question. I probably use it about one hundred times a day, in meetings, one-to-ones, you name it. Erin paused. I could see that her body language was contemplative—it suggested that there was something she'd left out and she was wondering if it was really important to include. "Well, I remember when I was at IDG," she said after a while. "The internet was really just taking off, and I was a part of a small group there that was tasked with figuring out our internet business—how we would monetize in this new digital world. There was no playbook, no set way to organize, no set way to do anything. Beyond that, within IDG we were a vanguard kind of group . . . I mean we really *mattered*. That meant a lot, but the biggest thing there that I think back on, and what made this truly the happiest time of my career, was that we built something from nothing. Was that important?"

The happiest I was in my career was when we built something from nothing. Wow. Erin was *going to skip that*. She asked if that was important the way a surgeon might hold up a kidney she forgot to reattach after an operation and ask, "Hey, is this important?" I knew at that moment that Erin's future would have to include something entrepreneurial—you know, *building something from nothing*—and I wondered to myself if she knew that, too.

Sometimes our "patients" just aren't in touch with the things that really, deeply make them tick. But patients lie for other, more nefarious reasons too. The worst thing that I see, and I've seen this a bunch among the high-achiever types I've worked with at Google and Twitter, is that they are trying to live out their parents' values more than their own. Yikes. My friend Darcy is a nurse, and I made this point one time to her, and she said, "Yeah, 75 percent of the doctors I work with are miserable. All of them would rather be playing guitar and writing poetry. Invariably, when I ask them why they're doing this thing that makes them miserable, it can be traced back to some notion of trying to live up to their parents' expectations."

Another type of lie is when someone tells you what they want you to hear. Early on, I asked one of my direct reports if I could run one of her highest performers, Eugene, through this process. At the time, I thought it would be a good way for me to get to know Eugene better, and I had hoped that he would see it as a benefit and not a punishment. Sort of like, "Hey, you won a career conversation with Russ!" and not, "Dude, my condolences for having to do one of those career conversations with Russ."

Eugene was an outstanding employee. Great guy, good

teammate, kind soul, but there were probably four or so layers of management between him and me. I have never been the kind of guy that wields or even draws attention to the authority derived from my position, but it's also naive to think others are not acutely aware of it. Going into the conversation, I was thinking that I was going to get to know a high performer dude to dude, but he had quite a different perspective. He was thinking of the meeting as a make-or-break opportunity. That's a little bit of a misalignment, and it certainly contributed to our less-than-compelling encounter. It was like he had memorized my full LinkedIn profile, made some guesses at the things I valued, and then parroted them back to me. He was either trying to feed my ego or remove all risk from the conversation. Most of all, he wasn't being honest. Google had some perceived elitist tendencies in its hiring back then, and Eugene came from a comparatively humble background. Sometimes folks worried that exposing that they hadn't gotten a 4.7 GPA in intermolecular quantum space brain rocket surgery from Harvard's Stanford Institute of Princeton Technology would somehow be used against them. I knew Eugene hadn't given me the whole truth, and I knew why. Fortunately, this taught me that I needed a better way to deeply understand what makes people tick.

The Life Story Conversation was the answer. People lie, but no one can lie through their entire life story. If you make them tell it and you really listen, you are virtually guaranteed to have a Dr. Gregory House, MD–style epiphany.

How to Run This Conversation

TIMELINE STYLE

"Starting with kindergarten, tell me about your life."

I admit it, this feels like a weird thing to say to a coworker, at least the first time you say it. Nonetheless, it is the sentence that

I recommend that you start with. If you aren't explicit about the fact that you really want to hear the full story from way, way back in the day, you run the risk that they will focus on a much later stage in their life. You have to make it clear, "Oh, yeah, baby . . . we're goin' *all* the way back."

If we zoom out for a moment, the way to think about this conversation is to loosely organize it around major periods of time. For example:

1. Elementary/primary or middle school
2. High/secondary school
3. Undergraduate university (if applicable)
4. Earlier career
5. Graduate school/previous role(s)
6. Current role

If you're aiming for an hour or so of conversation, you're looking at somewhere around ten minutes in each major period. This is not meant to be a rigid prescription; more of a guideline for productive facilitation and to provide a sense of how deep you're going to go in each area.

This is almost always regarded as a super fun, engaging way to learn some amazing things about the people you work with, and it's also an extraordinary display of showing someone that you care about them. We shouldn't forget, though, and also in the context of this overall career conversations approach, that this particular conversation does have a specific purpose, and to achieve that purpose, the conversation need not go beyond an hour. Promise. In fact, forty-five minutes is possible. My only caveat here is that perhaps your first couple tries at this you might bleed to seventy-five or ninety minutes. All good. Keep trying to get this dialed into sixty minutes or fewer. Having an approximate mental map of the major buckets of time in someone's life can help you keep track of where you are, assess your progress on the fly, and ultimately deliver on the full promise of a productive, fun, and efficient conversation.

HELPFUL FACILITATION QUESTIONS

Over the years I've uncovered some helpful facilitation questions. Just reading them gives you a sense of how this conversation should go. One note of caution: this is not a checklist. You're having a conversation as opposed to an interrogation. These are meant to get you unstuck.

Precareer

- *How did the people around you view education?*
- *Anything to share about your family? Siblings? Community?*
- *Tell me about your friends.*
- *Did you participate in any activities in school? What did you get out of those things? What did you love about them?*
- *Describe your high school life.*
- *Did you work during high school?*
- *Why did you choose that university? That major?*
- *Why that internship?*
- *What did you learn about yourself in college?*

Previous Roles

- *Tell me about your first job—how'd you end up there? Why did you end up there?*
- *Why did you leave? Why did you choose your next company?*
- *When was the last time you said "I love my job" or felt that way? Why did you feel that way?*
- *What aspects of past jobs have you loved the most?*
- *What aspects of past jobs have you hated the most?*

Current Role

- *Why did you come to this company?*
- *What do you love about this company? What do you hate?*
- *What's the best part of your week?*
- *What makes for a great day around here?*
- *What kinds of things get pushed to the bottom of your task list?*

TAKE NOTES LIKE YOUR LIFE DEPENDS ON IT

I recommend taking copious notes.

In a notebook.

With a pencil.

Seriously.

OK, maybe not the pencil, but the rest . . .

There is a really big difference between information and intelligence. As Joshua Goldfarb, director of product management at F5 and regular contributor to *SecurityWeek* magazine, put it, "Information is merely data. Data by itself doesn't include any context. It doesn't help us understand how to apply it to a specific problem." We don't want mere information; we want intelligence.

Understanding the life story is effectively an exercise in processing bits of information to see patterns emerge over the course of someone's life. Any single story or insight is merely information. Some of that information is extremely valuable and telling, and some of that information is less so, even if it's super interesting. The key insight, though, is that it's often impossible to know until after you've heard the full life story. Then each piece of information has full context.

With that in mind, there are a bunch of reasons for taking notes like your life depends on it. The first reason is that taking loads of notes puts you in the best possible position to achieve the ultimate desired outcome of the life story career conversation: five to ten values as evidenced by the pivots someone has made throughout his or her life. It is extremely difficult to tease those out if you just sit and quietly listen. When someone talks about their life story, they will cover a lot of ground quickly, and I can fully attest that while you are in the moment it's easy to miss something that matters. Note-taking can actually slow the process down a bit and make it more deliberate, which can ensure that you fully experience all the moments and pivots that matter.

Also, when you are in the moment, you lack the context of *the rest* of their life story from that point on, which can make identifying something that matters very, very difficult. It's not a terrible thing to say, "Sorry, can you give me just a minute. This is good stuff, and my note-taking is lagging behind the conversation." I do it all the time. Some managers prefer to sit and listen, and while this is natural, pleasant, and fun, you should be conscious of the fact that you are less likely to be able to string together useful intelligence.

I also specifically recommend taking notes in a notebook and not on a laptop. Some people insist on putting everything into Evernote, GoodNotes, reMarkable, etc., and if that's how you keep yourself together, then I say go for it, but if you are not religious about Evernote or digital notes in general, I suggest the notebook. A few big reasons for this. First, the laptop creates a physical barrier between you and your employee. Also, not everyone has the discipline not to take a peek at Gmail, Twitter, Jira, or Salesforce while their computer is open. That's a cardinal sin! Further, it's much easier to "mark up" your notes to create the final product of this conversation when they are in paper form. One practical tip: I went through a phase of using an iPad with GoodNotes and the Apple Pencil, and this combination is lit, fire, *en fuego*. The iPad does not create a physical barrier, and

GoodNotes has a few critical features, such as handwriting-to-text conversion. My Apple Pencil went missing, and that was that, but the reMarkable 2 is a great device too. Both are great solutions for digital note-taking.

Many people think the act of note-taking somehow makes you seem less present. I actually think the opposite is true—even if you're using that dreaded laptop. What better way to show that you care than to demonstrate it clearly and physically right in front of your employee? By taking notes on just about everything you hear, you are fully immersing yourself in their life story. I'm not sure I can name a time at work when we're more present for our people, more clearly demonstrating that we really care about what they have to say and that we really care about who they are. There might not be a greater expression of active listening, either.

EXTRACT FIVE TO TEN VALUES AND SHARE

Once you reach the end of the Life Story Conversation, you might feel a little tired, or you might feel completely energized. It probably depends on a lot of things, but one thing I can almost guarantee you will *not* feel is clarity on your employee's values. You now have a big giant book of information, and you need to turn it into intelligence, which is something you can both act upon.

I recommend you start the process of teasing out five to ten core values immediately after the conversation is done. Once you get good at facilitating and analyzing this conversation, you can usually knock this out in fifteen to thirty minutes. Because the story is so fresh, I will often schedule myself thirty minutes immediately following the conversation to give myself the time and space to do this. Below are a couple of real-world examples of what this looks like in my notebook—one example in a physical notebook and one example in GoodNotes. The circles often were drawn during the note-taking to flag a hunch that whatever story or pivot the person is explaining is going to tell me something about what they really value. By visually flagging it in this way, I can go back later and start to highlight the items that support a pattern.

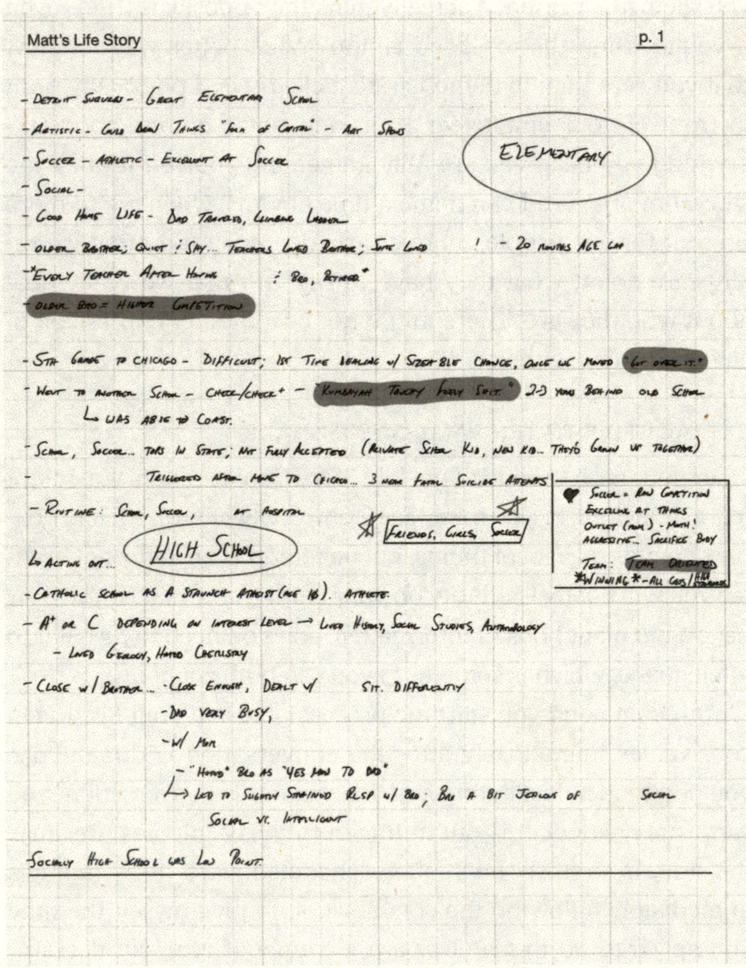

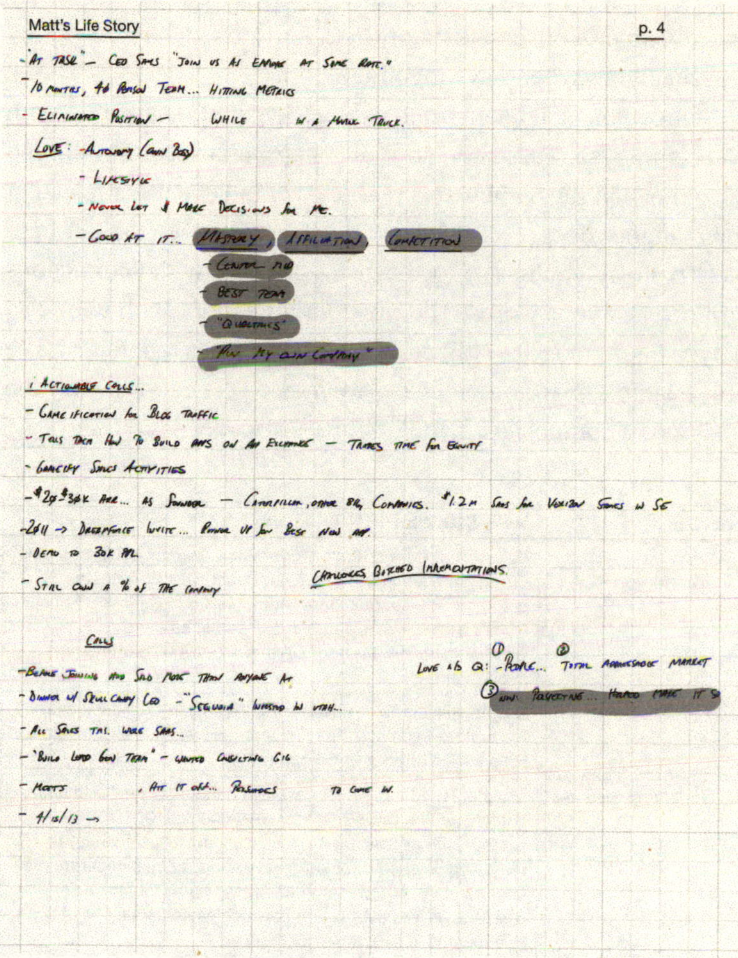

Matt's Life Story
p. 4
Love:
- Lifestyle
Mastery
Affiliation
Competition
Calls

Once you have some signal, write down five to ten core values, maybe in a Google spreadsheet or in a table in a shared document, and back them up with evidence. For example, you might write down "Autonomy—Given a lot of freedom at a young age, she made many of her own critical decisions as early as her freshman year of secondary school." I've developed a Coda-based (www.coda.io) product for keeping track of the entire Career Conversations process and have shared it on my website, www.whentheywinyouwin.com.

Once you document what you've learned, share this with your employee. These are, after all, *their* values, so they should have the final say on how this reads, but I believe it's crucial that the manager does all of this hard work as a service to their people. That way, you're saying "I heard you fully" with your actions and not just your words. The product you share with your employee might look like either of the two examples that follow. The first example is from one of my former direct reports, and the second is a composite I made up for this book.

VALUE	WHY DID WE PICK THAT VALUE?
Global View	Italy in fifth. German (age 9), French + German in high school, Claire. Experience living on East Coast. One Dartmouth quarter in France, one Dartmouth quarter in Germany. Nepal. COMPANY XYZ—involved in many areas, enjoyed "global view" of company, broader context with visibility into other departments.
Mentorship	Taught skiing in CO, "never doing that again" . . . did it again. Big brother, big sister, Tutor. Nepal teacher. Poisonwood Bible. Miss having a team at Company XYZ.
Exploration/Adventure	"Buena Serra"—:) Loved travel. One rationale for Dartmouth: stretch outside CA, stretch for relationships. OUTDOOR—outdoor club at Dartmouth, rock climbing (chose ww kayaking!). Cog Science enabled "exploration" across departments. Colorado Sophomore summer. Always had a job, extra cash—to never have to turn down doing something bc of $. Five months in Nepal. NZ sabbatical.
Lifetime Learner	Reading on car trips, "good at school," valedictorian, magnet puzzles, freshman skier = slow and scared, moved toward mastery "clear improvement"—"really liked training for skiing." Math minor, German minor. Favorite thing about Company XYZ—always a new, exciting project, always learning.
Competition	State spelling bees, math competition, homeboy Lyle who is "so smart, but we tied," "real" valedictorian :), beat the hot shot ski girl, "yeah I'm super competitive."
Relationships	5 Friends elementary school = friends today, Best friend from second grade = best friend today. Our homie, Lyle. High school friends not based on arbitrary criteria (proximity), but on substance (smart people, people who share global view). Dartmouth: tight-knit floor (Hoth outpost).

VALUE	WHY DID WE PICK THAT VALUE?
Lifetime Learner	Reading on car trips, "good at school," valedictorian, magnet puzzles, freshman skier = slow and scared, moved toward mastery "clear improvement"—"really liked training for skiing." Math minor, German minor. Favorite thing about Company XYZ—always a new, exciting project, always learning.
Hard Work	Performance Grade: "I got a performance grade and an effort grade in high school. Interestingly, my parents were in many ways more proud of the effort grade, and perhaps predictably, so was I."
Autonomy	"From a very young age, I was expected to make my own decisions and I quickly grew to love this, and got quite good at it fast. My decision to leave college to become a [leader] in France was not something my folks were excited about, but they let me do it, and I followed my passion around the world outside of Michigan."
Build Something from Nothing	"I loved my job at XYZ because I built something from nothing, and we were pioneers—and regarded as thought leaders in the industry."
Outcomes Matter	Swimming>Cheerleading—"Swimming so much better than cheerleading because hard work led to tangible outcomes."
Relationships	I met my lifelong best friend, Adrian, when I was in third grade, and we're still best friends to this day." "I don't enjoy the process of sales, or cold-calling, but I love building relationships."
Mentorship	Taught skiing in CO, "never doing that again" . . . did it again. Big brother, big sister, tutor. Nepal teacher. Poisonwood Bible. Miss having a team at Company XYZ.

Benefits

IT'S FUN!

You really should enjoy this. I mean it. If you go through this process once or twice and you don't enjoy this, you should seriously consider turning in your manager badge, and I'm not kidding. Take your lack of enjoyment as a sign from the universe that you are absolutely not supposed to be managing people.

> [Steps off soapbox.]

The vast majority of managers do enjoy this, as do most employees. One important point, though, is that we are really stretching our people. Most folks are pretty guarded at work, and this process goes pretty deep. Let's be sensitive that, at least initially, this could feel intrusive. The predominant emotion for the employee heading into this conversation tends to be one of anxiety, like they are going to be assessed and judged. One of my people at Google, anticipating our meeting, joked, "You got a couch in there for me to lie down on?" Employees don't usually know what this is going to be used for, so there's some anxiety there as well. I also recommend that you start out doing this with your more influential and up-for-anything employees. People will talk, and these folks will usually put a positive spin on it and help settle other folks down.

But with all that said, employees almost always end up having a much better time than they expected. Sometimes they ask, "Can we run this on you?" because they want to get to know their manager the same way the manager has gotten to know them. I say *go for it,* but I recommend a separate meeting, set up by the team and not by you, and you should have the whole team pull your life story out of you at once rather than scheduling a bunch of independent meetings. It could be fun to set up a room with chairs in a horseshoe, manager naked (figuratively, please), alone, and under a spotlight in the middle as the team members fire up the inquisition.

IT'S EFFICIENT!

Offsites, if I'm being honest, kinda suck for many people. They generally exist to help teams build a little camaraderie, let off a little steam together, and help them get to know each other. Not a terrible set of objectives. I just question whether those objectives are systematically achieved. I will ultimately focus on that last objective, the whole "getting to know people better" thing, with an eye toward the manager and their direct reports. But first . . .

We live in a world in which diversity is no longer enough. Inclusion is a critical component of a fully harmonious workplace. Offsites, ironically, are intended to include people, but they very often have the opposite effect. Just think about it for a second.

One time at Google, we had a committee responsible for coming up with offsite ideas. This was a committee for the people and by the people, so they were all in their mid-twenties, and for some inexplicable reason, they were all male. They brought forth an idea that we'd take the whole team to a water park. *Bzzt. Wrong answer.* "Guys, I don't think everyone is going to be comfortable stripping down to what is essentially their underwear in front of all of their coworkers, bosses, employees, etc. Can we sharpen our pencil . . . and maybe get a female on this committee?"

Imagine you want to organize a sporty type of offsite. It's going to be fun, right? We'll play soccer, but it will be on a short field with one of those four-foot-tall, beach-ball-style soccer balls, and everyone will have a blast! *Bzzt. Wrong answer.* Congratulations, you've triggered all of the insecurities of the people on the team who were shy, unathletic types as children, consistently picked last on the playground. Thanks for the reminder, Phineas!

Okay, well, happy hours aren't controversial, so we'll just plan one of those. And to spice it up, you know, really get people having fun together, let's put together some college drinking games. Of course we won't get wrecked like we did in college (probably), but you can't go wrong with drinking, cornhole, and beer pong. *Bzzt. Wrong answer.* In 2015, Twitter got hammered in the press because a number of female employees complained about a frat party–themed offsite. The guy who planned it was one of the most competent, thoughtful, skilled leaders at the company. He just didn't have any representation on his planning team and made a big mistake.

Happy hours, go-karts, bowling . . . may be fun, might work.

But let's be very clear that a few minutes a pop with each employee in a noisy environment, standing there with the beer-at-the-breastplate pose, folks checking in and out with Snapchat and text messages, is simply not going to help anyone learn about the things that really make each other tick.

And don't get me started on axe throwing.

DEEPENS YOUR PERSONAL CONNECTION

Having Life Story Conversations connects you more closely to the individuals on the team, strengthens their relationships with you, and generally helps stitch the team fabric more strongly so everyone feels like they're a part of the group.

It's impossible to walk out of this conversation not feeling more connected to your direct report. You will have discovered commonalities and major differences in your lives that will connect you in a more personal way. You will become more invested in their futures, and they will feel more supported. Once at Twitter, I knew that one of my direct reports, Dale, was conducting this conversation with each of her direct reports. After doing a little calendar spying, I took Justin, one of her managers, aside after she'd met with him and asked him how it had gone. (Importantly, Justin didn't know this was my model.) He responded with enthusiasm: "I have never once had a career conversation so focused on *me*!" It felt to him like a massive investment in him, his future, and his relationship with Dale. We have so few things available to us in the workplace that can achieve that kind of connection.

Gotchas and Pitfalls

NOT ABOUT YOU

The thing to keep in mind is that this is *their* life story, not yours. Recognize a couple of dynamics that could possibly be at play.

First, sometimes, managers may tend to "take over." Second, because of the power differential—and because your teammate might initially be uncomfortable—they are primed to let you keep talking once you start. Taken together, these two things can cost you as the manager fifteen minutes of precious time simply because you overshare.

Throughout this conversation, you will certainly find some moments that you strongly relate to. "No way, you played high school soccer too?" or "Oh, wow, I was also in chemistry club!" During these moments, go ahead and make the connection, but make it briefly, and then get right back into their life story.

DROP THE IRON CURTAIN: RESPECT BOUNDARIES WHEN THEY ARE PRESENTED

A common question is, *What if people aren't comfortable with this conversation?* In my experience, people aren't—in the end—uncomfortable with the conversation, though they might be uncomfortable with sharing certain parts of their lives with a work colleague or the boss. This is okay! People need to understand that they have freedom to skip anything they feel like they need to, but let's not miss the forest for the trees. Even people who go in with misgivings nearly always report afterward that they had a good experience.

In 2013, while at Twitter, I rolled this out for all the managers in global sales. Months later, I got a call from a Twitter HR person who was doing an investigation because an employee complained their manager was trying to get too personal. The intrusion, as it happened, occurred during a Life Story Conversation, when the manager decided it was really important to probe deeply around this employee's parents' divorce.

I explained that probing a little bit was a part of the process but that a parents' divorce would almost certainly be irrelevant. First, it's not an active choice or decision that was made by your employee, so it wouldn't give you insight into what they might value. Second, it's not at all clear what kind of value you might uncover by pushing so hard on that particular element of their life. Last, if the employee is uncomfortable sharing certain personal aspects, you should just let them drop the iron curtain and move on. You can skip meaningful sections of a person's life and still get a great result. If the end result is really their core values, it doesn't matter what story they skipped or what decisions they omitted on the way to the insight. The values will still have appeared.

At one company I worked for, I ran this process with one of my high performers, Tom. During the conversation, Tom shared with me that he was transgender and talked openly about some of the ways that his life was affected by this. I rolled with it, didn't push too hard, and was happy that he had shared this with me.

At the end of the conversation, he paused and said, "Wait, how is this going to be used again?" I explained that the conversation was used to tease out a handful of core values so I could better understand what Tom cared about in his work and be a better guide to him. As I mentioned earlier, he said, "Okay, that's good. But I just want you to know I've never told anyone at work that I'm trans—you're the first person I've ever said that to. . . . I just got talking and it sorta came out, and wow, now *I* came out at work!" I assured Tom of a couple things. First, the entire contents of the conversation would remain between us—to this day, maybe ten years later, I have still not shared what I learned about him. Second, I assured him that even as I documented his core values, I would not include this particular point in order to reduce any risk of the document getting shared by accident. Your secret is still safe with me, brother!

I share these stories to help guide you through those tricky moments when you must recognize the need to move on—to move away from certain sections and offer your employee an out. At those times, you must make it safe for the employee to move in a different direction.

If I were to point to the top two reasons people don't have this conversation and, therefore, don't kick off the model, the first reason is time. If you have ten direct reports, let's say, you are in for over ten hours of work on this alone. The second reason is that you risk uncovering personal things and thus make employees feel uncomfortable.

This is probably a good time to help you understand risk. Risk is an equation in which you multiply the probability of an event times the magnitude of the event. Humans tend to really focus on magnitude. Example: an airplane crash versus a car crash. Which is higher risk? Most folks will reflexively leap to the airplane crash because pretty much every airplane crash is catastrophic—a giant tube tens of thousands of feet in the air, loaded with jet fuel and hundreds of people. Huge risk, of course, but if you do the math, you realize that while the magnitude of an average car crash is much smaller than the magnitude of the average plane crash, the probability of a car crash is far greater. So which is higher risk to you day in and day out? Almost all of us know someone who absolutely will not get on an airplane, but very few of us know someone who absolutely will not get into a car.

The probability of an employee panicking during the conversation or an HR operative getting involved in an investigation because you went too far is also very low. On the flip side, the magnitude of this conversation—the impact on your relationship and your ability to be a great career guide—is enormous, which means the risk of *not* doing it is substantially higher, in my view, than any set of mercantile concerns that might cause you to hold back. Don't allow the small risk of a misstep cause you to incur an enormous opportunity cost in your relationships with your people.

PRODUCTIVE QUESTIONS VERSUS CURIOSITY QUESTIONS

Once you get rolling in one of these convos, you will have a million questions about this person's life. People are extraordinary, and their paths are interesting. We agree. But if you primarily service your curiosity throughout the conversation, you will not end up achieving your objective, which is to develop a shared sense of five to ten core values as indicated by this person's life pivots. The key, then, is to focus your curiosity on moments that you think might indicate a value. It's hypothesis testing, really. You hear something like, "And that switch from cheerleading to swimming made a huge difference." You, like any normal person—are primed to ask, "Why?" That's great, but I would just add a layer. Ask "why" only if you believe that this might lead to insight around a value. The reality is that to fully understand someone's full life story, in every detail, could take, well, as long as whatever their exact age is at that moment. Simple prescription: just make sure you are working a theory.

SLOPPY FACILITATION: SPENDING TOO MUCH TIME EARLY

If you are forty-five minutes into this conversation and you are still talking about grade school, you have, alas, mismanaged the time. Spending too much time on the earlier parts of folks' lives presents us with a major problem. Not only do we miss potentially large swaths of a person's life story but we also miss the most important parts, the parts in which they are more fully formed, in which they are far more likely to be expressing their real values.

I realize this seems obvious when I say it like that, and yet it happens all the time. The reasons are predictable and intuitive. To state the obvious, this is a chronological story and needs to be facilitated, conveyed, and digested as such. In the context of our objectives for this conversation, it's very difficult to contextualize their last role, say, without understanding how they got there first. The other reason is because the earlier part of the conversation will often feel more delicate to you, and you'll be less inclined to weigh in and facilitate. Between people showing up a few minutes late and the small talk you share while they're settling in, it's easy to lose fifteen minutes, particularly if the person sitting across from you is long-winded and not paying particular attention, *and* you are not pushing the agenda along. If you prioritize the objective of extracting core values, you will certainly serve all the other objectives around investment and showing you care. Promise!

15

Conversation 2: Using Dreams to Get to Vision Statements

Larry was an extraordinary talent. After receiving his electrical engineering degree, he served as an engineer at Intel, became a product manager at a company that eventually went public, transitioned to being a senior business development guy for Sony Pictures, earned a graduate degree from Harvard, and worked as a consultant at McKinsey. When I met him, he was having a really nice run at Google. Those credentials are nice, but Larry also had a unique ability to get shit done.

Larry was a strong people manager, who cared deeply about teams and challenged them with high expectations. A ruthless prioritizer, Larry was willing to say "no" and focus on the very small number of things that really matter. His teams always had clear goals, and Larry would step in front of a freight train to protect them. But every once in a while, he would kind of freak out about his professional lot in life, with a particular emphasis on whether it had been fair. Even though we all know that past performance does not predict future success, it's pretty obvious that Larry had a track record of achievement. Nonetheless, he was obsessed about where his career was headed and worried that he was stuck in the ranks of middle management because he didn't play the kind of political games that seem to get other people ahead.

Larry's sensitivity to fairness makes sense. I get it . . . now. But it took me a while because I didn't fully understand him or Google's culture. I can recall vividly the first time that I participated in Google's quarterly review, rating, and promotion process. As I mentioned earlier, in the Marine Corps most junior promotions were not so much a function of merit as one of tenure. I had also worked in my own small company, Pathfinders, and we weren't big on promotions. Some folks got some raises and recognition, but promotion just wasn't a big deal.

Promotions really mattered at Google. But I had quite a rude awakening when I started to give people their great news. Expecting joy, I got misery. Many people were jealous. Others had more rational but still surprisingly negative reactions, mostly centered on some notion of "why her and not me?" There's an awful lot to unpack there, of course, but the root of all the concern was a sense that things were unfair. It was the beginning of my education in the importance not just of fairness but of *perceived* fairness.

Earlier I mentioned the work of David Rock, author of *Your Brain at Work*. Rock developed the SCARF model, a handy acronym to help readers remember a collection of social threats in the workplace. It stands for Status, Certainty, Autonomy, Relatedness, and Fairness.

Recall, that at its simplest, the brain has two parts: the limbic system, which includes the amygdala and brainstem, responsible for emotions and survival instincts, and the prefrontal cortex, which is responsible for problem-solving. As Rock notes, these two parts of the brain don't operate together—they compete for resources, oxygen, and glucose specifically. One of my students at GE Ventures was an actual brain expert, and he offered me this clarification: not only do these two parts of the brain not cooperate, but the limbic system actively interferes with the problem-solving part of the brain by bathing it in chemicals designed to help the person prioritize the flight instinct. All of this together is why, for example, it's so hard to think (prefrontal cortex) when you are scared or angry (limbic system). "I was so mad, I couldn't think straight." *Correct.*

Rock makes the point that these social threats—SCARF—manifest in the same part of the brain as physical threats, like being chased by a pack of wolves, and similarly make it hard for people to think rationally. People experience each of the SCARF social threats differently, of course, but for Larry, any real or perceived unfairness drives him up a wall.

So, one sunny California afternoon, Larry came into my office. His body language signaled that he was upset. "What is it?" I asked.

"I feel like I'm stuck and not making any progress," he said.

This surprised me quite a bit, because he was running a national enterprise services organization for a recent and highly strategic acquisition we'd made, he'd received a highly coveted promotion to director, and, after I'd worked to rectify some historical compensation inequities for him, his pay was fair. In short, he had a huge job, and he was crushing it. "Say more," I prompted.

"I am questioning what I'm doing here. It's just not clear to me that this is taking me where I want to go, and I feel like I'm constantly losing ground in my compensation, both relative to my peers and relative to what I want."

Larry and I had had similar conversations a bunch of times, but I finally saw a thread I could pull on. I told him I didn't think we could do anything about his peers and how his progress compared to theirs; I don't like to encourage that kind of thinking when I have confirmed there is no systemic inequity at play.

I suggested that we focus instead on where he wanted to go. Larry agreed—I asked my assistant to clear my schedule, and with that we were both all in.

"Where do you think this is all heading?" I asked him. Larry was initially confused by the question. Remember, he'd come in to complain about his compensation, and here I was asking him about his long-term vision. It was probably a little jarring. "It sounds to me like you have a strong sense of where your career is heading, and that it's not where you want it to go," I explained. "I think I can be a better advisor to you if we have a shared sense of how you envision your future. Does that make sense to you?"

Larry and I trust and respect each other—even now, some fifteen years after we met, we're pretty tight. So he gave me the benefit of the doubt and answered my question.

"My dream is to be a CEO."

Boom. I was simultaneously stoked and embarrassed. I was stoked because I could immediately feel that this had the potential to be a game-changing conversation with one of my highest performers. I was embarrassed, though, that I'd never asked the question before and never even picked up on the signs. For example, Larry frequently talked about Jeff Bezos, Lou Gerstner, and Satya Nadella, clearly having studied them, their styles, their challenges, and their achievements. At that moment, it hit me that I just needed to get really explicit with all my folks about their dream jobs.

"What is it about being a CEO that is appealing to you?" I didn't quite realize it yet, but I was helping Larry bring his dream into focus.

"Hmm. Good question. I think there are a few things. First, I just like the clear accountability. Whatever happens, it's on you. I think second is that I like the variety of activities a CEO takes on—from managing a range of functions to external communications to dealing with the board of directors . . . I don't know, that just seems like a really fun way to spend my time. Last, this idea of managing the functions . . . it almost seems like you're a symphony conductor, trying to create harmony among the strings, brass, percussion, and woodwinds. . . . Does that add up?" This was an incredible set of insights into what Larry really cared about in his career, or said differently, the things he valued. I would later understand where those things came from when I retroactively did the life story exercise with him.

I told him his explanation did indeed hold water for me. Based on what I knew about his strengths and his background, on how he went about his business each day, I could see him with crystal clarity as a CEO. Larry was into the conversation, and so he served the ball back, "Cool, what else can I tell you?"

I puzzled this out for a split second. I couldn't exactly articulate it, but I was struggling a little with the fact that "CEO" wasn't the most actionable articulation of the future. I was encouraged that we'd come this far, but I felt like there was still some work to do to bring this dream into focus.

"I guess I'd like to get a feel for some of the dimensions of that, Larry. For example, being a CEO of a huge company is really different than being CEO of a startup. Being a CEO of a nonprofit is totally different than being a CEO in tech, which is different than being a CEO in the military-industrial complex."

This got Larry thinking. Keep in mind that he was a five-tool player. This is a term used in baseball to describe unusual players that have "five tools," meaning they can hit for average, hit for power, run fast, field, and throw.

To the uninitiated, it might seem like every professional baseball player has all five tools, but baseball is actually pretty specialized. For example, it's very common for a power hitter—someone who can hit a lot of home runs—to be a big, slow, lumbering guy, so they don't usually run well. It's also common for great power hitters to strike out a little bit more often than the people in front of them in the lineup, so they don't always hit for average. Last, it's unusual for a power hitter to play shortstop or second base—prized defensive positions—not only because you have to be very quick to play them well but also because the fielding difficulty and intensity is much greater than at, say, first or third base. The read here, then, is that Larry is an extremely versatile guy. In his day-to-day work, this means that Larry could simultaneously operate at a very strategic level—concepts and big blue arrows—and also at a very practical level—tactics, priorities, and daily/weekly goals. Larry immediately recognized that I was taking the conversation from big blue arrow to something more tactical. He grabbed the baton, excited and sensing we were onto something, even though he wasn't exactly sure what it was.

"Okay, Russ. Maybe we can just talk about some of those details."

"Let's do it."

"Cool, I think it's easiest to say that I want to be in tech. Most of my career is here, and I have a strong interest in computer science applications for people."

"Which kind of people, Larry?"

"Well, users . . . consumers. One of the things that makes me uncomfortable about my current role is that we don't really touch consumers, we're all B-to-B," which is tech shorthand for business-to-business-focused products and services.

"I see, so would it be more complete to say that you want to be a CEO in consumer tech rather than in B-to-B tech?"

"Yeah, definitely."

"Okay, that's huge. Any specific areas in consumer tech?"

"You know, the stuff Google's involved in. Web apps, native mobile apps, mobile web. Since I did that business development job at Sony, I acquired an interest in consumer video. Does that help?"

"Yeah, a ton. So, fair to say that you want to be a CEO for a consumer-video company? Something like that?"

"Yep. That's it."

"Mind if we try to put a little bit more meat on the bone here? I think it's worthwhile."

"Let's do it."

"Okay, just going back a bit, should we think about the size of the company at all? I mean, do you want to found something? I guess to be CEO of a startup, seed stage, for example, you would probably need to found it. Also, I'm guessing that the criteria for being a CEO of a startup is different than for CEO of a Fortune 500 company, so, you know, that's why I want to press on that a little bit."

"Yeah, that's a tough one. I don't think my risk profile suits a full-on startup here. My wife and I are starting a family now, and I think that might be too much. I don't know—does that make any sense?"

With deep appreciation for his candor, I replied, "Of course it does. Makes no sense to aim your guns at something that you don't even really want to do, so for the sake of progress, let's go ahead and eliminate the startup path."

I had a passing familiarity with the stages of companies in tech. There was seed stage, which was really about raising venture capital money, often in the $3 million range, and then series A, which was more like $7–10 million, and so on. Larry had been building a strong and sophisticated operational career that felt to me like it lent itself better to larger companies.

"Okay, so on the one hand," Larry continued, "tiny is out, but a huge company also seems like not where I want to be, so I guess midsize?"

"Well look, I think that by eliminating 'enormous' and 'startup' we've zeroed in on the idea that the company has some maturity—product-market fit, an operating company, and probably is starting to scale somewhat. I don't think we have to be a ton more precise than that, right? I mean, that's probably a good place to start, and I suppose we can backward plan off of that."

"Right," Larry finished.

"Okay, so here's what I think we have: CEO of a midsize consumer tech company, possibly focused on video. Did we nail it?"

"*Yeah!* Man, that's great. I don't think I've ever said that out loud. Those ideas have been bouncing around in my head forever, but I never took the time to assemble them into something coherent and communicatable." Larry was not even sure if *communicatable* was a word (it's not), but it didn't matter. We were rolling; both of us were eager to figure out what was next. We still had a lot of work ahead of us, but we had made an incredible amount of progress in a very short time.

Larry bebopped out of my office, a spring in his step, and, at least for rest of that day, the hand-wringing and brooding were over. He had caught a clear glimpse of his lighthouse; the next step was to plan his path to get there.

A common error that I've seen managers make is that they get out of the gate strongly with the Life Story Conversation but then fail to capitalize on all that goodwill and momentum. There are two major problems with this. First, the most important part of these three career conversations is not the life story, no matter how fun and engaging it is. Far more important is the conversation that follows it, in which you help your people zero in on their dream job—what they want to be doing at the peak of their career—and then turn that aspiration into a crisp vision statement that makes it tangible enough to grab hold of. Remember, the core idea here going forward is to align your employees' short-term actions and investments with this long-term goal, which is simply not possible without a vision statement. Also, recall the data at the beginning of this part—managers who complete the entire CAP process not only score higher for overall effectiveness but also enjoy a significant halo effect in how they are seen by their teams.

The best way to start this conversation is simply to ask your employees to talk about their dream job. But of course, that's easier said than done. As we saw with Larry, adults with jobs and careers have some trouble doing this, but most kids do it naturally. I saw a dramatic demonstration of that fact in Qualtrics's offices not too long ago. One of my coworkers, Josh, runs a church group for late middle school and high school kids, many of them non-native English speakers. So many young people get their ideas about what offices look like literally from TV's *The Office*—they imagine cubicle farms, energy-sapping lighting, dingy walls, drop ceilings, vinyl floors, beet farming, Toby Flenderson, and a general malaise toward work. Josh thought it was important to show them that "No, being in an office can be pretty cool" and arranged to have them come in one evening, accompanied by some of their parents.

He asked me if I could do a session with them on career planning. My first reaction was "What the hell?" but when I thought about it, I realized there was an opportunity. First, this thing Josh was trying to do for these kids was itself worthwhile for me to invest in. Sometimes, kids need to see it to believe it, and it's only then that they can achieve it. Second, it was a chance to try out career visioning on some young 'uns. The most consistent pushback I get around career conversations is, "I'm young, and I don't know what I want to be when I grow up." I always *thought* that was crap, but after working with these kids, I now *know* it is.

There are a bunch of reasons adults resist talking about their dreams and their dream jobs in particular.

- Some just don't take the time to put their long-term interests front and center, as they are entirely focused on the here and now.

- Others fear they will be locked in, not realizing that having a vision of a long-term goal doesn't mean that you can't pivot or change later on. They forget that we are not chiseling these vision statements onto their headstones.
- Others don't feel that they can be completely honest with their boss about their future aspirations.
- Some, sadly, have learned not to dream.

But in reality, people almost always have a dream job in their heads. It might be fuzzy, but in my experience, it's there. Indeed, I have been through this process more than a thousand times, and with one exception that I will describe below, I have successfully facilitated everyone I worked with into at least one dream that they could refine into a coherent vision statement, and it's a good thing too because I cannot offer a shred of useful career advice without a vision. Absent a shared sense of what you're working toward, my advice is as likely to be arbitrary and useless as it is to hit the mark. I just won't do it.

Getting back to Josh and the kids, the session I ran with them lasted about an hour. The basic idea was to get them to state their career vision and then articulate an action plan to achieve it. I had them each write down their dream job, then I matched them with partners and taught them how to challenge each other to understand "Why is that your dream job?" After that, I had them write down one specific action they were going to take within the next three months that would even slightly contribute to the realization of their dream. Finally, they partnered up again and made promises to their partner and to Josh that they would take this action. Simple. Effective. Unbelievably cute.

My point is that these kids—people who the world has not yet taught to stop dreaming—attacked the exercise with vim. Their enthusiasm was infectious. In that room, we had not one but two future zoologists, a future master auto mechanic, a doctor, and a professional soccer player—because "I want to show off what I can do for big crowds of people and make a lot of money."

There was a bonus moment too. I didn't expect the parent chaperones to be engaged. In fact, I didn't realize the parents were participating until I asked for volunteers at the end to share their dream job and one action they were planning to take. The kids were predictably reluctant to share at first, and when someone finally raised their hand, it was one of the moms. Through mildly broken English, occasionally corrected by her future soccer star son, she shared that her dream is to be a nurse. Her one action was to restart her evening classes at Utah Valley University so she could work toward her nursing degree. I was so moved by this and everything else I saw happen that evening.

By now I suspect I've made my point. We have to push people to bring their dreams forward and develop them, creating the time, space, and accountability to do it or it just won't happen. We need to insist. You may worry that you don't have a clue about your *own* long-term goals, which might in turn cause you to feel unqualified to help others. You don't need to have all the answers. You can still guide your people through this visioning process and help your folks identify the right people and places when you reach the end of your rope. We can't accept "I don't know" from ourselves or our people, but how do we do this?

Let's go back to that image of the lighthouse. Remember I talked about laying a path to it? But first, you have to bring it into focus. Once you do, you start to notice some of its finer details. A large seabird is resting on its roof—a pelican. Every so often she descends to the sea, strafes the surface, plucks a fish, and brings it to her nest, where she has two babies. The roof tiles are red and rounded. The sides of the lighthouse are stucco, cracked in several places and supporting several large vines of English ivy. Along the black boulders at the bottom, there's a colony of sea lions.

Hopefully by now the metaphor is clear. Remember from the "Commander's Intent" section that the primary way that our marine knows what action to take in the moment is because he understands the path behind him—the five-paragraph order, if you will—and he has a clear view of the lighthouse in the distance, which is the envisioned outcome of the mission. He takes relevant action right now in the context of those two items. You need to do the same in your career.

We just need to give a bit more treatment to the idea of focusing on the lighthouse. In the metaphor, we used binoculars, but in real life, it's not that simple. I recommend the following approach. Start with a fuzzy image, which means to just say the dream job out loud. Not a single detail matters. As a coach, manager, mentor, you can ask some clarifying questions to begin the process of describing it. I recommend you spend a fair amount of time just trying to understand the dream before you explicitly try to bring it into focus.

Once you and your coaching patient have bathed in that fuzzy notion of a dream job, you can use the three questions below to home in on it further, so you can turn this nebulous dream into a crisp Career Vision Statement.

1. What industry?
2. What size company?
3. What role?

WHAT INDUSTRY?

The most obvious reason for this question is to help your folks home in on what industry is most interesting to them. But it also gives you an opportunity to use what you learned during the Life Story Conversation to pressure check what they're telling you now. For example, did they convey anything about a sense of mission? How do the companies in this industry tend to manifest mission? Did they spike on service, which might make them good candidates for government or nonprofits? Did they convey anything about innovation? Tech companies frequently believe they are "inventing the future." Inclined to save the planet? Maybe they'd be happiest working for one of the many renewable energy companies emerging these days or getting involved in the electric car space.

The bottom line is that you want to be certain that your employee's ideas for their future align, at least at a high level, with what you've learned that they value most.

WHAT SIZE COMPANY?

I think this is the most important variable to push your people's thinking on. To help, I think it's worth familiarizing yourself with generally accepted stages of companies. A quick Google search will give you any number of terms; it doesn't matter which ones you use as long as both of you are clear on what they mean. For example, consider:

- **Seed stage:** Pre-product, pre-product-market fit. Turning the idea into reality. Order of magnitude: five employees.
- **Series A:** Post-product-market fit. Expanding operations. Has shown an ability to create and grow revenue. Order of magnitude: low tens of employees.
- **Series B:** Market expansion, have a strong customer base already. Order of magnitude: high tens of employees.
- **Series C/midsize:** New products, new market expansion. Order of magnitude: low hundreds to thousands of employees.

- **Large/mature company:** Well-established products and markets, mature operations. Order of magnitude: thousands to hundreds of thousands of employees.

This is the most important variable because the size of a company likely determines its pace, its agility, and the difficulty of its day-to-day operations. I, for example, learned that I'm not really a seed stage guy. I love the idea of a tiny number of people trying like hell to make something new, but the idea is much better for me than the reality. My skills, it seems, are more suited for companies with substantial operations who need to be able to scale, or more precisely, deliver more and more units of output per unit of input. The goal is to help your folks clarify for themselves what environment they not only will thrive in but also be happiest in.

WHAT ROLE?

The last question to answer is: What role do you envision? This is often the least comfortable question for folks to answer, and I've never figured out why. It's also the one most likely to inspire the "It's not really a role for me, it's more of a 'concept' answer. Yeah, yeah, yeah. So annoying. Look, I have guided my career by two simple ideas:

1. Work on hard problems with good people.
2. Do something that matters, *for* something that matters.

I get the concept idea, but still, the next question I will ask after you lay it out is: "Okay, well, what role do you think gives you the best shot of realizing your conceptual vision of your dream job?" I can imagine a number of reasons why people try to work around this particular question, but I push back really hard. The harder we work to clarify a vision statement, the more likely it becomes that we drop that first flagstone in the right place. Also, remember that you can keep a little wiggle room. Both things—being specific and tangible but also allowing for change—can coexist. Remember Sergeant Luhrsen—you gotta have a plan, even if you might not stick to it.

Sometimes, our visions will have flaws, and we will only learn about them through experience. But however impermanent it might turn out to be, you still have to have a crisp vision statement.

REAL PEOPLE VISIONS

I have conducted career conversations with thousands of people, and there was only one instance, with a woman named Katherine, where I could not help to produce a tangible vision statement in a single session. We spent ninety minutes talking through a number of options for her long-term vision, and we just couldn't quite land on a quality vision statement; this was mostly due to Katherine's hesitation to commit to what, to me at least, was an obvious choice. One clear lesson is that you can't force "the right" answers on people. Eventually I had to get her a professional assessment. So I turned to CareerLeader.com, which is a website that helps people get closer to their career visions through a questionnaire and years of research connecting people's life interests with the jobs that make them happiest.

I have found the CareerLeader assessment to be great at uncovering categorizations for your vision but not necessarily a precise vision. It might tell you that you're well suited for a particular career theme and then offer sample jobs that are more likely to make sense for you. Here's how it works. You fill out a questionnaire that surfaces your *deeply embedded life interests*

(DELI), which range from "Enterprise Control" to "Theory Development and Conceptual Thinking." The team at CareerLeader has kept track of thousands of students over the years and monitors how the different life interests correlate with job satisfaction in various professions. So, they might learn that students who spike on "Enterprise Control," like me, have been happiest in senior management roles. They can then pass on that insight to people who are taking the assessment—"Hey, one of your primary DELI themes is 'Enterprise Control,' so you should think about senior management." The assessment uncovers a number of other personal insights, but I found this to be the most useful—tying these deeply embedded business-oriented interests to a likely good fit down the line.

A few weeks after Katherine went to CareerLeader.com, we regrouped and realized that we'd come darn close in our original session. We actually had it, but she'd needed something else to help "prove" she was on the right track and to help her really commit. Now that we had a shared sense of her long-term vision, we were able to get busy building a path from here to there.

Below are a few fun examples of well-crafted Career Vision Statements. Note that each of them contains an answer to all three of the clarifying questions above. See if you can spot them:

- Frontline home builder for Habitat for Humanity or similar organizations
- COO of a boutique interior design firm
- CTO for midsize consumer tech company
- Own and operate my own spirulina farm
- Found and run a nonprofit focused on childhood obesity
- Lead all sales for Coca-Cola
- CFO of Disney
- Software architect for a midsize B2B tech company
- Editor for books with bestseller potential

- News anchor for a German television station (Got this one from Sarah, who was working in digital advertising in Sydney, Australia, at the time!)
- Artist (One of my favorites because the person who said this, Cindy, was an ultra-high performer working on the DoubleClick for Advertisers product, a deeply technical role, helping advertisers run campaigns. Yes, she was making campaigns fly, but she wanted to be an artist. . . . and she did it.)

The Career Vision Statement is simultaneously the most difficult and most important part of the entire model. This is why it seriously bothers me that so many people have false-started with the model—gone hard after the Life Story Conversation and declared themselves finished. Wrong. If you do nothing else, you must develop the vision. I've provided some space on the next page for you to refine your own Career Vision Statement. Once you have your vision in place, the rest is relatively easy. Now, for the rest.

CAREER VISION STATEMENT

16

Conversation 3: Career Action Plan

WHAT TO WORK ON

Now that you and your teammate have done the hard work of understanding the path behind—Life Story Conversation—and the envisioned future—Career Vision Statement—you are almost ready to help them develop their Career Action Plan (CAP). In this part of the process, your employee does the preponderance of the work. The idea is to begin to take tangible actions, no matter how small, toward their long-term vision while aligning with the values derived from the Life Story Conversation. With a tangible goal, you both now possess a commander's intent to guide their decision-making.

But there's one final half-step before you move fully into conversation 3 of the model, maybe step 2.5 or so, which is to help your folks determine the high-level organizing principles that their CAP will flow from, or more precisely, *what areas they need to work on the most*. But first, you guessed it, another metaphor.

Imagine a giant boulder sitting in front of you, maybe 30 feet tall by 30 feet wide, or if you prefer, 10 meters by 10 meters, reasonably uniform and roundish. You are the captain of a team of 130 people. Your job is to turn this boulder into finer-than-fishbowl gravel as quickly as you can, using handheld, human-powered percussion tools, such as sledgehammers, rock hammers, and the like. One other thing: you may only have as many of your people working as there are distinct pieces of the rock. So, one boulder, one worker, and 129 people on the bench. Two pieces of boulder, two workers, and 128 people on the bench, and so on.

What should the first worker be trying to achieve in order to break this huge boulder into gravel as quickly as possible?

The answer for many is obvious. The first person should be trying to break the boulder roughly in half. Now there are two workers and two still very large pieces of rock. Each of those two workers should be trying to break their half-boulder in half again. Now four workers should be trying to break their halves in half to get to eighths, and so on. This is the most efficient way to take this boulder down to gravel because it gets the most workers engaged in the shortest amount of time.

The boulder is the vision statement. It is, by and large, somewhat unaddressable in terms of present-day action. But when we break it down first into the big rocks and over time into pebbles, then we have something to work on, and, crucially, the pebbles only exist because the boulder and the large chunks of rock once existed.

In order to achieve your employee's vision, they will not only need to build their actual skills and capabilities, which I call the "engineering reality," but also clearly demonstrate to others that they have the skills and capabilities to do the job, which I call the "marketing promise." In business, there is almost always a small gap between the marketing promise (what's presented to the market about a product) and the engineering reality (what the product can actually do), and I've found that is also often the case with humans seeking new roles. Your employee's goal should be to shrink that gap as much as possible over time so that they have the demonstrable skills they need to be considered for the roles they want.

Below I've included a sample set of skills that you might tap into for a particular functional vision or that you might "mix and match" in service to a different, more general management type of vision. These are intentionally broad and represent the big rocks in our rock-crushing metaphor. Take a look below for the kinds of functional areas where one might need to demonstrate competency.

Let's say the vision is to be a chief human resources officer, or what I will now call a chief people officer (CPO) because humans absolutely are not resources. To be considered for a CPO job, a candidate will likely need to demonstrate at a high level that they have experience working in and with various People Ops functions. "People Analytics," of course, is not a skill, but it is a critical discipline—a big rock, if you will—in a modern People Ops organization. The skills underneath that are wide-ranging, but when it comes time for you to go for that dream job, no one is likely to ask you about your Excel macro and R skills.

GENERAL MGMT	CS ENGINEERING	MARKETING	SALES	PEOPLE OPS
Product Mgmt	Coding Language	Content/ Creative	Forecasting	Recruiting
Sales	Architecture	Research	CRM	Payroll & Benefits
Marketing	Design	Analytics	Client Relationships	Talent Brand
Business Dev	Code Review	Go-to-Market	Negotiations	People Analytics
Corp Dev	Debugging	Marketing Strategy	Presentations	Diversity & Inclusion
Finance	Front-End	Brand Architecture	Closing	Performance Mgmt
People Ops	Back-End	Paid Media	Sales Methodology	Leadership Dev

Once we have a feel for their big boulder—their career vision—it's time to prioritize the big rocks, or skills, from a list like the one above. The big pieces of rock are broad, communicable skills. I recommend prioritizing via a simple framework:

1. What is most important?
2. Where do you have the most room to grow?

Let's say that a modern People Ops organization leans heavily on Leadership Development, People Analytics, and Employee Experience Management. Those might emerge, then, as the priority big rocks. Let's say someone has lots of experience in People Analytics and Employee Experience Management, but virtually no knowledge, skills, or abilities in Leadership Development. This might signal, then, that this is the big rock to focus on because they have minimal capability both in terms of the engineering reality as well as the marketing promise. It's important, and they have low skill.

The high-level idea here is just to help you and your folks organize and prioritize broad investments to grow toward their vision. The specific actions, or the pebbles, come in the Career Action Plan, but those pebbles should be children of these big rocks. So this step is to generate a high-level, easy-to-understand master list of skills and functional capabilities and then prioritize them according to high importance and low capability. This won't be perfect or comprehensive, but it is a way to move forward in an organized, thoughtful, intentional, and logical way.

Along these lines, let's check back in with Larry. Once Larry and I had his vision in mind—to be the CEO of a midsize consumer tech company—we turned to the whiteboard, and I said, "High level, what kinds of things do you need to show competency in to get this kind of role?"

Larry started to answer by listing out the functional areas

of a business. What follows is not exactly what Larry and I discussed but a reasonable facsimile just to help teach the concept. Little lies for pedagogical purposes.

Larry's Vision: CEO of a late-stage consumer technology company		
Strategy		
Sales		
Operations		
Marketing		
Product		
BizDev		

Larry and I talked about each of these areas until we had a strong, shared sense of what each area means. After we identified the big rocks, or broad skill areas, Larry might need to show competency in, we then stack-ranked them.

Larry's Vision: CEO of a late-stage consumer technology company		
	IMPORTANCE	
Strategy	2	
Sales	4	
Operations	3	
Marketing	6	
Product	1	
BizDev	5	

Don't pay too much attention to the rankings right now. If you are a marketer and you stop reading because you're pissed that we put Marketing sixth, you've got the wrong idea. Larry and I had a detailed discussion about this at the time, and we knew why we listed each item where it was. Bottom line is that some large percentage of tech industry CEOs come from a product management discipline, and so we felt like this was the most important thing to focus on. Strategy, or more precisely, competitive strategy—which according to Michael Porter's *What Is Strategy?* is about determining how you will differentiate, or rather, how you will compete—seemed pretty important because a midstage company is more likely to be in a competitive situation. Lo and behold, we went through this exercise in 2006 or so, and if you look at the landscape today, the consumer-video tech market is highly fragmented and competitive. #NailedIt! Operations generally meant running large-scale, customer-facing operations. Running a company, after all, is about running an operation, and Larry and I felt this was important. Finally, I'll talk about sales. In any company, the overwhelming majority of people are either making something or selling something, so sales ends up being pretty important. You get the idea. However imperfect, we had a shared logic that was derived from a rich and detailed discussion.

Our next step was to evaluate Larry, thinking simultaneously about the engineering reality and the marketing promise. The goal is to be conservative, not self-loathing, and *consistently* conservative, meaning that there's no reason to be extra conservative in one area and less conservative in another. Here's what we came up with:

Larry's Vision: CEO of a late-stage consumer technology company

	IMPORTANCE	ABILITY
Strategy	2	●
Sales	4	○
Operations	3	◑
Marketing	6	◕
Product	1	◔
BizDev	5	●

Larry had been a strategy consultant for McKinsey and Company, so we gave him a full "moon," or a score of one, if you are so inclined, on Strategy. Larry had never once had revenue responsibility, so we gave him a new moon, or a score of zero, on Sales. Larry was running a pretty big customer-facing operation for me at the time, but it was only a US-facing operation. For full credibility to run a midsize company, he would need to understand how to run a global operation, so we gave him a half-moon in Operations. Finally, on Product Management, Larry had done about a year as a product manager at a company called Green Dot. Despite that experience, which is meaningful, we decided that we should go conservative, and so we gave him a quarter-moon, or a 0.25.

If you eyeball this, you can almost immediately tell which big rocks Larry needed to work on. Product Management was most important, and he had very low capability in that discipline. Operations, with a global focus, ranked third, and he had only a half-moon of capability. Last, you probably noticed that sales was ranked fourth and that Larry had no capability. Larry was clear with me at the time that he absolutely did not want a sales job. We agreed that he shouldn't do anything he didn't want to, but I also made him promise that he would reevaluate if his lack of quota-carrying experience ever emerged as an obstacle to the achievement of his vision. So Operations and Product Management were the two big rocks we picked.

Larry's Vision: CEO of a late-stage consumer technology company

	IMPORTANCE	ABILITY
Strategy	2	●
Sales	4	○
Operations	3	◑
Marketing	6	◕
Product	1	◔
BizDev	5	●

Now Larry and I were ready to build his Career Action Plan. By going through all of this together, we understood with deep and crystal clarity how we arrived at all of our conclusions. This shared context would allow us to adjust quickly and pivot our thinking as time went on, new information emerged, and Larry's skills grew.

FOUR-PART CAREER ACTION PLAN

Larry and I had done it. We'd identified his big rocks and were ready to take action. At the time I was developing this Career Conversations methodology, the best People Ops person I had ever worked with was a woman named Sally Anderson. I shared with her that I had stumbled onto a revelation with Larry and was reaching for a way that we could organize our action planning. Sally had an HR best practices planning document at her fingertips, which helped to organize our thinking around skill development in a handful of mutually exclusive, and collectively exhaustive (MECE) areas. I liked the model well enough, but I could see it required some small adjustments. After Sally and I made them, I started to brainstorm about Larry's Career Action Plan. The four MECE areas we decided to organize the CAP around are as follows:

- Make changes to current role
- Develop your skills . . . formally
- Identify the next job
- Activate your networks

I'll offer a brief explanation of each area, as well as an indication of what Larry and I did in each area.

Make Changes to Current Role

Of the various ways they can support an employee, managers often overlook the power of making changes to an employee's current role. I once worked with someone who wanted to be the CFO of Disney. Diane, our future Disney CFO but currently a customer support rep, was very junior, so this was not likely to happen in the short term, but one small thing her manager could do for her at the time was give her responsibility for the team budget. At first glance, this seems like an inconsequential step that may or may not really support the long-term vision. However, if we take a deeper look, we recognize that running the team's budget would require her to interact with the finance organization, which is the organization that a CFO manages. She eventually would be involved in developing and planning the budget, which would give her a clear view of how a financial planning and analysis (FP&A) team forecasts revenue and costs and invests revenue back into the business. That experience alone would help Diane learn whether finance was even a path she wanted to pursue. In the best case, she not only would have a front-seat view of what a finance organization is all about, but would also build real capability, supporting other elements of the Career Action Plan.

For Larry, recall that one of his two opportunity areas was in Operations. He was running a large-scale US-focused operation, but we felt as if he needed a little bit more global experience. The operation would benefit from a more global outlook as well, so by making only minor adjustments to Larry's role, we were able to solve a problem for both the business and the employee.

Too many companies focus on attrition as the premier measurement of People Ops or managerial success. That can lead to a "retain at all costs" mentality. We will all be better managers if we support people and help them get to where they need to go.

That said, if we can retain folks for the right reasons for both the individual and the company, we all win. When a manager and an employee get creative about things they can do together in the current role—small changes, given the long-term vision—the employee has a two-part incentive to stick around. First, the employee will likely realize that this is a differentiated manager, and while everything in the current role may not be perfect, the employee might say, "Well at least my manager has my back." And second, the employee has real opportunities for learning and growth right now, the lack of which is one of the biggest drivers of attrition. This is such a simple way to align what everyone wants—employee, manager, company—so let's be careful never to skip this important first step.

Develop Your Skills . . . Formally

Let's start by acknowledging that there are many ways to build skills. Ideally, you learn on the job, gaining new scope in your current role or taking on new challenges in a different role within the same company. But there are times in which formal skill-building is also helpful. This is where a Learning and Development team can really lean in and add a lot of value, perhaps even playing a consultative role in assembling your own learning path. What's important is to identify the courses, degrees, conferences, seminars, or certifications that promise to advance both the engineering reality and the marketing promise. One of my favorite examples of formal skill development is the MBA. I have been asked hundreds of times, "Should I get an MBA, and if so, where should I get it?" As with most things, I don't have an easy answer, but here's roughly how I tend to guide folks through that decision. Notice the contemplation of both the engineering reality and the marketing promise in what follows.

There are three "dimensions of return" you should evaluate when considering whether you should invest in an MBA.

1. **Learning Return**—At great schools, the professors are both deep experts on the body of knowledge that already exists and creators of new knowledge themselves through their research. This is the case at pretty much all schools, but it tends to be more systematic, dynamic, and impactful at the elite ones. Add in hundreds of very bright, very curious students who have an incentive to participate in class, and you have a vibrant "learning network effect" that is awfully compelling. Because I'd heard so many people talk about the MBA's value solely in terms of "the network," I was under the impression that no learning at all went on during the program! When I got my MBA a decade or so into my career, I was pleasantly surprised—and rudely awakened—by the academic rigor of the modern MBA model.
2. **Interestingness of Opportunities**—To describe the MBA's primary value in terms of "the network" not only shortchanges the total value of the degree but also misses the mark on what "the network" actually describes. It's not that you become a member of a club with special privileges. Think of it this way: Every person, every organization makes prioritization decisions. Companies make prioritization decisions in their recruiting efforts. They cannot recruit at every school. So, they tend to recruit at the schools that do the "best job" of due diligence on their students, and those schools tend to be the elite ones. This model effectively gives a company a lower probability of false positives, or mis-hires, while increasing its probability of false negatives, or the act of passing on great people simply because you never saw them. Most firms are comfortable with that tradeoff. When

advising people, I will point out that it does not matter if this idea that "elite schools do a better job of due diligence" or "average student quality is higher" is a perception or a reality. Companies have to make prioritization decisions, and those interested in hiring MBAs will often prioritize around school rankings. That said, an MBA from any school can open up new and more interesting opportunities. In C. S. Lewis's *The Lion, the Witch, and the Wardrobe,* there is another world that the characters can only access through a wardrobe cabinet. The MBA can be that wardrobe, opening up a world of opportunities that were previously inaccessible.

3. **Financial Return**—Financial return on an MBA is not a slam dunk. Prior to entering school, your earnings trajectory will have some slope above zero. When you exit school, your earnings trajectory should have a steeper slope, although you might actually start out making less money than you did before you entered school. This is okay as long as you believe the slope has forever changed. In addition to the hundreds of thousands of dollars you'll spend, you will also have a two-year opportunity cost on your earnings, meaning you will not earn a penny for two years—the proverbial "double whammy" of no income plus big debt/big expense. So, as far as I can tell, the expected slope change should be very compelling and clear. If, for example, you are independently wealthy, you probably don't really care about this dimension. If you're not, you should run some "what do you have to believe" about that post-business-school slope to make the investment worthwhile. Here's a way to evaluate not only the possible financial return of an MBA but also any expenditure you might make on formal training.

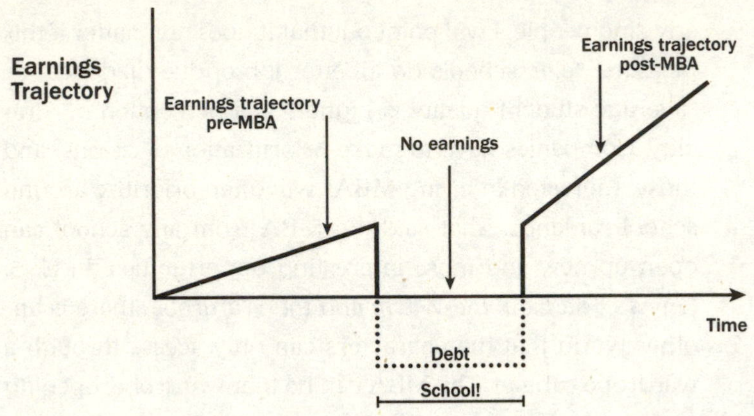

Given that I was a former marine and an entrepreneur with a small supply-chain consulting company who had an undergraduate BS degree in geography from a middle-tier state school, an MBA was probably a necessity for me if I wanted to achieve my long-term vision. Sure, there were people out there who would look at my résumé and think "Impressive!" but there were a lot more who would look at it and just scratch their heads. The pre-MBA Russ Laraway *marketing promise* held little, well, promise. How about the engineering reality? I was still in my twenties, owned my own company, and was delivering real value to real customers. If my career was represented by a brick wall, I'd built it pretty high, but that wall was missing so many bricks. I didn't really understand the symphony of functions that add up to a successful business, and the MBA filled in a lot of those blanks in my knowledge.

The bigger takeaway from all of this should be that you need a robust framework for evaluating whatever investments you might make in formal training opportunities. I used the MBA example since I have personal experience and have been in a position to counsel hundreds of folks on whether they should consider getting one. But there are a lot of other investments you can make in your skills and capabilities, and those need to be carefully evaluated as well.

Larry and I skipped this portion of the Career Action Plan. He already had an engineering degree from the University of Maryland and an MBA from Harvard Business School. I like this example for that exact reason. There are no rules or absolutes here. For Larry, additional formal training wasn't worth the investment of time or money given his existing experience and path.

If we think about Diane, though, this would definitely be something for us to talk through. Diane, if you recall, wants to be the CFO of Disney. Loads of CFOs have advanced degrees, or at least CPAs. So for both the engineering reality and the marketing promise, there are a number of investments in formal training that Diane might want to make in order to maximize her chances of realizing her dream.

Identify the Next Job

In thinking about the lighthouse in the distance and our need to build a path to it, there are few things as important as the very next step. Too few managers talk openly with folks about what their next job should be. Don't use a conversation about a promotion as a cop-out either, please. I think managers have invented all kinds of reasons to not talk about the next job with folks. *It's not my job* or *Retain at all costs* or *They're all good!* are some of the most common mistaken perspectives. I get it. We invest a bunch of time and energy in our people, and we want to maximize that return. This is why it's unnatural for most managers to invest time to help their people move on to another role. The simple insight is that your investment in them should never be only about what you need or what you want. Helping them move on *is* your job, and if you believe in serving your team, here's why you should rethink.

Remember that "gravity-assisted" slingshot I talked about? You likely only have your employees for a brief time, maybe two or three years if you're lucky. While you have them, your job is to use your "gravity" and be that slingshot that propels them into the far reaches of their careers.

The next reason is that your employees absolutely are talking to *someone* about their next job. If you're lucky and they're lucky, it's someone smart who is helping them think through their next step in the context of their long-term vision, but in reality that person is probably not doing that and might actually be doing your employees—whom you are supposed to be serving—a disservice. You have a choice here. You can bury your head in the sand, or you can engage smartly and safely. Your primary objective should be to help your people make good decisions rooted in their long-term vision. Help them avoid a grass-is-greener misstep or, if it's appropriate and the opportunity arises, actively help them make that next great job happen. That's what people who care about each other do.

Larry and I were crystal clear that his next job should be a role in the product management organization. We targeted about twelve months out, because we felt like he really needed to run this global operation with me for some time to affect the engineering reality and his marketing promise around the Operations big rock. In terms of being ready to secure a product management position at Google, he had already done most of the heavy lifting with his past education and experience. The idea would be to build his network in the product organization so that when the time was right, he had relationships he could lean on to make the transition smoothly.

Activate Your Networks

In *The Career Manifesto*, Mike Steib wrote, "If you are like most well-adjusted people, the word 'networking' evokes images of awkward meet and greets, uninvited solicitations, and disingenuous interactions. Networking, the way most people do it, is kind of gross." Yeah, we're not gonna do that.

This is about identifying people who can *inform and influence* your future career moves and aspirations. This can take a lot of forms. For Mike Steib and me, it is not at all about so-called "networking events," which are the bane of my—and all introverts'—existence. This is about learning from people who have a perspective to share. Years ago, I came across an article in *The Harvard Business Review* by Linda Hill and Kent Lineback, "The Three Networks You Need." It forever changed how I think about networking, and I recommend you give it a read.

The gist is that you really have three networks you should be maintaining at any given time:

- operational network
- developmental network
- strategic network

The *operational network* is more or less the one you take for granted. These are the people you work with day in and day out. You are intertwined with and dependent upon one another. So how about that, all you networking haters? You're doing it all the time. The *developmental network* is composed of people you trust, people you rely on for advice and to safely talk you through your professional options. Last is your *strategic network*. These are the big guns that you don't want to overly tax. Keep that powder dry, captain. "A strategic network is about tomorrow," say Hill and Lineback. I like this model because it's fluid. To explain it,

I want to tell you a bit about four people and how they've shifted as parts of my network:

- Kim Scott
- Sheryl Sandberg
- Jared Smith
- Dick Costolo

As I mentioned earlier, Kim, Jared, and I all worked on the same team at Google back in 2005 and 2006. Jared and I reported to Kim. Back then, they were both in my operational network. We worked together every single day. When Kim left to go to Apple, she moved into my developmental network until years later, when she and I cofounded Candor, Inc. and she reenlisted in my operational network. Jared followed a similar path, moving to my developmental network after our time together at Google and then back to my operational network when I joined Qualtrics. Now, as he begins his new life after Qualtrics, he's moved into my strategic network. I know I can call him any time, but I will wait for just the right moment so as not to overburden him.

Sheryl was Kim's boss in 2005. She was for sure in my developmental network back then, and she took that role—a developer of leaders—very seriously. Once she moved to Facebook, she was still in that same network, but as time wore on, she became a larger-than-life executive in tech, and now she's resting quietly in my strategic network. I know if I absolutely needed something from her, she'd be there, but I also know she's busy, with thousands of mouths to feed, and I refuse to be disrespectful of her time. Keeping that powder dry.

I had met Dick Costolo briefly at Google when we acquired his company FeedBurner. He was obviously a good guy, but he was in for a cup of coffee and out the door pretty quickly after the acquisition. I didn't know it at the time, but Dick had slid into my strategic network. Fast-forward a few years: I was preparing to leave FreeMonee, and I reached out to Kim, who linked me up with Dick, then the CEO of Twitter. I went into his office at Twitter, and before I could even take a breath, he laid out three potential roles for me; I ended up taking one of them. At that moment, he moved to my developmental network, and at times at Twitter he was in my operational network. Today, he's in my developmental network, and we have explored ways that I might work with his venture firm 01A to advise Series B CEOs on how to lead for engagement and results.

I need to offer just a couple caveats. First, I don't think about my network in this transactional way day in and day out. In fact, I almost never think about it. I'm trying to make Linda Hill and Kent Lineback's point about fluidity and changing relationships. The second caveat is that I consider Kim, Jared, and Dick good, good friends, and while "friend" might be a stretch in describing my relationship with Sheryl, I know her to be a good human being and think of her that way, not as a vehicle to create successful outcomes for Russ. I need to make this caveat because my clinical portrayal of people moving through "my networks" could potentially come off as Machiavellian, and it's not at all how I think about these human beings. I like them and care about them and choose to be around them, not because of what I can get out of them but because they are good people who like to work on hard problems, which, as you recall, is something that I value highly.

When Larry and I nailed down that he should be looking to move into product management, I thought of my colleague Neal Mohan, who came into Google through the DoubleClick acquisition and was running YouTube at the time. I introduced them, they had lunch, and they agreed to continue the relationship with a periodic touch-base. Larry treated the relationship with respect, and they both understood that at least one of the underlying purposes of their regular meetings was to smooth Larry's eventual move into the product management organization. It helps that they are both unbelievably likeable and accomplished guys and genuinely hit it off.

Larry ended up getting a job in product management under Neal at YouTube, as Neal led all product management for that business. At the time of this writing, Larry leads a team and has a pretty big scope there. He's had chances to move on and has even come close to his dream job, but he likes Google, likes what he's doing, and isn't in a hurry. His story is yet to be fully written, of course, but it's worth pausing for a bit and seeing this ten-year-plus Career Action Plan playing out quite nicely.

Putting It into Practice

17

Managers

We just covered an awful lot of ground together, and if you stuck with me this long, truly, I thank you. Remember, if managers explain 70 percent of employee engagement, and engagement leads to better results, then we need to employ a leadership standard that measurably and predictably produces those two things. To inspire a team to do great work and be totally psyched while doing it, the best managers provide employees with three things that the worst managers do not:

1. **Direction**—they ensure that every member of the team has clear direction
2. **Coaching**—they coach people toward both long- and short-term success
3. **Career**—they invest in their people's careers in a way that considers their humanity, not just their next promotion

Your reward for your patience was intentionally buried deep in this book. Managers, I will now share the handy acronym version of the leadership standard with you, because, hey, what kind of business book doesn't have some handy acronyms in it? Behold the CARES model, developed by Will Adams, a talented people system analyst, and Dave Dequeljoe, a former combat F-14 pilot. Both were close colleagues of mine at Qualtrics.

Managers whose teams are most engaged, and whose organizations produce the best results, systematically:

- *Create a Culture of Candor:* A culture of candor is one in which we regularly give and get feedback to enhance our team's and our own performance. If you do nothing else but enable the success of the people on your team, you'll crush it as a manager. Coaching is your most impactful, most available, and cheapest tool to do just that.
- *Actively Prioritize:* Prioritization is an exercise in subtraction, not addition; it's equally crucial that your teams know what *not* to work on, each day and each week, as it is that they know what they *should* work on.
- *Respond to Ideas and Concerns:* You don't have to take action on every piece of feedback about your leadership you receive, but you should always follow up with the person who provided it so they know why you did or didn't take action. It's a great opportunity to teach your people about the broader context while giving them a better understanding of your thought processes. Try asking, "How can I help you have more success?"
- *Establish Explicit Expectations:* When you take the time to clearly communicate the behaviors and results you expect from your team members, it increases their certainty, reduces their stress and worry, and increases their probability of success. It's also a critical inclusive leadership behavior, as you tend to communicate most clearly with those who are

like you. Do this well for everyone on your team, and you set everyone up for success.

- *Support Growth and Development:* When leaders take the time to have our three patented Career Conversations with their teams, they experience incredible results. We've seen it and tracked it, over and over again.

18

Planners: People Teams, Learning Teams, Leadership Development Teams

I hope it's pretty clear by now that the managers in any organization are the ones holding the keys. So the first question any leader should be asking is, "How can we ensure that we are recruiting, promoting, and otherwise developing the best managers possible?"

The answer is another framework with an easy-to-remember acronym: STAC: select, teach, assess, coach.

1. *Select* managers for disposition, mindset, and skill in accordance with your organization's leadership standards and the specific factors that lead to employee engagement and results.
2. *Teach* them—formally—what the leadership standard is, and set the expectation that they will need to adjust their behaviors to meet it.
3. *Assess* them on how they're doing relative to that leadership standard and from their employees' perspectives.
4. *Coach* them in real time to help close the gap between teaching and assessment and to help enable behavior change.

Think of coaching and learning as basic, ongoing hygiene—brushing and flossing around leadership.

Here is a quick primer on each of these actions. You've read most of it before, scattered throughout the book, but all of it bears repeating:

SELECT

We often select managers like we're competitors in the great Monty Python's "127th Upperclass Twit of the Year Show at Hurlingham Park." According to Gallup's 2013 *State of the Global Workplace* study, we get manager selection wrong as much as 80 percent of the time in the United States. Why? There are many factors, but the most persistent and, therefore, most nefarious one is that we tend to select managers based on how good of an individual contributor (IC) they are. This is simultaneously an unreasonable approach and also somewhat understandable. First, if you don't have any other signal to use, of course you would use this signal. Second, it's very hard to tell your top-performing—or worse, most-tenured—IC that they are not getting the leadership gig and that, say, the lowest performing IC on the team is getting it instead, even if you had perfect information that the lower-performing IC would be a superior manager. Tough message—takes courage.

Remember, the activities that will make you successful as a manager look nothing like the activities that make you successful as an individual contributor. Flatly, the work is different.

To select the best managers, you must first clearly define your leadership standard, hold it to measurable accountability, and then use it to guide both your internal promotions and external hires. At Qualtrics, we published a document called *The Leadership Hiring Guide,* a rubric that includes the questions we ask potential managers and the good and bad answers to them. This extra step of including good and bad answers helps ensure that we are selecting leaders based on our shared leadership standard and not the arbitrary standards of each interviewer. We further set the expectation that while more junior, less experienced managers might have, say, 15 percent or so compliance with the leadership standard, very senior managers must have nearly 100 percent compliance. It's not that we're looking for groupthink, but we just can't have one salmon swimming upstream. We have a strong sense of what works, so why would we tolerate much deviation from that standard? Senior managers are much more leveraged, so it creates much more damage when you install a sociopath in that role. Even though it's tempting to skip the assessment for senior folks, we actually put them through a more thorough examination, and we insist that they demonstrate much more sophistication in their approach to managing people. Simply put, we're more risk averse on senior hires and promotions and more risk loving on junior hires and promotions. The blast radius is different.

It's worth reemphasizing that this applies to internal promotions as well as external hires. A strictly defined leadership hiring rubric provides a strong test of the skills and disposition of your candidates. Hiring managers should assess candidates themselves, which has the benefit of forcing them to constantly revisit and therefore relearn the leadership standard, inspiring conversations around what is expected as a people leader that can bring about further refinements of it. I prefer a formal test—but if it's all I can get because perhaps the internal candidate saw the answer key ahead of time, I will take a good hiring manager's assessment, provided that all the requirements are duly weighed.

Finally, developing criteria for a job before you start searching or interviewing is a critical step in reducing the unconscious biases that can lead to inequitable outcomes. In a study titled "Constructed Criteria," Eric Uhlman and Geoffrey Cohen of Yale University took a look at people's biases when evaluating candidates for, say, a traditionally male role, such as police chief. Joelle Emerson, founder and CEO of Paradigm, summarized the study and its key upshot finding perfectly in a Medium blog post:

> Researchers showed participants resumes of two hypothetical candidates, one with more education ("book smart") and one with more experience ("street smart"), and asked participants to choose which candidate was better qualified for the role of police chief. When the resumes were anonymous, participants chose the book smart candidate. Then the researchers assigned the book smart candidate a male name and the street smart candidate a female name. Participants again chose the (now male) book smart candidate. But when the genders were switched—the book smart candidate was assigned a female name and the street smart candidate a male name—participants for the first time chose the male, street smart candidate. In each scenario, participants justified their decision by explaining that the selected resume had the most important qualifications for the role. Participants unintentionally adjusted their opinions about the skills necessary for the role to match their gender-biased assumptions. Interestingly, researchers identified an effective method of reducing this bias. By asking participants to decide in advance (i.e., before looking at any resumes) whether book smarts or street smarts mattered more for the role, and *then* giving them the two resumes, the bias disappeared and men and women were evaluated fairly.

TEACH

Even if you select people leaders according to a clear and explicit set of standards, it's not fair to expect them to consistently manifest the right behaviors unless you've formally taught them what they are. I know every Learning and Development professional is doing the wave, raising the roof, and cheering in full throat at that sentence. You're welcome. We have to teach every manager what is expected of them, and I say this while harboring a now well-documented great deal of skepticism about noncore job-related training as an answer to anything. I don't have strong opinions on the "how" of that. I prefer in-person classroom, exercise-heavy training, but I also understand that's not always feasible. The pluses and minuses of various teaching methods and approaches are pretty well established at this point, and they are far outside of my expertise since I am absolutely not a curriculum designer or training professional. The bottom line is that you have to be a special brand of dense to think that the leaders in your organization will regularly and enthusiastically manifest the right behaviors if you haven't made explicit to them what those behaviors are and why they matter.

There's another side of this. Not only do you have to teach the leadership standard, but I also believe you need to actively keep out the stuff that just doesn't matter. As we've covered in detail, there is no shortage of content on leadership you can offer to your managers. But does it *work?* Remember, we've defined *works* to mean that the leadership standard measurably and predictably delivers engaged employees and incredible results. Before hiring someone to come in and speak or developing a new leadership module that your managers will be expected to pay attention to, just ask yourself if you believe that this addendum to your leadership standard is truly worth their time. Ask yourself whether it *works*.

One cohort to watch for is the "I already know this shit" crowd. These people live directly under my skin. They've been around the block, have had some success in the past as people leaders, and generally think *I've got this figured out* or *I know what works for me*. Please call bullshit on them unless they have measurable evidence that "what works for them" is real. By the way, they almost certainly don't have this evidence because it's hard to develop, and very few companies even attempt to establish a leadership standard let alone hold that standard measurably accountable.

I worked with a fairly senior manager once who truly believed he didn't need to go to the training where the core leadership standard was presented. His manager effectiveness score was low. His team was confused about their direction, charter, and performance standards, and, predictably, they were beginning to leave, frequently citing his leadership as a reason for departing the company. Further, in a system of about six to eight lateral stakeholders, only one was happy with the delivery from this failing manager's organization, and that particular stakeholder happened to be this failing manager's direct boss. You absolutely cannot make this up.

The arrogance required to reach this conclusion—that "I don't need this shit"—is staggering. This manager assured me he would get things fixed, and after a few coaching sessions, his engagement and manager effectiveness scores went up a few points. Two weeks after he wrote me an email in which he somehow simultaneously spiked the football, took a bow, held up the trophy, and sprained his shoulder patting himself on the back, one of his top people put time on my calendar to tell me she was leaving, in large part—mostly, in fact—because of him.

Everyone needs to be taught the leadership standard. Junior or senior—no difference. Leadership by example never goes out of style. The full standard needs to be taught formally and consistently. Otherwise, you should not expect folks to comply with it, and you will have no reason to believe you will see happy results.

ASSESS

If you don't assess people, they won't change. Leadership is often very personal to people, so "what I think works" reigns supreme over more objective versions of "what leads to engagement" and "what leads to results." Of course, absolute objectivity isn't really feasible. It's hard enough for people who *want* to change their behavior to change it, and it's way harder when there is disagreement about how far a person needs to make changes, which things need to change, etc. The first step toward getting someone to change nearly always involves some gentle teeth pulling.

An assessment helps people find the will to change while plainly identifying the skill gaps that need to be closed. At Qualtrics, we used a manager effectiveness (ME) score, the twelve-question composite already covered thoroughly in these pages. The ME score across the company is a measurement of how well our managers are doing relative to the leadership standard. The full picture of a manager includes delivery of the expected results and their teams' employee engagement scores, but those things will generally follow if the manager manifests the right behaviors with his or her team.

When using an assessment, it's important to provide evidence and, therefore, confidence that making these changes is "worth it." This is especially true in high-growth companies, where managers are stretched particularly thin and it is flat out hard to find the cycles to invest. That's just reality. If you are going to use the assessment as a mechanism to reward, it's even more critical that the standard has been proven to make a difference and is not just an arbitrary flavor-of-the-month metric from some senior executive or learning professional.

We would use the assessment at Qualtrics primarily as a coaching tool. We might, for example, look at our bottom scorers and quietly reach out to them so we can gain context and offer them help. Often, the person is already working with their manager on improvement because they've evaluated their results in their manager effectiveness dashboard. We further use the ME score as a consideration in performance ratings and promotions. Don't read that this is the only consideration we use—because it's not—but it is a factor we discuss openly in ratings calibration meetings and promotion committees. Most important is this: we assess you from the perspective of your team . . . you know, the human beings we're all fighting to attract, develop, and retain. While it might not seem like it, your team telling you all about your leadership shortcomings—measurably—is the greatest gift you can receive.

Some folks push back a bit on this because they worry that asking employees to evaluate their managers is akin to running a popularity contest. Maybe a super cool manager gets high marks, and maybe a manager trying to refurbish a failing team gets hammered. This is a fair risk to flag, but I don't think it usually plays out that way. First and most important, if you use manager effectiveness questions that are oriented around whether a behavior was demonstrated, an employee has *to lie* to cause a score to be too high or low. Sure, occasionally an employee will give their manager too much benefit of the doubt (or too much doubt of the benefit), but it's rare that all of them will. If you do believe that all your employees are lying, then you are manifesting extremely low trust, and if that is the case then you should reconsider your talent acquisition methods to make sure you are hiring more honest people. I think the reality is that some scores are exaggerated up and some are exaggerated down for any number of easy-to-articulate reasons, but at scale it all comes out in the wash. Your employees will rise to the occasion and give their best evaluations far more often than not.

Of course there are flaws; no human system is perfect. The question is whether those flaws are substantial enough to justify not gathering this perspective from the employee, and my strong opinion is that it's not even close. You can control for dishonesty with behavioral questions and confidentiality thresholds, where employees are assured of anonymity if the manager has, say, fewer than five direct reports. Be careful about using employec-generated evaluations punitively, and certainly don't make them the only evaluation. Creating and using a Manager Effectiveness Index is critical, so don't let perfect be the enemy of good.

If you use this evaluation primarily as a coaching tool, you can simultaneously avoid dishonest responses and also help managers and their teams become more successful and less miserable. One time, I reached out to one of our senior sales executives because one of his leaders—still pretty new to our company—had the lowest ME score in the whole company. I asked if there was anything I could do. This senior executive was all over it. He had already diagnosed the issue as primarily a span-of-control problem—the leader was managing a complex region and didn't have a team in place yet that allowed him to fully nail it. The diagnosis resonated for me. We had learned recently that a manager was much more likely to manifest the right leadership behaviors if she had a span of control of no more than seven direct reports. This particular low-ME-scoring leader was well beyond that as he terraformed his organization. The senior executive and I agreed that decent, planned organizational hygiene would solve most issues and gave the problem a six-month timeframe to turn around. In the meantime, the executive would use the ME assessment to coach the sales leader on how to be his best, given the current state of the organization. I was pretty happy with that. The executive had already diagnosed the issue, had a reasonable action plan, and was willing to commit to a timeframe for improvement. I'll take that all day long.

Another example. We reached out to a very low-scoring manager, Sylvie. Her first reaction was a little bit defensive, along the lines of "Back off, I got this." We made it clear that we were all about partnership, not punishment. Once she saw we were on the same team—and interested in her success—we were able to move on to problem solving.

The assessment helped us prioritize what to solve. We looked at areas that were not only low scoring but also meaningfully impacting engagement. We coached her on how to gently approach the team and, with their help, clarify the specific areas in which she could improve. Finally, we put a simple, commonsense action plan together and set her loose.

Her turnaround was swift and astounding. She went from one of the lowest-scoring managers to one of the highest in a single quarter. Her team's engagement skyrocketed; today it is generally acknowledged as a team that gets the hardest stuff done, so much so that it has become something of a SWAT team, deployed to address some of the company's toughest challenges.

None of this would have been possible without the assessment. Openness and receptivity to change tend to be ghosts without an understanding that our leadership standard will produce results.

COACH

I'm not the biggest fan in the world of coaching accreditation. It has its value, but let's be careful not to lose sight of what we are trying to accomplish, which is to get another perspective on how well our leadership or performance matches the standard. It's very difficult to see yourself unless you hold up a mirror. Good coaches have a lot of mirrors and they may or may not have a certificate of authenticity.

Years ago, when I was putting together the Radical Candor workshop that we sold to companies, I got a little help from Stephanie Soler, a professor at Stanford's Global School of Business. She gave me the idea for what became our "Feedback Triangle" exercise, in which we challenged one participant to give feedback to a second participant while being observed by a third. Role-playing exercises are not unique, of course, but our spin on this one was because we told the feedback receiver to act like a complete jerk. This makes the exercise raw and stressful and drives home the need for crystal clarity on the message. We allow the exercise to transpire for a few minutes, and then we take a few minutes for the other two participants to coach the feedback giver—feedback on feedback, if you will. After more than three hundred or so repetitions on this exercise, I've learned a number of things, mostly because I've asked participants a number of questions, including whether the coaching they got from their randomly chosen partners was "any good." The answer was always a resounding yes. I suppose they *have to* say that because those same randomly chosen partners are sitting right next to them, and it would be awkward to respond with "Meh." But I think the sentiment is genuine, mostly because after some of the more enthusiastic "yes" responses, I would make people prove it by probing further. "Wait a minute," I'd say in a voice that was dripping with sarcasm. "Do you mean to tell me that these . . . these . . . *laypeople* are capable of giving you good coaching around this crucial and difficult skill when they've had *no training* beyond what we've covered here today?" Even so, they almost never changed their answers. Turns out that the folks around us have a pretty strong feel for how we can be better, but often lack (a) the mandate to tell us and (b) the know-how that would empower them to share their insights with us. I've learned that if we just give regular old folks those two things, they can all be pretty darn good coaches.

After attending any training, only a very small number of people are capable of a very small number of behavior changes. Following up on training with good, solid coaching on their real-world leadership challenges, derived through careful assessment, helps bridge the gap between training for the standard and achieving it.

Epilogue

THE DREAM

My dream is that readers of this book will join me in my quest to rid the world of assclown managers everywhere. Like Star-Lord and Gamora, you are the Guardians . . . of the Employee Experience. People deserve to be led well. If every manager begins to lead in the ways I describe in this book, we could expect global engagement to increase from its embarrassing 15 percent to something much greater. Just imagine how the billions of dollars of recaptured opportunity could be used by companies, educational institutions, governments, and nonprofits to invent new things, cure diseases, solve problems, and lift more people out of poverty. There are tens of millions of managers in the world. If every last one of us decides to lead better, we can instantly put humanity on a better path. Our shared lighthouse is this: our people doing extraordinary work and being totally psyched while doing it. When they win—and only when they win—you win.

A fair question from managers might be, "Where do we start?" This is difficult to answer because this is designed to be a coherent leadership system, but I will offer you three ideas on where to begin, as long as you promise not to stop there. The first place you might start is the Life Story Conversation outlined in chapter 14. There are so few things we can do to improve our human connections with our employees quickly and meaningfully, and this is one of them. More to the point, it strengthens the foundations of our relationships with our people, and the stronger those foundations are, the more easily and soundly we can build on top of them.

The second place one might start is with the quarterly goal-setting and daily/weekly prioritization I describe in chapters 6 and 7. Are you sure your teams know exactly what is expected of them, and has it been articulated to them in clear, measurable terms? Go through the process of stripping down your team's quarterly goals to a tiny number of highly measurable, unambiguous ones. Couple this with the installation of a fifteen-minute daily standup meeting to discuss each person's priorities for the day/week.

The last place one might start is chapter 9, where I talk about praise, or *continue coaching*. I gave a talk in April 2021 to about forty managers at a company that had just gone public. When I told them about the five-to-one praise-to-criticism ratio, one of the managers asked the common question, "What about the risk of setting an expectation of constant and limitless praise?" I've heard this before. Look, I just don't think most of us are at risk of overpraising, but if you're not convinced, here's how to avoid it. First, remember, it's five to one, not ten to one, twenty to one, or infinity to one. Second, hold yourself to *Radical Candor*'s standard for quality praise, which is that it must be both specific and sincere. I think with just that discipline, you can mitigate this phantom problem of overpraising and begin to transform your relationships with your teams. Remember, they are probably doing an awful lot more well than they are doing poorly, and my evidence is that you are not walking around firing everyone.

For planners, it's my sincere hope that you will build on what is in this book.

Greg Glassman, the founder of CrossFit, was interviewed in 2015 by Sharyn Alfonsi on *60 Minutes*. There's a specific part of that interview that I think is highly germane to the theoretical underpinning of this book:

"You know, you didn't invent weightlifting," she challenged.

"Nope," he agreed.

"You didn't invent calisthenics," she continued.

"Nope," he offered without hesitation.

"You didn't invent gymnastics," she asserted.

"Nope," he said with great consistency.

"So what did you do?" she asked.

"I invented that doing lateral raises and curls while eating pretzels is dumb. That's what I invented," Glassman offered, simultaneously taking a shot at poor diet and a couple of traditional yet relatively useless weight room movements. Recall from earlier in this book that Glassman first defined fitness and then set about developing a regimen that measurably and predictably delivered better fitness results within that definition of fitness.

I've done something similar. I didn't invent setting expectations or coaching or career development. I certainly didn't invent leadership or engagement. What I invented is the simple idea that we should evaluate and determine the full worth of a leadership behavior or a composite or set of leadership behaviors based on whether they measurably and predictably drive better engagement and better results.

That is the big opportunity: to advance the understanding of the leadership behaviors that drive both engagement and results. A note for statisticians and analysts: What I believe to be most unique in this book is that we've analyzed leadership by measuring behaviors and creating a Manager Effectiveness Index. We then set this Manager Effectiveness Index as an independent variable, with the two things we expect to come from good leadership—engagement and business results—as the dependent variables. The opportunity to advance this study and inject greater and greater sophistication and rigor into it is right there, just waiting for you to pick it up.

For HR folks, I want to offer you an analogy. In digital advertising, a common rule of thumb is that you should spend your first, second, and third dollars on Google search advertising. And then you should keep spending your money at Google until you can't spend anymore or you're not getting any more value out of each incremental dollar. Only when you reach that point should you consider any of the other major platforms. Similarly, I would ask that you evaluate whether you have appropriately allocated your investments, time, and attention to improving your organization's leadership culture at scale. It is an absolutely critical investment, and most of us are way undercommitted because we're focused on a bunch of traditional, low-impact HR activities because that's how we've been trained or because that's what the boss expects. My hope is that you can use this book to justify shifting your investments.

If we all do this together, we can not only put an end to assclown managers everywhere but also create a world in which millions of people care deeply about their work and deliver far greater results. Happier people, at least at work, and more opportunity. Sadly, and I believe justifiably, we no longer think of our institutions as a realistic force for good. Heck, we hardly trust them at all, but if we could just improve the way their people are being led, systematically, with managers deciding to be better and planners committing to support them, we can change the world for the better. I truly believe that, and I hope that now or very soon, you will see that I'm right.

The Definitive Leadership Library

Below are twelve books on management and leadership that I have come to view as my Definitive Leadership Library. The first eight, from *Conscious Business* to *Extreme Ownership*, deal primarily with your managerial mindset. Don't misunderstand, their pages feature heaps of tangible skills too, but much more importantly these books will help you get your head screwed on straight so that you can learn, grow, and succeed as a manager. The next two, *Built to Last* and *Measure What Matters*, serve as critical underpinning for part II of this book, "Direction." The final two, *Your Brain at Work* and, of course, *Radical Candor*, give you some extra help with coaching.

Below, I've given just a tiny taste about why I find each one useful.

MANAGERIAL MINDSET

- *Conscious Business* by Fred Kofman. This is my only business "bible." Chapters on "Authentic Communication," "Impeccable Coordination," and "Unconditional Responsibility," which features the Victim-Player model, a simple way to understand how to avoid the victim mindset (one of powerlessness) and how to migrate to a player mindset (one of powerfulness), are all must-reads in learning how to become a great manager. It's this book above all others.

- *The Leadership Moment* by Michael Useem. If you enjoyed the story about Wagner Dodge and the Mann Gulch firefighting disaster and want to learn more about it, Dr. Useem has you covered. He also brings a profusion of lessons through eight other leadership stories, which range from Fortune 100 company Merck to the *Apollo 13* mission to an all-female ascent of Annapurna, one of the most dangerous mountains in the world.
- *Mindset* by Carol Dweck. Do not let someone tell you that you can't be a great manager because you are X or because you lack Y . . . it's a discipline, and to be great only requires focus and practice. Don't be afraid when you don't have all the answers (i.e., always); instead, recognize that you have to work to find out where the answers are.
- *Grit* by Angela Duckworth. You shouldn't listen to Angela Duckworth solely because she graduated from my Olympic Conference rival high school, Cherry Hill East. Listen to her because she discovered that talent and intelligence matter less for success than perseverance, hard work, and goal setting. Former president of the United States Calvin Coolidge presciently summarized Angela's work: "Nothing in this world can take the place of persistence. Talent will not; nothing is more common than unsuccessful men with talent. Genius will not; unrewarded genius is almost a proverb. Education will not; the world is full of educated derelicts. Persistence and determination alone are omnipotent."
- *A Message to Garcia* by Elbert Hubbard. Fastest read among nonchildren's books in the history of books. This is the first

required reading for every USMC 2nd lieutenant, and it harshly conveys through a simple story the value of taking initiative. Of the Marine Corps's fourteen leadership traits, I believe that *initiative* is the most important. Things don't happen because we sit around and wait for them. They happen because we take action, even in the face of great ambiguity.

- *The Servant as Leader* by Robert Greenleaf. Don't just use the "inverted org chart" cliché. Show up to truly serve your team. Serving does not mean going easy. In fact working with the team to set and deliver on high expectations might be the greatest service you can provide them. Remember that if they are clear on their expectations and you do little more than enable their success—by serving their needs—you are most likely to serve the company and yourself.
- *Multipliers* by Liz Wiseman. Speaking of setting high expectations and challenging people to do their best work, Wiseman helps us understand that Multipliers get two times as much out of their teams as Diminishers. She then goes on to help you increase your own inner Multiplier and work on your Diminisher tendencies. The section on the accidental Diminisher is tops because it shows that we often diminish folks with our best intentions on full display—a painful reminder that we're never done learning.
- *Extreme Ownership* by Jocko Willink and Leif Babin. I offered you a story from the Marines to help put into perspective what it means to truly own outcomes. You are responsible for everything your team does or fails to do. No wink-wink. No nudge-nudge. It's critically important to leave excuse making and finger pointing behind. Willink and Babin use war stories and business case studies to teach you how to admit mistakes, check your ego, and delegate work but never responsibility.

DIRECTION

- *Built to Last* by Jim Collins. Collins offers us a much deeper dive on core ideology—values, purpose, and vision—and helps us see the way those things have contributed to the success of some of the most iconic companies and teams.
- *Measure What Matters* by John Doerr. Learn more not only about OKRs but also the tactics required to help people focus, commit, and align their objectives with the company's. Most successful Silicon Valley companies use OKRs to help coordinate the organization from top to bottom, so if you want to tap into a little Silicon Valley magic, this is an excellent place to start.

COACHING

- *Your Brain at Work* by David Rock. In part III, I gave you a high-level overview of how the brain functions in the context of giving and receiving tough feedback. Rock not only covers this in more detail but also defines a model for understanding and overcoming the five common social threats we feel in the workplace.
- *Radical Candor* by Kim Scott. Kim and I founded a company to teach Radical Candor and to help people have better relationships at work, so yeah, I'm a little biased. Her two-by-two should be committed to memory. She teaches so much through stories from places like Google and Apple.

Get yourself one of each of these, and then—with *When They Win, You Win* already in hand—you will have all you need to become the manager you've always dreamed of being.

Acknowledgments

The Leaders of the Bands: Mom & Dad (Russ & Re-Re), Tracy & Don, Cheech & Margie, Jim & Denise, Sue & Brian, GG & Starks, War & Frank, Ryan & Amy, Gene & Donna, Bill & Mimi, Tom & Ginger, Shar & Dan, Yvonne & Rick & Chuck, Joey & Brandy, Matt & Kristen, Liz & John, Laura & Mark, Lisa & Mike, Michelle & Andy, Richard & Erin. Love yuz.

The Big 3's Magnificent 7: Alexis Lopez, Will Adams, MK Ryan, Dave Dequeljoe, Keagan Case—the five people most responsible for helping understand whether, and then demonstrating that, this 3→E↔R model is valid. Can't leave out Heather Carpenter and JacQui Walker, Hangar Bay copilots. I am so grateful to you.

Editing team: Lindsay "the Winger" Logan, Dave Dequeljoe, and Arthur Goldwag. Thanks for getting me ready for the big boss. Anne Mercogliano, Kim Scott, Ryan Neading, Alexis Lopez, Dan Greene, Mike Steib, Brian Marquardt, Joe Wolf, Anant Singh, Rachel Kay, Ben Saitz, Amy Schoemehl, Shaunda Zilich, Ben O'Rourke, Joe Scaravaglione, Melanie Shar Adams. You all made this book better. Thanks to my niece, Alyssa Adams, who helped design the original cover concepts. Rachel and Shar—thanks for the sensitivity check and helping make sure I wrote an inclusive book. Ryan Masteller—wow. The detail orientation you brought to the table here. I can't express my appreciation. I really felt like you *owned* the manuscript, and as you might gather from having read the book, that's among the highest compliments I can offer. Thank you so, so much. Kevin & Alice—thanks for your expert quarterbacking of the production process. No you, no book.

Of course, the big boss editor, Tim Bartlett. You and I have been on a journey, friend, and I can't express enough my gratitude to you for agreeing to edit this thing. We each did our part—five years ago, you challenged me to improve the ideas, and when I finally did, you were right there ready to go. You and I are always gonna have two things: this book and Super Bowl LII. #FlyEaglesFly, #HereTheyCome, #RingTheBell, #Anytime-Anywhere.

Kim Scott—I don't know what I did to deserve the universe steering you in my direction, but thanks for all of it. I joke a bunch that the worst job in the world is being my boss, and you are the only manager I've ever had who actively farmed for dissent, which I readily supply . . . in large quantities. Didn't realize how important that was to me at the time. Your advice at key moments during the writing of this book was spot on every time. You are a walk walker.

Jared Smith—for the opportunity at Qualtrics and the charter to "do HR differently" . . . and to really mean it. Can't express how appreciative I am of the bet you placed on me, how happy it made me to reconnect with you, and how happy I am for your personal success. You are a walk walker. Dambisa Moyo—your encouragement, guidance, and insight in the summer of 2019 was invaluable and meant more than you know. At that time, I could not even get an agent to respond to my emails. You laughed at me for thinking that mattered, and then simplified the whole process. By doing those things you injected a renewed confidence. For you, an easy fifteen minutes. For me, a sharp change in optimism and direction.

Dick Costolo—I hope you don't get tired of me saying this, but you are the ultimate walk walker. I learned more about leadership watching you as CEO of Twitter than almost any other single person. "The more difficult the message, the less clear you become." Just one of your many pearls of wisdom. You also took a bet on me, and for that I am more grateful than I can express. Adam Bain and Richard Alfonsi—thank you for the opportunity at Twitter and for putting people at the center of all you do. Adam, thank you for being so nice. Kelly Kovacs—love working with you, and I am so glad we're still connected after all these years. Thanks for your encouragement. Ravi, Joe, Dale, Anne, Vinay, Barry, Em, Stephen, and Aliza. I learned so much from all of you. You're all walk walkers.

Colonel John Boggs—"you know what I know, old man." "What do you know, and who are you telling?" "Hollywood good looks." Thank you for letting me command Alpha Company, First Battalion, 5th Marines. You are a walk walker.

Alexis Lopez—You taught me so much. Who would have guessed the two of us would have such a bond, especially given your college football rooting interests. We will not forget Dale Lopez, a great manager (and dad and grandpa) in his own right. "It's about time." Love ya, friend.

David Rosenblatt—thank you for your mentorship and guidance. Your support and advice were very important to me, and I am grateful. You are a walk walker.

Jim Levine—my agent. We're a couple of Jerry Maguire and Rod Tidwell coconuts. Anyone in this business knows Jim is the biggest baller agent around, but more important for me, Jim is a walk-walking people manager. Throughout the process, he continually referred to my book as “important.” I bet he says that to all the Tidwells, but I sure hope he’s right. His confidence in these pages had a meaningful effect on my motivation to nail it.

Kylan Lundeen, Julie Larsen-Green, Blake Tierney, Jay Choi, Jeremy Smith, Chris Beckstead, Rob Bachman, John Thimsen, Zig Serafin, Ryan Smith, Julia Anas, Kelly Waldher, Brain Stucki, and Amy Bates—thanks for putting people at the center of all you do. Chris—thank you for your expert guidance and partnership. You are one of the highest integrity people I have ever worked with—and I just want you to know that I appreciate you very much. You, sir, are a walk walker.

Qualtrics’s best managers: The OGs, Adam Marre, Vicki Tisdale, and Cody Guymon; v2: Alexia Newgord, Austin Nilsson, Jason Matthews, Mary Kynaston, Michael Page, Shellene McKendrick, Stephen Kelly, and Thomas Karthaus. Thank you for delivering at the Q by putting people at the center of all you do. Walk walkers, the lot of ya.

To the ACs: Amy, Anant, Archana, Ben, Brian, Eric, Erin, Estee, Goots, Joe, Kate, Lauren, Maya, Sally. I hope you all like the transformation story in the introduction—full credit to all of you. I’m grateful to have been your manager/partner and I am so thankful we’re still friends. I miss you all, and I hope you can see your impact in this book. Thanks for being such strong people leaders and for showing me through your actions that the ideas in this book work. Never forget that bereavement discount the SF Giants gave us for the “Goodbye Russ” message on the big board. RIP Russ. Lauren, my original eyes and ears, you’re also a savage negotiator.

The core posse at the Q: Krista, Steiger, Stride, Laura, Meg, MK, Heather, JacQui, Dave, Lexi, Shaunda, Farren, Brandon R., Julia, Bernal, and partner in anticrime, Sydnee. You are all so wonderful, and I am so lucky to have worked with you. I think the next *Kung Fu Panda* movie's posse should be loosely based on all of you (cc: @pixar).

Claire Johnson, Michael Comerford, Laura DeBonis, Kim Scott, Hal Bailey, Jared Smith, Stacy Brown Philpot, Tim Malley, Bryan Schreier, and Sheryl Sandberg—thanks for hiring me into Google. I know you weren't sure about me, and I know you placed a bet on me. I hope that you feel like that bet paid off. H/T to Tom Pickett and Scott Sheffer. Two of the best peers I have ever had. I learned so much just from sitting alongside you two. I've never been in a healthier, more robust "debate, decide, and commit" environment than when we were together. Miss you guys.

Scallywags: Randy, Bill, Jim, and Shane. Love you guys. Grateful for each of you and looking forward to the next Scallywag Convention. Let's just hope there isn't a cold puddle on the ground in Kentucky or else Shane won't be allowed to come. May what little wisdom we have be forever contained and protected by our scallies. Scallywag v1 was the second- or third-best $64 I ever spent.

The few and the proud: Mike Moran, Ben O'Rourke, Shane Tarter, Ben "Looch" Luciano, Gary Wright, Brian "Sancho" Sanchez, General Mike "Chilli Mac" McWilliams, Bryan Patterson, Brian Hilyer, Chris Griffin, Eric Hamstra, Kelsey Thompson, Chas Holler, Chris Yates, Mike Buckingham, Don Gallagher, Greg Grizzle, Roy Estrada, Mike Wiley, Owen "Flash" Frederic, Jason "The Great Kornholio" Kornmueller, Jeff O'Neill, Jim "Wigdeer" Brigadier, John "Stinkin" Lincoln, Sean "Hairy Bug Wings" Berg, Giles Russell Boyce, Bill Gray, Steve Luhrsen, Scott "Big Mac" McMillan, Tony "Dirt Merchant" Ede, Mark Thieme, Walt Yates, Greg Funk, Staff Sergeant Anderson & Staff Sergeant Acosta (OCS '93) and so many more. Semper Fi, Marines. Thank you for all you taught me.

My family. V—thank you for never doubting this would be

a real book. That optimism mattered, especially when I couldn't even get a real-estate agent, let alone a book agent, to respond to my emails. Your confidence in me at times feels unfounded, but it's there, it's real, I feel it, and it helped me push through when I was stuck. What an against-the-odds life we've built! I love you. Anthony, Chas, and Starks—this is for you. Each of you is precious to me. Remember that *success comes when opportunity meets preparation*. Luck + skill. It will be your grit and resilience that determines your success in all things and not your innate smarts or talent. Please try your best to make the most of your opportunities, and please help others, the best you can, along the way. And remember, there will come a day when the only friends you have are your brothers. Cherish each other.

P.S. Do you guys wanna get haircuts? We ready to roll?

Index